STILL AIN'T SATISFIED

Still Ain't Satisfied!

CANADIAN FEMINISM TODAY

Edited by

MAUREEN FITZGERALD

CONNIE GUBERMAN

MARGIE WOLFE

The
Women's
·Press·

CANADIAN CATALOGUING IN PUBLICATION DATA

Main entry under title:
Still ain't satisfied
ISBN 0-88961-074-6

1. Women – Canada – Addresses, essays, lectures.
2. Feminism – Canada – Addresses, essays, lectures.
I. FitzGerald, Maureen, 1942-   II. Guberman,
   Connie, 1955-   III. Wolfe, Margie, 1949-
HQ1453.S74   305.4'2'0971   C82-095085-8

Title from song by Bonnie Lockhart
Cover and book design by Liz Martin
Illustrations by Gail Geltner
Lithographed by union labour at the Hunter Rose Company, Toronto
Printed and bound in Canada
Published by the Women's Educational Press
16 Baldwin Street
Toronto, Ontario, Canada

CONTENTS

STILL AIN'T SATISFIED

BY BONNIE LOCKHART

CHORUS:

And I still ain't, woa they lied,
And I still ain't, woa they lied,
And I still ain't, woa they lied,
And I still ain't satisfied.

*1. Well, they got women on T.V.
but I still ain't satisfied.
'Cause co-optation's all I see,
and I still ain't satisfied.
They call me "Ms.",
they sell me blue jeans,
Call it "Women's Lib,"
they make it sound obscene.

*2. Well, they got women prison guards,
but I still ain't satisfied.
With so many still behind bars,
and I still ain't satisfied.
I don't plead guilt, I don't want
no bum deal.
I ain't askin' for crumbs, I want
the whole meal.

*3. They liberalized abortion,
but I still ain't satisfied,
'Cause it still costs a fortune,
and I still ain't satisfied.
I'm singin' about control
of my own womb,
And no reform is gonna change my tune.

*4. They give out pennies here and there,
but I still ain't satisfied,
To set up centers for child care,
and I still ain't satisfied.
And while we work at slave wages,
They brainwash our kids at tender ages.

5. Well, they got unisex fashion shows,
but I still ain't satisfied.
For all the dykes that no one knows,
I still ain't satisfied.
They say, "All right,
we'll sell the Butch Look,"
But they won't put queers
into the text book.

6. Well, this world sure don't look my way,
and I still ain't satisfied.
'Cause women get raped every day,
and I still ain't satisfied.
They say, "OK,
we'll give you a street light,"
But they get uptight
when we learn how to street fight.

*7. I've got some pride,
and I won't be lied to.
I did decide that half way won't do.

8. They say we have the right to strike,
but I still ain't satisfied,
'Cause we lose our jobs
each time we fight
and I still ain't satisfied.
My job pays half
wage for a whole day
Then I cook and clean
at home for no pay.

*Original verses by Bonnie Lockhart
Verse 5 by Elaine Magree
Verse 6 by Robin Flower
Verse 8 by the Red Berets

ACKNOWLEDGMENTS

A project the size of this anthology cannot be attributed solely to the work of three editors. It was a collective project and we owe our deepest appreciation to many women. Jane Springer, our editor, is the first person we'd like to thank. Her skills, commitment and good humour throughout were indispensable. To Liz Martin, who designed the book, and who once again bore the brunt of a much shortened production schedule, we are equally grateful.

Through the entire development process, members of the Women's Press Collective have provided insights, support and encouragement. Meg Luxton came up with the idea of an anniversary anthology back in 1979, and she and the rest of the social issues manuscript group – Wendy Donner, Bonnie Fox, Genevieve Leslie, Peggy McDonough, Brenda Roman, Judy Skinner, Jane Springer and Lynda Yanz – were helpful in commenting on the issues, providing direction and in making organizational suggestions in the early stages of the book. To the collective staff members, Liz Martin, Judy McClard and Lois Pike, who excused our occasional hysterics and were always patient and encouraging, and to Daphne Read, who calmed us at harried editors' meetings, we owe a special debt. Karen Alliston, Joan Armistead, Beth McAuley, Sharon Nelson and Stephanie Stone assisted with typing and general preparation of the manuscript.

We are grateful to many other women for their contribution to the anthology: Gail Geltner added a touch of grace and wit through her illustrations; Sandra Sorenson, Carolyn Egan, Barbara Williamson, Lynda Yanz, and Press Gang publishers, particularly Diana Smith and Pat Smith, provided us with introductions to and contacts with many of the authors; Susan Bazilli, Sherrill Cheda, Freida Forman, Charlene Gannage, Patti Kirk and Carol Zavitz helped us focus individual articles; Bonnie Lockhart was generous in granting permission to reprint her song, "Still Ain't Satisfied"; and our friends at Women's Healthsharing allowed us to develop the article by Marianne Langton that originally appeared in their magazine.

To all of the marvellous women listed above, and to the writers –
whose unstinting commitment made this project possible – we are
sincerely grateful. And finally, we thank our friends, whose caring,
patience and understanding provided a constant source of much-needed
support.

Maureen FitzGerald
Connie Guberman
Margie Wolfe

EDITORS' INTRODUCTION

TEN YEARS AGO, in 1972, the Women's Press published its first book. *Women Unite!* was an anthology of writings on the issues, debates, demands and strategies of the developing Canadian women's liberation movement. This year, 1982, the Women's Press is celebrating its tenth anniversary as a publisher. And in celebration of its survival and the survival and strength of the women's liberation movement, the Women's Press is publishing *Still Ain't Satisfied*. This book is a sequel to *Women Unite!* The articles – all but three of which were written especially for this collection – reflect the development and maturation of the women's liberation movement in Canada.

The issues chosen for discussion in the anthology are representative of the areas in which women have been struggling throughout the decade. Ideally we would have liked to cover every concern addressed by women during these years. But this, of course, is impossible in a single book. Obvious omissions are specific articles on Québécoises, the family, the right, microtechnology, the anti-nuclear and peace movements and the special problems of welfare, older, adolescent and disabled women. This collection does, however, reflect the diversity of issues, the ideological differences and the multiple strategies involved in feminism in Canada.

Choosing the articles for this book was a difficult task, and arranging them proved equally so. Any division or section title we came up with seemed artificial because all the articles, irrespective of grouping, focus on women's mobilization and activism. Specifically though, articles featured in *Out of the Bedrooms* deal with issues that have traditionally been considered the most private and personal, those in *Into the Work Force* address the questions around women and work, and those in *Onto the Streets* focus on women's organizing and mobilization. The progression throughout the book mirrors the development of women over the decade towards increasing visibility and collective strength.

Still Ain't Satisfied is not meant to be a history or survey of the women's movement in Canada but rather an evaluation of feminist activities over the last ten years. Authors were asked to focus on major areas of women's activity and participation, to pinpoint the current priorities and characteristics of the movement and also to provide a background for determining aims and strategies for the future. They were encouraged to discuss how our struggles of today reflect the issues and practices around which we organized in the early years of the decade.

As editors we wanted to provide an overview of how feminist perspectives have changed. Both as editors and activists we were concerned to offer an analysis of how these changes have influenced our practice, the major obstacles to be overcome, the successes that have been won and the possible directions for the future.

Readers will not find a singular or cohesive description or analysis running through the articles. The women's movement in Canada does not have a single voice, and there is no one ideological line to which all activists adhere. The authors here mirror that diversity.

This book was undertaken to provide a comprehensive resource for both activists and those new to feminism trying to understand what this movement of ours is all about. We hope that *Still Ain't Satisfied* will stimulate discussion and debate to aid in building feminism and achieving liberation for us all.

◆

The Last Ten Years

A PERSONAL/POLITICAL VIEW

BY NAOMI WALL

Each of us has a personal history with the women's movement and each of us reflects on the movement with a perspective informed by that experience. In this article, Naomi Wall weaves a personal chronology with an analytic commentary on some of the changes in the Canadian women's liberation movement over the last decade. She traces the beginnings of the movement from the chiefly university-based women caucusing in new left organizations in the late Sixties to the present more diversified movement that addresses the concerns of a much broader range of women. Along the way she considers the kinds of organizations formed by feminists during the decade, the various currents within the women's movement and the recent convergence of socialist and radical feminists around specific issues. This article is not meant to be a comprehensive overview of what has happened everywhere in Canada, but in whole or in part, it reflects the experience of many of us.

*I*N LATE SPRING 1969, *I attended a conference of anti-war activists in Montreal. We had come from across Canada and the U.S. to coordinate our various areas of work around our efforts to bring about the end of U.S. intervention in Vietnam. Most of the women at the conference were working in the anti-war movement – they had cut their political teeth in the new left of the Sixties and had developed a keen understanding of their oppression within that movement. They came to the conference in Montreal determined to be heard.*

On the final day, when we met to present resolutions outlining our common goals, all hell broke loose. Women refused to discuss the resolutions or the war until every woman present who had something to say about the conference was heard. The men went wild. How could these women insist on addressing their concerns as women when men were dying in Vietnam, when the U.S. and its imperialist designs in Southeast Asia went unchecked? Who gave a damn whether they were listened to or whether they were given the right to speak? They were irresponsible, disruptive and ignorant of the real purpose of the conference. They should shut up and let the conference organizers (the men) get on with it.

The women refused to sit down, refused to keep silent and redirected the focus of the conference around their demands as women. Within an hour's time, the women had taken over the agenda, recorded their demands and called a recess in order to organize for their presentation, which they would make later in the day. All women were invited to attend this planning meeting.

I went back into the conference from the planning meeting exhilarated. We voiced our demands and they went into the minutes and became history. I had never been part of a women's caucus before. I learned, at that conference, that women all across Canada had been cursing and caucusing and giving voice to their oppression within their new left organizations for many, many months. For me, it marked the beginning of my awareness of both the need for and the possibility of an autonomous women's movement.

This was my experience in one sector of the emerging women's movement in Canada in the late Sixties. The rising of new left women marked the advent of what came to be known as the women's movement in Canada – an issue-oriented, politically diverse, primarily middle-class grouping of women that reflected an ideology rooted in the struggles of women who had organized before us, as suffragettes or as trade unionists – for equal pay, birth control, the right to unionize and to strike, child care and an end to violence against women.

The majority of the women who began caucusing together within new left organizations during the late Sixties were middle-class, university-based women. The sharing of their experiences as women, their common rage and frustration, gave rise to the phenomenon of consciousness-raising groups. CR groups, as they came to be known, encouraged women to share stories from their lives and enabled them to develop the understanding that these were not isolated events in the lives of individual women, but that they reflected a common oppression. Every woman's experience was rooted in a system that depended for its survival on the exploitation of women – as homemakers, as sex objects, as submissive and dependent pillars of the family.

When I was 23, as yet unmarried, my younger sister became engaged. I was dating a guy, but we never discussed marriage. When my sister set her wedding date, my father asked me about the intentions of my young man. I was mortified, but it never occurred to me to protest or to make counter demands or to insist on my right to remain unmarried. I knew I didn't want to get married, but I thought it would be better to do the "normal" thing and hopefully I'd adjust afterwards. Several years later when I joined a CR group I did it because I thought I was crazy not to be satisfied as a wife and mother and I wanted some kind of therapy to help me adjust. Instead I discovered the roots of my "madness" were in the system and not in me at all. I met so many women going crazy just like me – and for the exact same reasons.

For many of these women, political action seemed extreme, but they carried with them through the decade to come – and passed onto their female children – the conviction that anything boys can do, girls can do just as well, if not better. Consequently, there are many young girls today who possess self-images that I would have given my eye teeth for when I was a girl growing up in the Fifties.

This very personal sense of rage we felt as girls – and then as women – was allowed to surface and find expression in the atmosphere of sisterhood provided by consciousness-raising groups. However, the benefits of participating in these groups were reaped by a minority of women in Canada. Canadian mainstream institutions like the media and the schools did carry bits and pieces of this newly-discovered awareness to women who were never participants in CR groups. However, most of the women directly affected by the process and therefore able to act on what they learned from it, were middle-class and professional women. This is not to underestimate the impact of consciousness-raising on women who remained outside its framework. But women who were able to strike out on their own or to make new demands on their husbands and families for equal consideration had access to support networks and the entire array of privilege that comes to women of the middle and upper classes. The vast majority of women in Canada could not make this leap towards their personal liberation.

Women who chose to work politically during the late 1960s and early 1970s had at our disposal a legacy of experience and struggle. To this legacy we contributed, very early in the decade which concerns us now, diverse theoretical bases for organizing around issues of concern to us. These varying theories regarding the roots of our oppression – and relating to our practice in terms of the strategies and tactics we would apply to our work – created a fragmentation within the visible women's movement in Canada. As early as the mid- and late Sixties, women who identified themselves as socialist feminists put forward a class perspective and distinguished between women along class lines, insisting that the reality, and therefore the demands, of working-class and poor Canadian women were different from those of middle and upper-class women. Other women disagreed and believed that all women were oppressed by the patriarchy, regardless of class, and our concerns were the same. Though these different analyses divided these two groups of feminists, they shared a fundamental belief that women's oppression could only be overcome through a radical change in the structure of our society. Other women who were active in the early years of the Canadian women's movement believed that women's liberation could be achieved within the present system. Thus they lobbied and organized for confrontation with government representatives and in this way attempted to redress their grievances.

It is no small matter to agree that it is only through a fundamental overhauling of our system that women's liberation will be realized. Because of this radical perspective, socialist feminists and radical feminists distinguished themselves from women who were primarily reformist in theory and practice. However, regardless of the affinity

between socialist feminists and radical feminists, the work of organizing around issues, through various ad hoc committees and groupings
of women across the country, was approached from different
theoretical points of departure. This resulted in conflict and confrontation and for many years over the past decade our movement has
been characterized by its fragmentation and its political diversity.

Political action relating specifically to the concerns and demands of
women and centering on issues related to reproduction and sexuality
became the focus of activity for hundreds of Canadian women as the
decade of the Sixties closed. Believing that women's right to control our
bodies was fundamental to our liberation, women from civil rights
groups, new-left caucuses and university campuses began an all-out
campaign for free and accessible birth control information and con-
traceptives. And then, in 1970, feminists initiated a national action for
free abortion on demand. This demand grew out of the experiences of
women who had worked in the birth control and abortion counselling
centres. These women reached the conclusion that the abortion laws had
to be repealed, arguing that the existing laws discriminated against poor
and working-class women, left the decision as to whether or not a
woman qualified for an abortion in the hands of male doctors and
psychologists, and completely undermined the right of women to control our own bodies. The Vancouver Women's Caucus organized a
caravan to travel to Ottawa so women could present their demands to
the House of Commons. This action drew the participation of
thousands of women from across Canada and brought the issue of abortion into the foreground of the women's liberation movement.

Other issues related to women's sexuality and reproduction were
also the focus of political activity in the early Seventies. There were campaigns around day care, women's work both inside and outside the
home, the oppression of women within institutions such as schools and
universities, and sexism. But many women who had worked hard to
bring these demands into focus were dissatisfied with the limitations of
political action which centered on single issues. They were convinced
that a much broader strategy for women's liberation had to be
developed and that a theoretical basis for political practice was the essential component of this strategy. Many of these women looked to the
organizing of women in the work force – both in and out of existing

trade union structures – as the most viable focus for their political work. Others joined political parties or organizations, preferring to work in groups with men, as difficult as that might be, than in a women's movement which, in their minds, lacked a theoretical basis.

For women who could not find a niche for themselves in party or pre-party organizations – who preferred, for personal and political reasons, to work with women – and who had found a new and radicalizing approach to their work through the experience of fighting for demands of particular concern to women, there were feminist organizations. By the mid-Seventies these organizations existed in abundance. There were artist collectives, writers' groups, feminist therapy collectives, service organizations for women, feminist publications, feminist self-help groups, skills-sharing centres, health clinics for women, information networks and many others – all staffed, administered and controlled by women. Though the political orientation and theoretical bases of these various organizations differed, they offered women who chose to work within them the opportunity to grow as feminists, to experience the joys, frustrations and camaraderie inherent in women's shared commitment to collective work. One such organization was the Women's Press.

In 1975, after completing one year as a grade four teacher, I quit my job and moved from Toronto to B.C. I was floundering, politically and personally, and had heard that there was a lot happening in Vancouver. I did a lot of reading, mostly by feminists, and I looked for work. There wasn't any. B.C. had its share of unemployed teachers, so I returned to Toronto after only a few months. I did some supply teaching, but couldn't find a permanent job. I had only one other skill – I could type. I was on my own with two kids and no job. I didn't want to be a typist, but it was the only work I could get. A friend suggested that I enroll in a typesetting course at a community college, because typesetting was more interesting work than typing and paid better. Shortly after I completed the course I heard about a typesetting job at the Canadian Women's Educational Press. They needed someone with experience to typeset a book about the effects of population control on women in the Third World. I didn't know much about the Women's Press, except that it was a feminist collective that published books by, for and about women. I had never worked politically with an all women's group before. To me, it was a job and I didn't think about joining the collective. But from the first day, I knew I was in a situation totally unique for me. There were about fifteen women around all the time, talking, working, arguing, in and out of conflict, making decisions, relying on no one but themselves. No one seemed to be monitoring my work. Of course, I was not an experienced typesetter, but no one seemed to mind; in fact, the women who had experience in production were anxious to teach me all they knew. After eight months on the job, I not only learned how to typeset, but I learned all the aspects of production right up to camera-ready copy. When they asked me if I wanted to apply for membership in the collective, I jumped at the chance, not because the work situation was ideal, or because the atmosphere was free of conflict. In fact I had never before been in a work situation where conflict surfaced so quickly. But I wanted to join because I was so familiar with women's way of relating, at the best of times and the worst of times. I had heard about the women's movement, had been to demonstrations, rallies, meetings and had talked with women friends about feminism. But I had never really worked as a feminist or felt the incredible waves of energy generated by women's collective efforts. I had become so much more skilled than I had ever imagined I would be. And I had learned these skills from women, who, in spite of misunderstandings and painful confrontations, had nurtured me through my initiation into the realm of feminist consciousness. It was through my experience with the Press that my feminism found its practice.

By this time, feminists had created service organizations to meet some of the needs of poor and working-class women and of women in transition from brutal family ties. The campaign against violence against women, the advent of rape crisis centres and the response of women across the country to the issues of pornography and domestic violence indicated a rising feminist consciousness among women in Canada.

Many of these service organizations had a radical feminist base. The radical feminist attack on institutionalized patriarchy hit home with many socialist women who identified with these issues. As well, it struck a chord of truth in women who had repressed their rage for years, who had remained outside the organizational structures of the women's movement. The incredible extent to which the hostility of men for women finds its various forms of expression in our society was reason enough for a radical feminist perspective. Radical feminism drew women into the women's movement in Canada who had not been there before, women who relished the long-awaited opportunity to join with their sisters to take to the streets and let it be known that they'd had enough of the patriarchy.

From the time I was just a kid, I preferred to be with my girl friends. Boys didn't make any sense to me. When I was about ten I had a crush on a woman many years older than me and didn't think anything of it. I spent my first year in university living in a "girls'" dorm and had intimate relationships with women there. I never thought about being a lesbian. I was also going out with guys and fully expected to marry one of them. I didn't really think about it much. I guess I thought I was bisexual, but it didn't have any real significance for me. I didn't consider just being with women because I thought that would mean I wasn't normal. Bisexuality seemed normal to me, so that was my practice. Looking back on it years later after I came out, I could see that my relationships with guys were peripheral to the centre of my concerns, that my women friends, my girl friends, were everything to me. I've talked to heterosexual women who've told me the same thing. When I finally came out, it was a political as well as a personal decision. It was personal in the sense that I preferred intimacy with women. It was political in the sense that I recognized that lesbians face a particular oppression under this system and the women's movement did not address our uniqueness in this regard. I wanted to join the ranks with my lesbian sisters.

Lesbians have increased their visibility both inside and outside the women's liberation movement in Canada. As activists in the gay and lesbian movement they have radicalized other women and have become radicalized themselves. While recognizing that the women's movement in Canada has taken up many of their demands, lesbians are aware of the limitations of a feminist perspective that fails to make the link between sexism and heterosexism. Lesbian feminism is an evolving political position, which recognizes heterosexuality as an institution. It calls on the Canadian women's movement to expand its analysis of the lesbian reality from one which views lesbianism as primarily a choice or a particular lifestyle or sexual preference, to one which encompasses a demand for a non-heterosexist society. The right to be a lesbian must be every woman's right, whatever her personal choice. Lesbians share with their heterosexual sisters the common oppression of women. But their demand for the right to be lesbians puts them in a unique position politically and in making this demand they speak for all women. The advent of autonomous lesbian feminist organizations gives voice to their conviction that their liberation depends on their establishing their own communities as part of the women's movement, from which they can speak in a collective voice.

Lesbians are everywhere and always have been. We're working in solidarity groups, in trade unions, in the women's movement, both bourgeois and socialist, we're working 9 to 5 as clerks, secretaries, in factories, you name it. Some of us work politically, some don't. We reflect the same lifestyles that distinguish us along class lines as all women do. Some of us come out, others stay in the closet. The way we're oppressed, in spite of our new visibility, or maybe because of it, keeps most of us locked in the closet. But wherever we are or have been, in or out, we constitute an enormous threat in this society. We scream a resounding ''No'' to our lives being defined and controlled by men, through our sexual preference and practice. That's why we're under attack.

Throughout the development of the Canadian women's movement there has been an ongoing debate about the best way to broaden the base of the movement. Many women believed that a women's movement that lacked the participation of poor women, working-class women, native women and immigrant women also lacked credibility as a movement for radical social change and for women's liberation. However, in spite of the discussion and debate, the visible and popularly known Canadian women's movement continued to maintain only a narrow base of support. Many women working within the framework of the movement were socialist feminists committed to involving working-class women. But its tradition remained middle-class, whatever its aspirations. As the decade closed, poor and working-class Canadian, immigrant and native women began to create organizations, many of which were service-oriented, through which they have been able to address their own constituencies, thus broadening their bases and laying the groundwork for political discussion around issues of particular concern to them. The emergence of these organizations has had a significant effect on the developing movement.

In March 1978, the largest women's demonstration in Toronto's history so far was held to celebrate International Women's Day. The keynote speaker, representing the International Women's Day Coalition, made the following statement:

> . . .this demonstration is particularly significant because of the wide spectrum of women who have been involved in organizing and building it. I think that for the first time in Toronto we have women from the trade unions, the immigrant communities, women's services, the lesbian community, neighbourhood organizations, universities, high schools as well as many individual women, all working together. . . .The women's movement has grown incredibly from its small, isolated beginnings in the 1960s. Today it is a massive network made up of women with many backgrounds and perspectives, who are all fighting the varying aspects of our oppression. Every woman engaged in fighting against her particular oppression is part of the women's movement, whether she is in a women's group or in a mixed organization such as a trade union local.

Whether this "wide spectrum of women" was an accurate description of the participants at the demonstration, or whether it represented a bit of wishful thinking on the part of the organizers, the message was clear: as far as the activists in the Canadian women's movement were concerned, the base of the movement had broadened. For the first time, immigrant women, poor women, trade union women and lesbians were highlighted in a keynote address and their particular demands outlined. The issues which had for so long been the central concerns of so many women from varying theoretical perspectives were once again addressed. Control of our bodies, quality child care, an end to cutbacks in social services, lesbian rights and an end to violence against women were all accentuated in the speech, and significantly, these issues were placed in the political and economic framework of the burgeoning economic crisis of the mid- and late Seventies. And new issues were added to the list. There was a demand for an end to the deportation of Jamaican women, a demand for full native rights for native women, and full social, trade union and political rights for immigrant women. The oppression faced by poor women and sole-support mothers was described. The contribution made by women who choose to remain at home to raise their dependent children was recognized, along with the fact that welfare payments and old age pensions were far below poverty levels. The speech ended with a call to "consolidate and extend the links that we have made, to become an even more potent force, and to use to the fullest the power that is ours as women united'' (International Women's Day Speech, 1978, Convocation Hall, delivered by Carolyn Egan).

Has this vision of a unified movement of women in Canada been realized? Is it being realized? There is no doubt that trade union women have begun to confront their male-dominated committees and bureaucracies and increasingly raise the demands of women in their unions and on the picket lines. In the years since 1978, there has been a steadily developing relationship between trade union women and feminists. The support from the women's movement on picket lines, in the fight for equal pay, an end to sexual harassment, and against the use of hazardous and job-threatening technology has helped to build a movement that is broader based. But what of poor Canadian and immigrant women, native women and the vast majority of women in Canada who remain outside the movement's existing organizational structures?

In 1981 I was hired to coordinate the opening session of a conference on immigrant women in Canada. The focus of the session was to be poor and working-class women and I was given a pretty clear mandate to present, through print and audiovisual materials, the oppressive living and working conditions faced by these women. I worked with several immigrant women on the organizing committee and we spent many hours talking about women's oppression in Canada. Since I was a North American woman the question of the Canadian women's movement came up and I was asked to explain what the goals of the movement were and who the movement represented. Try as I might, I could not dispel what seemed to me to be a myth perpetrated by the mainstream media: that the Canadian women's movement was a bourgeois movement, that it reflected the concerns of middle-class women only and that it did not put forward a class perspective. I explained that there were women in the movement who were socialists, who recognized that the needs of poor and working-class women were different from middle-class women, that the movement was open to a dialogue with women from different sectors. And though most of the women I worked with during the conference came to accept the diversity of the women's movement in Canada, they maintained the view that poor and working-class and immigrant women would have to organize autonomously into parallel structures, and that their natural affinity would be with Canadian women of their own class. So, while the concerns of poor women can be reflected in the Canadian women's movement, they are not in and of that movement. Not yet, anyway.

Today, it is perhaps more accurate to refer to the movement of women in Canada than to the Canadian women's movement. If it is true, as was stated at Toronto International Women's Day in 1978, that "every woman engaged in fighting against her particular oppression is part of the women's movement," then there is little doubt that the movement has broadened its base since 1970. Across the country women are organizing within their own constituencies. It is true that there continue to be regional as well as theoretical differences. If the more visible women's movement in Canada seems less fragmented, the movement of women on the whole might seem more so. There are more issues than ever before, and a wealth of organizations to choose from. But, within this diverse movement, there are the seeds of unity. We've been working together for quite a while, coming together when our differences would allow it, to fight in a common struggle. We've influenced one another, back and forth, so that the barriers between us, created out of our different perspectives on women's oppression, have begun to give a little and our perspectives have begun to fuse. Our experiences – on picket lines in support of our trade union sisters, as witnesses to the economic brutality endured by poor women, and as workers who are gaining first-hand knowledge of a spiraling downward mobility – have broadened both our sense of the different realities women struggle against, and our vision for our future. Now it is no longer a question of whether or not a class perspective is a correct perspective, for it is clear that women's oppression is rooted in class oppression. We can see it out there in the world, from the reality of Third World women to the reality of women living in Canada. At the same time, we know – from the experience of working together against violence against women, against pornography, against the patriarchal institutions that create the conditions for the oppression that is common to all of us – that feminism cannot be subsumed within the class struggle. Feminism is a consciousness of the oppression we face *because* we are women, the political expression of this consciousness, and a fundamental underpinning of our vision of a liberated society.

It is true that the Canadian women's movement has effectively permeated the consciousness of thousands of women across the country – women from all sectors of the society. It is equally true that women's oppression in Canada takes different forms and that at this point in our ongoing and developing struggle it is time to widen the context of our discussion and debate, in order to heed the demands which a broadening base places on us. We need a new kind of dialogue, one that allows for controversy and creativity, one that welcomes the influence of women whose lives are rooted in realities different from our own.

N O T E S

I would like to thank Myrna Kostash for her book, *Long Way from Home* (Toronto: James Lorimer, 1980); Maria Teresa Larrain and Maureen FitzGerald for inspiration; Arlene Mantle and Amy Gottlieb for their critical support; and the Women's Press editing team for helping to shape the article.

Out of the Bedrooms

AS MUCH AS ANYTHING ELSE, feminism has taught us that the personal is political. It has provided the assurance that all those problems and doubts traditionally considered solely the domain of the individual are not: the discontent we experience is not necessarily a personal responsibility. Women have learned that the long-standing rationales that separate individual and social concerns are merely artificial barriers maintained to safeguard existing power relationships, ones which specifically obstruct the liberation of women.

For more than ten years now, feminists have been struggling to erode these barriers. Over coffee, in consciousness-raising and support groups, at public meetings, we've aired our frustrations and dissatisfactions. By examining subjects previously considered no one else's business, we have discovered that our individual experience is reflected in the lives of thousands of others. We have in fact built a political movement based on our commonalities. Women's liberation has essentially taken our doubts, burdens, supposed failings and aspirations out of our personal closets and placed them, if not always squarely in the political arena, at least in the open – to be mulled over, debated and reevaluated.

This section, *Out of the Bedrooms,* directly addresses women's politicization of the personal. While the state and the church have traditionally prescribed the moral and legal necessities concerning childbearing, it is the individual woman (and her personal support network) who privately carried the responsibility, doubts and problems of parenting. The demand for reproductive rights has transformed this supposed personal concern into a clear political issue. Until feminism recognized that society must be made accountable for violence against women, we also individually bore the pain, responsibility and humiliation of abuse engendered by attitudes that stereotyped us as sex objects, that advanced our subservience and that maintained the sanctity of men as all-powerful kings in their homes. The politicization of the personal is further reflected in our sexuality. There are few concerns that have been considered more private than those involving our sexual lives and relationships. Before the women's liberation movement spoke to the power and domination that played an intrinsic part in defining our sexuality, society had successfully secreted away our questions to the sphere of the very private and personal.

The articles in this section also illustrate the varying forms women's organizing has taken. Violence against women, for example, has become a clear issue involving mass action, demonstrations and ongoing lobbying. Response to the questions of our own sexuality has, however, taken a different turn. There has been no large-scale organizing and women tend to meet in small groups or informally. The low-profile nature of this struggle does not necessarily diminish the political nature of the problem, however. It indicates that women's sexuality has not to date been defined as an issue in the traditional sense and that in fact the very nature of the concerns intrinsic to it may always be resolved best through small group activity.

Women's struggle for independence, and the freedom to better determine the content of our lives, are implicit themes throughout this section of articles. The first chapter, dealing with reproductive rights, focuses specifically on the freedom of women to choose whether or not we want to give birth and raise children. The right to make this decision influences the content and quality of our lives. The middle articles on rape, pornography and wife battering make clear that as long as we remain subject to violent abuse simply because we are women, our freedom is undermined. Liberating and equalizing our sexual relations follows in the chapters examining women's sexuality. Without a clear reevaluation of ourselves as sexual participants, women will remain victims of the traditional power relationships which we've recognized as exploitative. Finally, the article detailing the fight for social services demonstrates both how women's options are dependent on the availability of a public support system and exemplifies the transformation of individual responsibility into social accountability.

◆

Claim No Easy Victories

THE FIGHT FOR REPRODUCTIVE RIGHTS

BY KATHLEEN MCDONNELL

The Abortion Caravan of 1970 brought the nascent Canadian women's liberation movement to its feet. This action was followed by heated debate about whether abortion should be the chief focus of feminists' attention. In city after city, feminists agreed that the women's movement could not neglect other issues – and we have seen a decade of proliferation of groups organized around different struggles. Those who continued to fight for better access to abortion have been dismayed by the hard times on which the struggle for abortion rights has fallen. Due to cutbacks in hospital quotas and opposition from anti-abortionists, it has been difficult to maintain even the status quo. Kathleen McDonnell takes a look at the reasons for this impasse, and asks some hard questions about the way that the women's movement has dealt with the abortion issue.

A BORTION IS THE forgotten issue of the women's movement in Canada. Despite its high-profile position in the feminist struggles of the early Seventies, abortion rights now seldom engages women in any significant numbers. There have been some victories since the law was liberalized in 1969, especially in Quebec, where Dr. Henry Morgentaler now operates his clinic without harassment, and where a number of other free-standing clinics (i.e., outside hospitals) have been established with the tacit blessing of the Parti Québécois government. And the dearth of activity around abortion is far from uniform across the country: in British Columbia, particularly, pro-choice forces have mobilized large numbers of supporters to fight attempts by anti-choice groups to gain control of several hospital governing boards. Nevertheless, it is safe to say that the Eighties have so far been a curiously calm period in the struggle for abortion rights in Canada.

This withdrawal from activity is difficult to explain in light of the highly restrictive situation faced by women seeking abortions in Canada. Over the years, numerous studies, including the federal government's own Badgley committee report in 1977, have documented the inequities and bureaucratic delays inherent in the Canadian abortion law. These constraints force untold numbers of women to forego abortion altogether, to have more hazardous second-trimester abortions and to travel long distances – in some cases out of the country – to obtain abortions. In recent years the situation has been steadily worsening. Agencies report growing difficulties in finding hospital referrals for all the women seeking the procedure. Hospitals across the country have cut back on the number of abortions they perform, and some have dissolved their therapeutic abortion committees and stopped doing abortions altogether. It is now obvious that Canadian women did not win the "right" to abortion with the 1969 revisions in the Criminal Code. Accessibility to abortion has depended entirely on a liberal interpretation of the "threat to health" provision in the law, and on the vagaries of individual doctors and hospital policies.[1]

So why aren't women in Canada rising up in great numbers around the issue? For one thing, the abortion "problem" in this country is largely an invisible one. The medical, social and economic costs of our restrictive abortion law are simply not obvious to the vast majority of people. It requires a specialized knowledge to get even an elementary grasp on the labyrinthine workings of the system. In contrast to the United States, where the Hyde amendment and the rise of the New Right have thrown the abortion struggle into dramatic and highly visible relief, the situation in most of Canada is vague, much less polarized. Instead of a clearly visible threat to abortion rights, what we have is a complicated, slowly eroding situation whose impact is difficult to convey to the public. In some ways the liberalization of the law in 1969 helped to knock the wind out of the sails of the movement. It left us with a half-measure, which does not safeguard our right to abortion, but which makes abortion just accessible enough to neutralize pressure for outright repeal and to thwart efforts to mobilize women in any numbers.

As well, other issues have taken centre stage from abortion. Workplace struggles for equal pay and against sexual harassment, the fight against rape and other forms of violence against women – these are the issues that currently stir large numbers of women to action. And the personal priorities of many longtime feminists appear to be changing. While the abortion movement sits in limbo, issues related to childbirth, such as home birth and the legalization of midwifery, command enormous amounts of energy and attention. Many of us for whom abortion rights seemed so central in the struggle to gain control of our lives in the early Seventies are now part of what seems to be a minor baby boom among women over thirty. While many of us may only be *thinking* about having children, that in itself influences the amount of time and energy we commit to an issue that may have a less immediate personal importance than it once did.

These are fairly obvious reasons for the present moribund state of the abortion movement, but I want to suggest that there are other, less apparent explanations. Abortion rights is an issue that, logically, should command the support of the vast majority of women, simply because it touches so many lives in such an intimate and determining way. Rare is the woman past the age of puberty who has not had an abortion or who does not know someone who has. The need for abortions cuts across class and cultural lines that divide women from each other in many other areas. Yet despite this, and the fact that opinion polls continually tell us that a substantial majority of the population believes abortion to be justified in at least some circumstances, the movement has rarely commanded the active support of more than a core of committed, activist feminists. The vast majority of women would not dream of going into the streets carrying banners calling for "abortion on demand." Why? Why are so few of the women who support abortion rights, or who have had abortions themselves, willing to take public action to ensure that it continues to be an option for all women?

A possible explanation is that they don't really believe they are entitled to that right. Abortion gives rise to powerful feelings of ambivalence in women. These feelings hit us at the core of our female socialization, which dictates that we sacrifice ourselves for others, that we not take control of our own lives or act in our own self-interest. And because of the way abortion is dealt with in our society – carried out essentially in secret, something we confide only to those close to us – these feelings rarely find sufficient outlet. We "get it over with." The shame, guilt and grief that we feel over our abortions is in most cases never dealt with. But the feelings themselves do not disappear. In fact, they have a tremendous influence on our attitudes and our behaviour, precisely because they remain largely unconscious and unresolved. Thus many women cannot march into the streets demanding abortion rights with any degree of confidence because their basic feelings about the issue are so wracked by ambivalence. They are not convinced in their guts that abortion is "right" – often despite the fact that they've had abortions themselves.

While this aspect of the abortion process is increasingly being acknowledged and dealt with in individual abortion counselling, recognition of women's ambivalence towards abortion has not characterized public discussion of the pro-choice position. Feminists are understandably reluctant to play into the hands of the anti-abortion advocates who so skillfully manipulate those very feelings. Our fear is that, by acknowledging women's contradictory attitudes about abortion, we run the risk of fueling anti-choice arguments. "There, you see," we can hear the pro-lifers saying. "Even the feminists feel guilty about abortion. So it must be wrong."

However, it is possible that by *not* acknowledging women's mixed emotions about abortion, we are skipping over some very important steps in helping them come to terms with it, both personally and as a political issue. In our firm conviction that abortion is every woman's right, we project an image of strength and self-affirmation (which many regard as "selfishness") that is inspiring for some women, but threatening to many others. Such women either shun involvement in the issue altogether, or succumb to the appeal of the Right to Life position, with its emphasis on self-sacrifice and its apparent moral superiority in championing the rights of the ultimate underdog – the tiny, defenceless fetus. We should not misunderstand or underestimate the appeal to women's altruism that the Right to Life ideology presents. Women have always viewed themselves as truly "pro-life" and anti-violence. We are the nurturers, the protectors of the weak and helpless, the guardians of truly human values. We feel a deeply ingrained sympathy for the underdog, partly because of our socialization and partly, too, because of our own history. One Canadian anti-abortion periodical is entitled "The Uncertified Human" in reference to a nineteenth-century U.S. Supreme Court ruling that blacks were not "human." The overt analogy is of course with the status of the unborn. But women know that they too were once, and in many ways still are, "uncertified humans." Such an analogy strikes a strong chord of identification.

Right to Life ideology has a particularly powerful appeal among certain groups who are little influenced by the women's movement, such as adolescents and women in highly traditional cultures. And the Right to Life movement, much to our discomfort, is itself a "women's movement." As U.S. feminist writer Deirdre English has pointed out, while women do not control the leadership of the movement, they make up the vast majority of its volunteer, kitchen-table support network. Should we assume that such women are merely misguided, too steeped in their female socialization to act in their own self-interest? Or is there a positive aspect to their commitment with which we can find at least some common ground?

If we have to some extent surrendered the *appearance* of moral superiority to the Right to Life movement, we have also allowed them to coopt the entire discussion of the morality of abortion and frame it in stark, black-and-white terms. Feminists have largely sidestepped the question and have taken the stance that "abortion is not a moral issue but a health issue." Do we really wish to argue that abortion is the moral equivalent of a tonsillectomy? If not, then we have to start dealing with the multitude of issues it raises – issues which are "moral" in the sense that they touch on some of the core values of our collective life. Do we wish to give approval to abortion in all circumstances? What do we have to say about couples who choose abortion after learning via amniocentesis that the fetus is the "wrong" sex? Could there be negative consequences for a society in which abortion is freely and widely available, as it is in the Soviet Union? There abortion is the chief method of birth control and women have an average of six abortions in their lifetime. Is the cheapening of the value of human life a real possibility with widespread abortion, or is this just a scare tactic of the Right to Life? If we fight efforts to enshrine the "human rights" of the unborn in law, do we also run the risk of undercutting efforts to ensure the protection of the fetus against environmental and occupational hazards?

There are no ready and simple answers to these questions, and there are many others which could be asked. Raising them will lead us down some difficult paths, and we may well find ourselves acknowledging that there is some truth in the Right to Life position. For instance, some pro-lifers have sounded the alarm about the link between abortion and repressive genetic engineering policies. Their concern is not misplaced: the population control ideologues of today, who generally favour liberal abortion and birth control policies, are the direct descendants of the racist proponents of eugenics, a pseudo-science of human "breeding" prevalent in the 1920s and 1930s. One population control advocate, biologist Garrett Hardin, is also known as a prominent spokesperson for liberalized abortion laws worldwide. Where feminists part company with the Right to Life, however, is in our belief that abortion, if kept distinct from such repressive ideologies and controlled by women themselves, can be both a humane, moral alternative and a tool of human liberation. If we truly believe that, we should not shrink from acknowledging the moral dimension of abortion for fear that such a discussion leads inevitably to an anti-choice position. An honest, even painful airing of the whole dilemma will ultimately win us the confidence of a great many more women, and allow us to reclaim the moral initiative that rightfully belongs to the struggle for abortion rights.

Besides undertaking a reevaluation of some aspects of our own position, we need to take a fresh look at the anti-choice movement itself. The current tendency is to lump the Right to Life in with a mixed bag of conservative, anti-feminist, anti-gay and "pro-family" groups popularly referred to as the New Right. This is by and large an accurate reflection of the political orientation of the movement. In early 1981, for example, various pro-life groups co-sponsored a national conference on the constitution with the actively anti-homosexual Renaissance International and a variety of other "pro-family" and fundamentalist Christian groups. Nevertheless, it is worth examining whether the anti-choice movement is as monolithic and unanimous in its outlook as we presume it to be.

One problem with our perspective is that it has not been based on an analysis of the Canadian situation, but has largely assumed that anti-choice forces in Canada parallel those in the U.S. Does the New Right have the same potential to gain electoral power in Canada as it has in the U.S.? Even there, Ronald Reagan's ascendancy has not resulted in the swift outlawing of abortion that pro-life supporters had hoped for. The most militant pro-life groups are reportedly bitterly disappointed in the Reagan administration's failure to legislate on the issue.

Recent events in Canada suggest that the anti-choice movement here is not a monolith; in fact, it faces significant splits within its ranks. In 1981, for instance, the Archbishop of Toronto, Cardinal Emmett Carter, publicly broke ranks with the Campaign Life organization on the constitutional issue. Though Carter's action in no way suggests a softening of the Catholic hierarchy's stance on abortion, it does indicate a rejection of certain aspects of New Right political strategy. Part of the disagreement focused on the tactic of "targetting" political candidates who refuse to publicly embrace the pro-life position. Targetting has been a favoured and highly successful tactic of U.S. New Rightists, most notably in the 1980 congressional elections. Yet at the time of Carter's action, which was in part a repudiation of targetting, at least one other Canadian pro-life spokesperson also stated that she was opposed to targetting, saying, "There are other issues besides abortion."

All this suggests that we should start viewing the anti-choice movement more creatively than we have in the past, and examining it analytically as a movement with a left, right and centre of its own. For instance, a minority of Right to Lifers are progressive Catholics, people who have deep moral convictions against abortion but who in many other respects hold views compatible with feminists and other progressives. Many of these people are active in the Nestle boycott (to protest Nestle's massive involvement in the Third World infant formula market), for example, and are critical of population control and other forms of exploitation in the Third World. Do we want to explore whether there are any possibilities for dialogue here, or make efforts to work together on those issues we do agree on?

There is little doubt that the events of the next few years will demand a revitalized abortion rights movement in Canada. Whether the New Right manages to make the sizable electoral gains here that they have in the U.S., their influence is clearly growing and will continue to have a significant effect on access to abortion. This could mean either a continuation of the steadily eroding situation we have now, or some more dramatic turnaround of events whereby abortion once again becomes virtually illegal. While the latter is still a distinct possibility in the U.S., the failure of the Right to win acceptance for the so-called "Human Life Amendment" to the Canadian Charter of Rights and Freedoms makes the total outlawing of abortion in Canada unlikely for the time being. But the anti-choice forces still have a wide range of other avenues and tactics at their disposal – hospital board takeovers, elimination of health insurance payments for abortion, stricter interpretation of the existing law. Campaigns to win a majority of seats on hospital governing boards have had a conspicuous and disturbing degree of success in British Columbia, for instance. Without any legislative change whatsoever, abortion in Canada could still become nearly impossible to obtain.

We will also continue to see New Rightists linking abortion with their other pet targets – feminism, gay rights, day care – in an effort to raise the spectre of social chaos arising out of the destruction of the nuclear family. How are we to respond to this growing threat – "new" only in its intensity and its enormous potential appeal for a society beset by upheaval and economic insecurity?

We need new ways of posing the issues if we are to counter the New Right offensive effectively and speak to the great masses of women and men who truly support reproductive choice but are beset by reservations and emotional ambivalence about abortion. One important step in this direction has already taken hold in recent years, and that is the emphasis on the notion of "choice" itself. While the mainstream media still routinely refer to "pro-abortion" and "anti-abortion" groups, we now take pains to distinguish ourselves from that terminology because it does not accurately reflect either our position or the issue. To support a woman's right to have an abortion is not the same as being "in favour of" abortion. Indeed, though the New Right likes to depict the "liberated woman" as happy-go-lucky about abortion, using it casually as a form of birth control, we know too well just how anguished and difficult the decision to seek abortion is for most women. By the same token, to be personally opposed to abortion is not the same as to be anti-choice, that is, to take active steps to prevent *all* women from having abortions. Italian women, in fact, made this important distinction by the thousands in their refusal to follow the Pope's dictum that they vote "yes" in the 1981 national referendum to repeal Italy's liberal abortion law. Said one who voted against the referendum, "I agree with the Pope about abortion. I am against it. But I do not want to keep others from having it." This insistence on the primacy of choice is more than a mere semantic exercise. It lends badly needed clarity and rationality to a highly charged issue, and allows us to dissociate ourselves from the distorted anti-child, anti-family picture painted by the Right.

But the emphasis on choice does not in itself go far enough, and in fact runs the risk of oversimplifying the issue. More and more we are recognizing that the decision to have or not have a child at a given time is not made in a social vacuum, but is rooted in a complex of forces which includes, among other things, a woman's economic options and career goals, the availability of support services and cultural expectations of what constitutes "a real woman." For the woman who is poor, for the single mother without access to adequate day care, for the native or immigrant woman under pressure from middle-class professionals to limit her childbearing, the "choice" to have an abortion is often no choice at all.

Dealing with this reality requires a rejection of the single-issue focus which has long characterized both sides of the abortion struggle. This means ceasing to treat abortion rights in isolation from the other factors which affect our ability to control our reproductive capacity – the availability of safe, effective birth control and the economic resources to raise a family, access to day care and other support services, and the presence of attitudes and policies that encourage or discourage childbearing on the basis of race or class. In this regard we might take our cue from American feminists, who are increasingly linking abortion rights with other issues like sterilization abuse under the comprehensive banner of ''reproductive rights.'' Though sterilization abuse has not been as important an issue here in Canada, we know that many of the same repressive policies and attitudes are prevalent in our family planning programs. By making the critical connections between these different reproductive issues, feminists in the U.S. have been able to expose the moral bankruptcy of the New Right: it is ''immoral'' for the government to pay for poor women's abortions, but ''moral'' for it to force sterilization on those same poor women. Thus the reproductive rights movement has managed to win the confidence and support of many working-class and minority women who previously had kept their distance from abortion and other feminist concerns.

The term ''reproductive rights'' puts the emphasis on a woman's right to control *all* aspects of her fertility, and presumes the necessity of conditions that allow her to do so. It is not meant to replace abortion rights in any and all circumstances, but serves as the context to which abortion rights must be referred time and again. By stressing our commitment to reproductive rights rather than simply the ''right to choose'' abortion, we dissociate ourselves from population control interests both at home and on a global scale. At the same time, we acknowledge the complex social context of women's childbearing decisions, and convey our commitment to changing those social and economic conditions that limit reproductive choice.

The coming decade will be a critical period for the reproductive rights movement. Simply holding on to the gains we have made will be a difficult struggle. But we cannot stop there: we must keep fighting to expand reproductive freedom. To fight that battle we need to develop new tools, new alliances and new ways of communicating the issues.

N O T E S

1. The legal grounds for an abortion in Canada are that continuation of the patient's pregnancy "would or would be likely to endanger her life or health." A Therapeutic Abortion Committee, consisting of at least three doctors, must approve an application for abortion on this basis, and the abortion must be performed in a hospital.

F U R T H E R   R E A D I N G S

Badgley, Robin F., D.F. Caron and Marion Powell. *Report of the Committee on the Operation of the Abortion Law.* Ottawa: Supply and Services Canada, 1977.

Gordon, Linda. *Women's Body, Women's Right: A Social History of Birth Control in America.* New York: Grossman Publishers, 1976.

Mass, Bonnie. *Population Target: The Political Economy of Population Control in Latin America.* Toronto: Latin America Working Group and Women's Press, 1977.

Watters, Wendell. *Compulsory Parenthood.* Toronto: McClelland and Stewart, 1976.

Whose Body? Whose Self?

BEYOND PORNOGRAPHY

BY MYRNA KOSTASH

One of the earliest actions of feminists in Canada was to express anger at the stereotyping of women as sex objects in beauty pageants. Pornography today raises much more than the concern we had then about objectification of our bodies. Now we are asking: is pornography inherently violent or has violence been grafted onto pornography? Whatever our answer to that question, we find the use of violence against women as a male sexual turn-on a chilling reminder of the horrors and fear we carry around with us daily. Pornography is sometimes hate literature against women. And, as Myrna Kostash's article points out, it is often difficult to know who our allies are in our attempts to combat misogyny. There is the dilemma of trusting state censorship when it is a state that seldom acts in the interests of women. And we reject an alliance with prudery. This article weighs the issue of sexual and intellectual freedom on the one hand with the atrocities that are committed against women on the other.

A NNALS OF THE BOYS' CLUB. When Larry Flynt, publisher of *Hustler* magazine, was convicted a few years ago of obscenity charges in the United States, several luminaries of the arts world, including novelist Gore Vidal and filmmaker Woody Allen, came to his defence. They called him an "American dissident," a designation which made their association of his tribulation with that of the Soviet dissidents, Andrei Sakharov and Alexander Solzhenitsyn, irresistible. "Look," they were saying, liberal banners unfurled, "the authoritarian Soviet state represses free thought, the puritanical American state represses sexual expression." The implication was clear: those who would defend the fastnesses of the human imagination must take a stand here, at the line where the bureaucratic thought-police decree their interests (in this case, sexual discipline) have been trespassed.

It shall be left up to the reader to judge the appropriateness of the comparison between the situation of Soviet intellectuals and an American skin-magazine publisher, but this much can be said: the possibility that a pornographer is a *victim* of society is the fruit of a mid-Sixties mentality. Which is to say of a pre-feminist mentality. For it is thanks to the feminist movement of the last decade that we are now in a position to understand that obscenity and pornography, far from being a release from the sexual repression that bedevils our culture, do in fact trade in the same coin: contempt for women and traffic in our sexuality.

Larry Flynt is no dissident. He is a pimp.

◆

Unfortunately, this perception alone resolves nothing. For women, the current debate about what does and does not represent sexual and intellectual freedom spins around a truly anguishing dilemma. On the one hand, the historical challenge (up to and including the sexual liberation skirmishes of the Sixties) to age-old taboos that govern sexual behaviour have been moments in women's ongoing struggle with the patriarchy – its family, its marketplace, its state. One has only to think of the exuberance with which the women's movement smashed the conspiratorial silence that had muffled the issues of female masturbation, female orgasm and lesbianism to understand how campaigns for the right to sexual self-expression have served us well.

When we have repudiated the received notions of "virginity" and "chastity," have denounced the sexual double standard ("Higamous, hogamous, women are monogamous; hogamous, higamous, men are polygamous"), have exposed the fallacies of "biological destiny," have censured the publicization of female masochism, we have in effect joined the struggle for the right to determine the nature and practice of our own sexuality.

In so doing, we have stood up in the same forum with those who, for instance, defended the publication of *Lady Chatterly's Lover* or *Body Politic,* or the distribution of *Pretty Baby,* or liberal amendments to the Criminal Code. This, then, is the anguish and the confusion: now *Hustler* and worse, have entered the forum, on the grounds that pornography too smashes taboos and constraints. Do we feminists contradict ourselves when we say we hate and fear it?

The dilemma is deepened by the compelling arguments of civil libertarians that the "freedom to read," and indeed the "freedom of the imagination," are in the public interest, even when these freedoms are employed to produce or consume pornography. This is all the more cogent when the freedom to read comes under attack, as in the case of Ontario school boards' banning of Margaret Laurence's *The Diviners* from school bookshelves; and the freedom to publish, as in parliamentary denunciations of the Canada Council's funding of publishers of "pornographic" poetry, "offensive to anyone with even a shred of decency," an idiotic allusion to Talonbooks and the work of poet bill bissett.[1] And when a small-town Ontario newspaper complains that such writers' "offerings are nothing more than a succession of gutter language, usually not even in sentence structure,"[2] we see how perilously close the attack on the allegedly pornographic comes to an attack on the artistic avant-garde as a whole.

Well, we say, *we* know what we mean by "pornography" and it isn't bill bissett; fair enough, but we are not in control of the public definition. *They* are, the MPs, the police, the judges – and feminists, as well as civil libertarians, have every right to fear that *their* definition casts a wide net indeed: shall we see public burnings of *Our Bodies, Our Selves?*

No, say the civil libertarians, not if we insist that the freedom to read and to publish is absolute and indivisible. Feminists cannot have it both ways – the restrictions on the distribution of "snuff" films, for instance, but the lifting of restrictions on, say, the Official Secrets Act.

On the other hand, of course, are the demands of the women's liberation movement. Reproductive freedoms: access to safe abortion and birth control and the right to give birth without trauma and insult. Freedom from rape and sexual abuse. Lesbian rights. Day care. Maternity rights, and so on. All those instances of the decolonization of our bodies.

How can we take these up and *not* hate and fear pornography?

Pornography: "the representation of sexual images, often including ridicule and violence, which degrades human beings for the purpose of entertaining or selling products."[3] The definition must be atttempted, just as the definition of other modes of oppression and exploitation – racism, sexism, imperialism – have been risked and from that have entered our political lexicon. Else we risk wallowing in the subjectivities of perception, ambivalence and other temptations of liberalism ("Obscenity is in the eye of the beholder"), as though pornography does not take place out there in society, in social transactions between men and women. Pornography: from the Greek "to write about prostitution." At its root, then, the mercantile notion of the (usually) female body as a commodity. The territory of a commercial transaction. Pornography: a graphic metaphor for sex as the power that one (male) person wields over the destiny of another and the hostility that such an imbalance of power provokes.

What are its elements? Sadomasochism: the woman's body is subjected to various bondages, abuses, humiliations, from which she is often seen to extract her own pleasure. Misogyny: contempt for the female and her chastizement. Fascism: the male "lover" is frequently costumed as a militaristic superman, triumphing over the female subhuman, particularly where she is non-Aryan. Phallocentrism: the pornographic scenario is organized, overwhelmingly, around the penis and its ejaculation. Voyeurism: the deployment of the woman's body so as to excite the viewer.

What is its message? That sexual violence is pleasurable to men and that women desire or at least expect this violence. That women are "bad," their femaleness ridiculous, even foul, their submission appropriate. That male sexual (and political) satisfaction requires the diminution of female energy.

The images. The female torso disappears into a meat grinder. The woman, bound and gagged, splayed across the bed. The concubine, trussed up like a chicken, and raped. The girl-child, receiving foamy "come" on her eyelids and cheeks.

Enough.

Now begins the hard part. Must not our definition – images of ridicule and violence – also include the ostensibly artistic, the "art" photography of a Les Krims (a breast, cut off, is stuck to a table and dribbles blood) or the "arresting" acrylics of a James Spenser (a woman in black lace panties, her languid nudity an advertisement for her availability and for the flesh's uselessness, her body long since deprived of animation)? Must not our definition – for the purpose of entertainment or selling products – include almost the whole of popular culture and mass advertising in which the fragments of the female body are made to represent the desirability of a given product for consumption or for sale? Must not our definition – that which degrades the human being – now also include all those representations of coercion in which one person loses power to another's (aggressive) will, images which are pervasive in a male supremacist culture, which is to say are present in the merely sexist and in the pleasurably erotic?[4]

The definition, it turns out – but has anybody another that is more useful? – includes just about the whole of the iconography of everyday heterosexual life. The question becomes: what is *not* pornographic?

The answer to that lies in the realms of the utopian, or at best in the purely intimate or in the pockets of feminist subculture. For the nonpornographic, or the erotic, is about our, women's, vision of the sexually *possible*. In the best of possible worlds how would we represent sex? (What would art look like? Publicity? Movies?) With tenderness, affection, respect, with humour, playfulness. We would take delight in the sensuous detail, we would caress, we would be open psychically to the "lunar," to that part of our nervous system which is intuitional, which apprehends patterns, which is artistic. The "erotica" which corresponds to this ideal would represent freely chosen sexual behaviour in which the partners would serve each other's (and Eros's!) pleasure equally and in which the "I love you" is made flesh. How does it go? "With this body I thee honour. . ."

Feminist descriptions of the non-pornographic are necessarily as vague, evasive, dreamy as this for we have only recently allowed ourselves the luxury of contemplating sexual happiness, as opposed to the sexual terror of our environment. It is not easily done. Everywhere we turn we see our need for "romance" distorted as the ostensibly "erotic," which is in fact a thinly-veiled invitation to further violence. I'm thinking of the movies in which "provocative" women are murdered; blue jeans ads in which young girls are offered up to adult men; fashion layouts in which the limbs of the models are bruised in the jaws of snarling dogs. This is the so-called "pretty porn," the means by which the pornographic fantasy, heretofore closeted in hard-core literature and imagery, acquires access to the broad public. "Pretty porn" softens us up, as it were; it creates a tolerance for the explicitly sadistic and, like a callous, dulls our nerve endings so that we are no longer repelled. The image has become normal. Full frontal female nudity – this used to be considered porn – is now a standard of the Hollywood film and *Playboy;* the horse we flogged in the early Seventies now seems positively pastoral compared to the stuff in cellophane wrappers. For women, such de-sensitization is grotesque: we have somehow to make our way through the city *as though* pornography had nothing to do with us. For to acknowledge that it does is to let in the nightmare: "to be unknown, and hated," as Susan Griffin writes.[5]

But let it in we must, for to know the nature of the beast is the end of illusion and the beginnings of politics. Consider: *Hustler* magazine has seven million readers a month; six of ten bestselling monthlies are "men's entertainment" magazines; there are 260 different periodicals available in the United States devoted to child porn; pornography, in short, is a $4 billion industry.[6] Is this a problem for women? It is true that, even in Canada, rape is increasingly accompanied by sexual sadism and mutilation. Now where do rapists get their ideas? While current research on the relationship between pornography and aggression is far from conclusive, one way or the other, we do know that more than 50 studies involving 10,000 children have demonstrated over the years a consistent relationship between the amount of television violence consumed by the child and her/his level of aggression.[7] We have it from

Drs. Neil Malamuth and James Check at the University of Manitoba that, when "effects of pornographic violence were assessed in responses to a lengthy questionnaire the findings indicated that heightened aggressiveness persists for at least a week."[8]

Of course, as it has been said, women do not need the "proof" of laboratory research to know that the pervasiveness of the pornographic image is a threat to our well-being. In the image is an education: by it, men and women alike are instructed in the power men have over women, a power which extends along the whole desperate continuum of male privilege, from conjugal rights to pimping, from sexual harassment to rape-murder. By it women themselves are blamed for what has happened to them: we are venal, we are stupid, we are uppity, we deserve what we get.

The *political* content of these representations of sexuality – that male authority is normal and can only be challenged at enormous risk – is obscured by the fact that, in our culture, relations of dominance and submission between men and women are seen as *sexy*. Power is an eroticized event, masked as titillation. Which is to say it is experienced as something intimate, domestic, personal. We literally don't see it. Two men are grappling on the floor, fingers at the throat, teeth biting into flesh: they are fighting. A man and a woman are grappling on the floor, teeth bared and her clothing ripped: they are making love.

◆

Having come this far in our disillusionment, our work is cut out for us. Some feminist groups, organized explicitly to challenge the *consensus* that the pervasiveness of porn represents, have taken the beast by the horns. In San Francisco, Women Against Violence in Pornorgraphy and the Media (WAVPM) have picketed shops selling *Hustler,* have conducted tours for women through the Tenderloin, the porn district (no more averting our eyes from the scenarios of our humiliation), have put together a consciousness-raising slideshow and guided women through the "speaking bitterness" sessions which follow. In Toronto, Women Against Violence Against Women (WAVAW) demonstrated at Metro and City executive committee meetings to demand that the film *Snuff*[9] be banned. Twenty men and women invaded the cinema, smashed the projector and staged a sit-in until five of their number were arrested. And all over North America similar groups have demonstrated to "take back the night" from the merchants of sexual ghoulishness, repeatedly making the connection between porn and all other violence done women – rape, battery, forced sterilization, back-alley abortions – that cements the foundations of our social structures.

Such campaigns immediately raise the hackles of those to whom the issue of pornography is one not of sexual politics (who has the power to do what to whom) but of society's right to uncensored opinion. Briefly, they argue that "the realm of the imagination should not be subject to government control"[10] and that one must always be careful to draw the line between "personal" rights (we do have the right to freedom from physical attack, say) and "intellectual" rights (we all have the right to say aloud what we think without fear of reprisal). Even those who are as nauseated as any WAVAW member by pornography point out that men do not rape just because they see pictures, for the pictures are simply "metaphors" for what is already taking place in society. Besides, as long as women have little political power *qua* women, the demand for censorship of pornographic materials reproduces our powerlessness: somebody else, not us, will be the censors. In any event, as Alberta's attorney general put it to the Alberta Status of Women, ". . .it is impossible to pass a law or laws governing every imaginable human activity. Laws unfortunately do not prevent all undesirable activity, but merely make them illegal."

In reply, feminists have argued that the claim that pornography exists solely in the realms of the imagination or of self-expression is specious: it is an extensively public phenomenon, an *event* in the social situation of the sexes. Certainly the Nazis understood this when, having occupied Poland, they flooded the bookstalls with porn to demoralize the population. And certain disenchanted Scandinavians understand it when, for all the availability of "liberating" porn, they still refer to themselves as "sexual invalids" and admit that from 1960 to 1978 rape was up 60 percent.[11]

Feminists have further argued that the right to "free speech" in practice extends only to those who have the money to buy it: the publishers, the producers, the politicians, the consumers. Those without money, women's groups for instance, must resort to other practices – leafleting, picketing, rallying, marching – which are, of course, denounced by liberals as "interferences" in the freedom of speech. Feminists ask: *whose* freedom?

All kinds of limitations already exist on "freedom of speech": laws relating to libel, slander, perjury, copyright, advertising, incitement. We accept them; we acknowledge that this freedom is not absolute. Therefore, the "right" to produce and consume pornography must be curtailed if our *women's* right to freedom from slander and injury is to be respected.[12]

In any event, it comes down to this: the women's liberation movement, like all collectivist appeals to social transformation, is impatient with the claims of civil libertarians. It seeks not mere individual rights but social justice.

Justice must be seen to be done. It is within the *realpolitik* of the streetwise women's movement that each woman activist make her own decision about what she is prepared to do to smash the gloomy tyranny of porn. Already the agenda is drawn up. Consumer campaigns, public education, vigilante squads, agit-prop (protests that provoke public debate). Feminist-informed research (to establish once and for all the connection between pornography and behaviour). Agitation for changes in the law relating to obscenity, as in "a law based on new standards which would entrench the physical and sexual autonomy of women and children within the law"[13] (although it is debatable how that which is not true in society – the sexual autonomy of women and children – can be guaranteed by law).

Feminists must also refine their arguments with their critics. There remains the longstanding liberal defence of pornography as an "isolated act," harmlessly "indulged in" by individuals free to choose their own "lifestyle." Feminists say: we want to live in an order where what we do and think has consequence. Leftists, ostensibly pro-feminist, have defended pornography on the various grounds that it is a "revolutionary aesthetic" (in which case it is the social protest of an idiot), that it is the "erotica" of the working class (in fact, pornography is a capitalist success story and is consumed overwhelmingly by middle-class men), that *Penthouse,* say, is anti-establishment (in fact, the fantasies purveyed by skin magazines *replicate* the deadening relations of the family place, the workplace, the marketplace). Rightists, lining up to burn skin magazines and smash rock records, are, however, on a moral crusade against sexual explicitness and are no friends of women. Against the feminist demand for women's right to sexual self-determination, the Right poses the stability of the patriarchal family, the iniquity of homosexuality and the sanctity of the chaste. We have been through that scenario before.

Through such refinements, women in the anti-porn movement may even come to a vision of what is possible beyond pornography. Pornography celebrates the atomization and irresponsibility of the person in the pretence that what one does as a sexual being has nothing to do with anything else, neither with the sexual partner nor with society. Beyond this morbidity, the gentle, laughing, administering embrace of sensual camaraderie presents itself: the longed-for alternative to the social tyrannies of passivity and mechanization. Beyond pornography lies the *polis,* the political space of the aggrieved in which we may finally overwhelm those forces that would circumscribe our vigour and our compassion.

◆

At the University of California in Berkeley I am sitting in a journalism class. The instructor, writer Valerie Miner, has invited a representative from WAVPM to present the "consciousness-raising" slideshow on pornography. We watch it in disbelieving silence. Then the class is split up – the male students are invited to discuss the presentation in a separate room.

The women talk. So *that's* pornography. I've never really looked. Do men *really* want it? You know, it isn't just weirdos buying this stuff, it's our brothers and boyfriends (six, ten, fifteen million a month!), they're harbouring these fantasies, it's like a, well, barrier between us, isn't it? Do we have to accept it? How do we teach our men that this stuff hurts us without alienating them? Wait a minute, there's a "porn" for women too: all those romances of the super-feminine heroine overpowered by the dark, passionate lover. Remember *Wuthering Heights*? (Giggles)

I am thinking: my God, women have to be *taught* to like and live with men; our first, instinctual feeling toward them is fear.

Fear. The discussion takes an interesting turn. Away from the pornographic images we have just seen to anecdotes about fear. One story after another. Of being followed. Of obscene phone calls. Of being afraid to live alone, to go out at night, to answer the doorbell. "Women are such scairdy cats," the women say, "why are we so dumb, so afraid all the time?" And then more stories.

Fear. Suddenly all the intellectual and political anguish provoked by the threat of pornography has dissolved into one simple perception. Pornography is about women being afraid. While there is pornography, we are not safe. It is not a question of learning to "live with it": we are dying with it.

N   O   T   E   S

1. Quoted in *ACP Notebook,* No. 13 (July 1978), p. 2.
2. Ibid, p. 8.
3. Valerie Miner, "Fantasies and Nightmares: The Red-Blooded Mass Media," unpublished paper, p. 3.
4. I am aware that almost all disccussion on the issue of pornography concerns itself only with the photographic image, as though we accept the written word and the painting as "self-expression" but the unmediated image – the ultra-realistic depiction of gross materiality, not form – as dangerous and offensive. The photograph seems to reproduce reality and erases the distinction between fantasy and what is actually possible. Since this is true of any photograph, the next question is: is *any* photographic representation of women in a male supremacist culture *ipso facto* sexist and exploitative? Two British writers pursue this. "Pornography is a site for the struggle over the representations of women. . . . Is it more acceptable to view the image of a woman at work than a nude playmate? Why?" (Mary Bos and Jill Pack, "Porn, Law and Politics," *Camerawork* No. 18). Perhaps because work, for all its exploitation of the worker's labour power, does not *as an image* deny the dignity of the worker. The image of the female, however, has carried the burden of meaning of everything from original sin to commodity fetishism. The image of the female connotes venality.

5. Susan Griffin, *Rape: The Power of Consciousness* (New York: Harper and Row, 1979), p. 51.

6. The figures are American. No Canadian ones are available.

7. Miner, op. cit., p. 11.

8. *New York Times,* September 30, 1980.

9. The film purports to show the actual mutilation and death of an actress.

10. The Writers' Union of Canada, "Obscenity Brief" (in respect to Bill C-51), January 1970.

11. Cited in "Fallout from the Sexual Revolution," *Maclean's,* 1981.

12. It is worth noting, however, that in the eleven years since the enactment of the Hate Propaganda Act (governing the "irrational and malicious abuse of certain identifiable minority groups" or an attack on such groups in "abusive, insulting, scurrilous and false terms") there have been only two charges laid under it. The first was against people distributing "Yankee Go Home" leaflets at a Shriners' Parade in Toronto.The second was against two men distributing anti-French Canadian handbills. In the latter case an appeal resulted in an acquittal. Cited in "Group Defamation in Canada," Jeanne Hutson, *Carlton Journalism Review,* Winter 1980.

13. Debra Lewis, *Kinesis,* April-May, 1979.

F U R T H E R   R E A D I N G S

BOOKS

Dworkin, Andrea. *Pornography: Men Possessing Women.* Don Mills, Ont.: Academic Press, 1981.

Griffin, Susan. *Pornography and Silence.* New York: Harper and Row, 1981.

Lederer, Laura, ed. *Take Back the Night – Women on Pornography.* New York: Bantam, 1982.

JOURNALS

Calgary Women's Newspaper, April/May 1980.

Canadian Forum, March 1980.

Kinesis, April/May 1979.

Home Sweet Home?

BY SUSAN G. COLE

An individual woman who is being battered needs to know she is not alone. All of us need to know the pervasiveness of "intimate" violence that is part of many women's lives. Along with rape, violent pornography and sexual harassment, "wife" battering forms the web that keeps us in our place. Ideology and sex roles reinforce the built-in economic dependency of women and children on a man's wage. Women's socialization and the sanctification of the family make it difficult for women to seek escape from violent domestic situations. Although hostel and shelter space is scarce, Susan Cole finds hope for change in the educational work that is being done by feminists. This education goes on among workers in the legal system, among social workers in the traditional social agencies and, most importantly, among young students in the classrooms. But, she points out that in the long run, change means the elimination of sex roles and the transformation of the family; it means alternative and economically non-dependent domestic situations for us all.

I F WE TAKE the avid advertiser at his word, the home is a happy haven, a place where all that has to be toughed out is a little ring around the collar. Right-wingers, particularly of late, have hammered away at the old line. They insist that the nuclear family is the last hope for keeping us all civilized, the institution that is guaranteed to keep male carnality under control.

It isn't working that way though, and evidently, male brutality is not so easily contained. Within the family, within this much-touted paradise, one out of every ten women is staggering. She is nursing broken bones and tending the bruises that are the result of assault at the hand of her husband or live-in partner. No fact smashes the myth of the happy family more than the one that estimates that 24,000 women in Canada are battered wives.

The extent of the damage goes beyond the use of profanity or the occasional slap of the hand. It means cracked ribs, concussions and miscarriages, the result of being kicked in the belly while pregnant. Over ten percent of the homicide victims in Canada are women murdered by their husbands. The facts tell us that the words ''home, sweet home'' are the fabrication either of a deluded fabulist or a skilled propagandist.

Two years ago, Margaret Campbell, then MPP for the district of St. George in Ontario, delivered this nasty truth to her colleagues in the Legislature. She was particularly interested in taking Attorney General of Ontario, Roy McMurtry, to task. Why were there no more women's shelters? Why were police refusing to lay assault charges on spouses who were beating their wives? Why did it all keep going on?

Mr. McMurtry, at the time a crusader preoccupied with laying assault charges on hockey players who couldn't keep their sticks down, hadn't thought a good deal about wife assault. He had known that the subject would come up on the floor and yet he sputtered and groped for words. Then, out of his mouth (and chronicled by the legislative record), came the ingenuous confession:

> People become so frustrated and disturbed with their lot in life, that they will lash out at society in general, and, for some peculiar reasons better understood by psychiatrists and psychologists than by lawyers, they tend often to use people of whom they should again be most protective as the most convenient target.

Lawmakers, especially those who stand for election, are inclined to mince words. Campbell's question concerned the assault of women at the hands of men and yet McMurtry insists on talking about the assailants as "people." He wonders why these "people" go after the most vulnerable targets. Women, after all, belong on the pedestal, not on the other end of someone's fists.

And so the attorney general would like to know why men beat their wives. Psychologists and psychiatrists, in spite of the confidence he's given them, have not discovered the reasons. It's been left to women – feminists, mostly – to grapple with the question. As it turns out, the answer is not "peculiar" at all, but rather is devastatingly simple. Men beat their wives because they are permitted to do so. And although, technically speaking, wife assault is no longer legal, there is enough strong cultural reinforcement of it to ensure that the assault will continue.

Every time a psychologist or a social worker tells a woman that she should be less "dominating" and try not to provoke the beatings, the counsellor places the blame on the victim and gives her husband an excuse for battering away. The victim is accused of having violated sex-role stereotypes and the husband is given carte blanche to punish her for her crime. The social working establishment's commitment to the preservation of the nuclear family has made it possible for the family to become a convenient arena for men to exercise total power.

Every time a wife batterer consumes pornographic material, an estimated 50 percent of which depicts women as the willing victims of violence, he is given reinforcement, cultural permission for the assault. He is reminded that women are objects to be seen and not heard, voiceless receptacles for his sexual pleasure or for release of his own violent tension. Pornography, as it plays its role as propaganda for male domination, tells the wife beater that his actions are appropriate, sometimes even to be celebrated.

Every time a police officer refuses to interfere in a domestic quarrel ("domestic" is another term badly misused: "domestic violence," for example, is a gloss for wife battery), he gives permission to the assailant to continue the attack. This refusal by the police to get involved has been an ongoing travesty of law enforcement. At worst, male officers, otherwise quite comfortable with breaking down the doors of private houses, suddenly become protective of the family's privacy when the crime is wife assault. At best, the police agree to walk the assailant around the block to cool him off. Seldom do the police press assault charges and then only when they have witnessed the attack.

A February ruling by the Supreme Court of Canada has made it impossible for the victims of wife assault to secure restraining orders from family court judges. Now they must go right to the Supreme Court in order to get protection in their homes from violent husbands. The cost and length of time required to secure the orders have escalated to the point that women are waiting weeks and spending much more money than previously on legal advice in order to secure protection.

The courts have betrayed women in other ways, for example, in many cases, by not letting an assault charge stick. Every assault charge finally pressed that does not result in conviction gives more permission to the wife batterer to carry on as he has. As the police and the courts continue to be lenient, the wife beater is convinced that the home is truly his castle and that no one, not even the uniformed cop or the robed judge, will brook his authority.

But let the McMurtrys of the world ask their naive questions. Those of us who are aware of the power of sexism and the prerogative given in a sexist society to brute force and male privilege know full well why men beat their wives and get away with it. As long as the media deliver their barrage of images of women as objects, as long as failure to comply with strict sex-role stereotypes is deemed a punishable offence and men are allowed to minister the punishment, as long as the police want to steer clear, as long as sexism is alive and well in our society, men will continue to beat their wives.

What we can't understand is why a battered woman would stay in her situation for more. In fact, she doesn't go back for more. Saying so assumes that *she* is giving permission to men to assault her. This is the single most important assumption to dispel.

The popular myth has it that the typical battered woman has a masochistic pathology, that she is a strange and different freak.

Actually, *she* isn't an anomaly at all. She is isolated in the home, usually with children, always with the desperate wish that her marriage work. Invariably she is imbued with any number of romantic notions, that love conquers all, for example, and that the best way to make the conquest is within the framework of traditional sex roles.

The first assault is likely to be verbal and will take her totally by surprise. The attacks will escalate in ferocity – from a slap, to a slam, to a pummel.

She has absorbed the myths of the family well, even if her own experience belies these myths. One out of four battered women experienced violence as a child. Far from being convinced that family life is lacking, she assumes that violence is a part of the family package deal. Marriage is her only lot in life, or so she thinks. If cuts and bruises go with it, so be it. And the scrapes and broken bones aren't so bad, especially when compared with the tenderness she receives after the attack. Wife batterers tend to do that, to be achingly kind and, apparently, sincerely contrite after the worst is over. These men don't exist in their wives' eyes as animals. They are fathers, lovers, friends. The violent side of them is perceived by the battered as the sad exception, something that can change and get better even though the attacks inevitably grow more intense with each incident.

Since the propaganda from media, from every institution, including the church, relentlessly preaches the virtues of family life, a woman whose life in the home is a violent nightmare believes that *she must be doing something wrong.* Is the food too well cooked? Is the table too dusty? Am I giving enough? Do I *love* him enough?

Even if she is able to place the blame somewhere else, she is convinced that the problem is her own. She is alone. She would be shocked to discover that her life is not atypical at all, that there are thousands of others going through the same turmoil, that her experience is a graphic reflection of the sexism every woman confronts.

She may get an inkling that she needs help and will go to a social worker. He or she might chide her for complaining about a perfectly normal situation and she will feel foolish. Sometimes she never gets the urge to seek help again. A variety of incidents may trigger the radical action of leaving home. Often the choice to leave occurs to her only when she's been hospitalized after an attack. Sometimes she thinks to flee only when her husband threatens her children.

Having understood the how's and why's of the battered woman's experience it is of monumental importance, politically especially, to know that this woman could come from any income bracket. She is as likely to be the wife of a professional architect as she is to be the spouse of a manual worker or of someone unemployed. Wife battery as a phenomenon crosses class lines and compels us to view women as a "class" dominated by specific social forces and restraints.

Chances are, for example, the wife of the upwardly mobile executive will have an encounter with a psychiatrist similar to the one the working-class woman has with a social worker. No matter the family income, the victim of wife assault shies away from relatives and friends who must not know what she believes to be true – that she is a failure.

Regardless of economic class background, the battered woman is usually dependent on her husband for funds and has no personal income to dispense. If the wealthier woman has access to a credit card, she may go to a hotel, but only for temporary shelter. For the most part, up until ten years ago, if a battered woman, even in spite of her intense socialization, was able to get to the point where she knew she had to get out, there was nowhere to go.

The first short-term solution to the problem of wife battery thus became shelter. The founders of Interval House in Toronto had a partial handle on the situation. They wanted to create a hostel, a place where women could come if they wanted out of a restrictive marriage or if they were in crises that forced them to move suddenly.

"It wasn't until the hostel was opened that we realized that women were running away from dangerous situations," confessed Trudy Don, now coordinator of women's shelters in Ontario. "We became aware as soon as the phone started to ring." It did not take long for the hostel to become a shelter for battered women.

Of course, a culture that permits wife battery is not likely to foster governments that will provide the means to rectify the situation. Jillian Ridington put it succinctly in her article on the transition houses started in Vancouver in 1970:

> Setting up an institution for the specific purposes of aiding battered wives implies that the problem is not only widespread but that it is a social pro-

blem rather than an individual one. It also implies. . . that women have the right to leave the men who abuse them. [1]

No wonder then that the shelter movement grew out of the non-traditional grass roots women's movement. It took clear-headed feminist thinking to devise a comprehensive analysis and a strategy to separate the government from some of its money. It helped considerably that the government in the early 1970s was given to doling out grants, part of its strategy to mollify rowdy radicals. Yet dependence on the state for funding has come back to haunt the shelter movement. Now that the state is much less generous, coordinators of shelters across the country yearn for more stable funding so they will not have to spend so much time looking for funds.

In ten years, 75 shelters have sprung up across the country, making available to battered women approximately 700 beds. Seven hundred beds for 24,000 physically abused women. The numbers speak eloquently for the desperate need for more.

Ideally, providing shelter for the battered wife is the first stage in her transition from dependent and battered to independent and secure. The shelters provide a woman with support. The workers inside describe to her the options and make the connections with welfare officers who can provide funds and a more permanent roof over the woman's head. Most important, the battered woman, once isolated, discovers that she is not alone.

"The transition house," writes Jillian Ridington, "facilitates the process of examination and reconceptualization by providing a social context in which alternative ideologies and behaviours are necessary and workable; a milieu in which women see other women acting authoritatively, behaving independently while making decisions." It sounds like the perfect environment, but it hasn't always worked out that way.

The seemingly ideal environment of the shelter can be enormously alienating for a typical victim of wife abuse. Out of her isolation she is plunged into a cooperative setting, a noisy one, with little privacy. For non-natives of Canada, the problem is exacerbated when few or none of the people inside the shelter speak her language. And while we may assume that seeing women acting authoritatively would have a salutory effect on a woman whose self-esteem is low, it can work the other way around. Many women seeking shelter have never really talked to women at all and think the exercise is useless. It's men's approval they are after.

Encouraged, and rightly so, to find economic independence, a battered wife throws herself onto a job market that is not hospitable to women and shows no signs of becoming so. In her frustration she turns to the welfare officer, who tells her that as a woman with two children she can receive $258 a month in benefits. She discovers that she cannot rent a room for less than $50 a week, which leaves her with $58 to take care of herself and her children. Suddenly the prospect of an independent life does not seem so appealing and her former situation does not seem so bad. She doesn't want to be alone. She already has a home, her own possessions and a life that she believes belongs to her.

Besides, many women come to a shelter for temporary relief only, to keep away from their husbands until the storm has passed. Yet we ask battered women to realize the necessity and desirability of making changes in their lives. Given the restrictions on staying periods in shelters, is it reasonable to expect them to make the changes in less than a month? More often than not, the battered wife does return home. The horror of her experience is underscored by the agony of the shelter worker who cannot work miracles, who can only grant the victim the right to choose and who must watch as a woman goes back home, possibly to be maimed for life. The battered woman returns three or four times before she decides that she can change her life.

◆

If the victim of wife assault has to transform before she can emerge, our whole society has to be shaken to its roots in order for wife beating to cease. In the face of it all, it is amazing that workers in the field have not thrown up their hands in despair and resignation.

But they haven't, largely because they have placed the issue in its historical context. Wife battery has been a fact of women's lives for thousands of years. A movement ten years old is unlikely to stem the tide of centuries of approval for men who beat up women.

As is the case with most feminist issues, women are working on all fronts. The short term has the priority, more so with the issue of wife assault than with some other feminist endeavours. Women's lives, after all, are literally at stake.

Shelter workers, sociologists and social workers agree that if we can't create a wholesale change in attitudes, we can at least affect the *behaviour* of people who come in contact with battered women. The campaign is being waged on two fronts specifically – within the legal system and among social workers in traditional agencies.

Roundly criticized for shrugging off domestic squabbles as incidents "outside of their jurisdiction," police have set up domestic response teams around the country, some of which combine the authority of the police with the service of social workers. Like any police initiative, the emergence of these teams should be viewed with a jaundiced eye. The motivation for the projects was the safety of police officers, not the safety of women. Police departments realized that 50 percent of their domestic calls involved wife abuse and that the lives of policemen were endangered when they were trying to drag assailants away from their victims. There are now seven teams across the country, in Restigouche, Toronto, Hamilton, London, Edmonton, Vancouver and Surrey.

Recent studies of the criminal justice system reveal that the courts and police are ambivalent about their dealings with wife abuse and accordingly have perpetuated the victim's cycle of helplessness. In London, for example, police refused to lay charges except in 4 percent of the cases they dealt with. Out of 40 cases in which women were advised to get medical treatment, only 6 charges were laid. Of 56 cases that went to court, only 23 defendants were found guilty and only 4 went to jail – all this in spite of the fact that the study showed that women were twice as likely to get assaulted again if charges were not laid.

The justice system has a long way to go, but the domestic response teams still serve three crucial functions. First, they give us a sense of what is going on out there. Toronto's domestic response team expanded into a new division and the number of reports of wife abuse tripled within a month. Police teams are helping to provide useful statistics that more accurately reflect how widespread wife battery really is.

The social workers who accompany the police explain to the victim her choices, that there is shelter, that there are people she can talk to.

The workers follow through by accompanying the woman to a shelter if that is where she wants to go or by setting up interviews with other social workers.

Finally, the policeman himself – or herself for that matter; apparently assailants become quite calm at the sight of a female officer – makes it plain to the attacker that what he is doing is against the law. To wife batterers who have flailed away with impunity in the past, this is important information. Now all that's left is for the police to put their real clout where their mouths are and actually press the charges they threaten to lay.

Practically every former victim of wife abuse has a horror story about a social worker or a psychiatrist who has blamed her for her plight. One of the vital components of a domestic violence project operating in Toronto is the education of professionals who have day-to-day dealings with battered women and who in the past, have not been able to give them meaningful assistance. Their failure has to do with the fact that social workers too have been overrun with the myths that surround the phenomenon of wife assault.

Deborah Sinclair and Susan Harris travel the country to lead workshops designed to bring the consciousness of the non-traditional shelter movement into the traditional agencies. At these workshops, Harris and Sinclair attempt to turn people's thinking around. They make it plain that because women do not like to admit that they're physically abused, the extent of the crime is greatly underestimated; that alcohol consumption doesn't cause violence against women, it excuses it; that women do not provoke the attacks but are sometimes even dragged from their beds to be beaten; that the victims of wife assault are not masochistic, but rather are resigned to their situations; that men should be made responsible for stopping their violent behaviour and that the sole responsibility of women is not to accept victim status; that the hearth is not so happy and that any social worker who encourages a woman to return to the bosom of the nuclear family and the institution of marriage may be sending a woman to her death. This last point is not rhetoric or hyperbole. Sixty percent of female homicide victims between the years 1961 and 1974 were murdered in the family context.

Harris and Sinclair are among a handful doing this kind of work and they are making huge inroads, given their small numbers.

Every shelter that has been opened in Canada over the past ten years has been filled within a week. That is not so surprising. If there were 1,000 shelters instead of just 75, they would be crammed just as quickly. The need for more shelters is painfully obvious. Women working inside are absorbed with dealing with the immediate crises of the women who come to them and it has been difficult to muster a full-scale campaign to get more government funding for transition houses.

Still, there has been a flicker of interest in government circles. The Canadian Advisory Council on the Status of Women funded a Canada-wide study of wife assault and the result is Linda MacLeod's fine overview entitled *Wife Battering in Canada.* The information in the study galvanized the research division of the federal government to produce more studies, one on service to victims of crime in Canada and another on the social service role of police in domestic crisis intervention. The danger, as usual, is that wife battery will be studied to death.

The federal Parliament, giving the impression that it had some interest in the matter, established an all-party committee that invited briefs and testimonies addressing the question of domestic violence and shelter. A total of 12 people have spoken to the committee. Three politicians, a male psychiatrist and a male legal expert, both sympathetic to the needs of abused women, are among them. Only three people working in the front lines of the shelters have made an appearance in front of the committee. There is fear that the committee will be useful only to those who want to make political hay out of the issue.

Worse still, if the issue isn't studied to death, it may be talked to death. But Trudy Don, one of the founders of Interval House in Toronto, is insisting that the front-line workers be heard. They are the ones who will cut through the verbiage. They are the ones who can state the truth succinctly – that there is simply not enough shelter for battered women, that 700 beds are not meeting the needs of 24,000 women who, if given the chance, could stagger away from their nightmare.

In May 1982, Margaret Mitchell (NDP, Vancouver) asked the House of Commons the same question Margaret Campbell demanded of Roy McMurtry in Ontario two years earlier. Why were there no more shelters? But the honourable members did not take the query seriously enough even to deliver the kinds of platitudes Ontario's Roy McMurtry had been able to muster. Instead, a ripple of laughter was heard, and from all sides of the House. No other single incident in parliamentary history so vividly conveys how firmly entrenched sexism is in Canada.

A furious response from women across the country forced an apology from the House to all Canadian women. Members of Parliament, in a fit of mortification, may move faster now than they would have had the parliamentary wheels been left to their customary slow churn.

But even if the all-party committee were to recommend to Parliament that legislation be enacted granting millions of dollars to shelters across the country, and even if Members of Parliament could stop sniggering long enough to take such action, we would only have put battered women on the mend. We will not have put an end to the beatings. Until sex roles are eliminated, until the family no longer serves as that convenient arena for male violence, until wife beating is no longer a logical extension of male domination, in other words, as long as sexism exists, the beatings will continue.

The eradication of sexism, of course, is no simple task and there is no simple blueprint for change. But two main areas have to be addressed. The first, naturally, is education, not only education within the legal system and traditional family agencies as they've been described here, but education within the classroom as well. One thing we know for certain is that men learn their privilege when they are young and women absorb the propaganda designed to keep them down at an equally early age. Unless young people are infused with a new set of values, the patterns of wife assault are bound to repeat themselves.

Second, the silence that surrounds wife battery has to be broken. The violence perpetrated against women in our culture is something that is not talked about often enough. And so, the activities of women organizing against violence against women take on a new significance. The act of political demonstration seeks to convey to the public the notion that violence is not a fantasy confined to the pages of a pornographic magazine and that women are angry about it. Of even greater import is the message this kind of high-profile political protest gives to women who are the victims of violence in the home. By emphasizing the pervasiveness of violence against women in our society, we tell women that they are not alone, that they are not the ones to blame and that they have support.

But none of us can be effective until we dispense with the baggage that clutters up our own view of the battered woman herself. The battered wife is not a testament to the frailty of women but to the power of sexism. In overestimating her ability to emerge, we underestimate the strength of patriarchy.

And that we must never do.

N O T E S

1. Jillian Ridington, "The Transition Process: A Feminist Environment as Reconstructive Milieu," *Victimology*, Vol. 2, No. 3/4.

F U R T H E R   R E A D I N G S

Kinnon, Diane. "A Report on Sexual Assault in Canada," submitted to the Advisory Council on the Status of Women, December 1982.

Lewis, Debra. "A Brief on Wife Battering with Proposals for Federal Action," Advisory Council on the Status of Women, 1982.

MacLeod, Linda. *Wife Battering in Canada: The Vicious Circle.* Advisory Council on the Status of Women. Hull, Quebec: Canadian Government Publishing Centre, 1980.

Support Services for Assaulted Women. "Wife Assault in Canada: A Fact Sheet." (P.O. Box 245, Station K, Toronto, Ontario.)

Breaking the Hold

WOMEN AGAINST RAPE

BY BARBARA JAMES

Rape, perhaps more than anything else, exemplifies the uneven power relationship between men and women. In their struggle against rape, feminists have put considerable energy into the establishment of community-based, women-run rape crisis centres and phone lines. These centres carry out the very important service to all women of providing support, information and advocacy about women's rights and the options that exist under the law. In this article, Barbara James points out the inadequacy of both current rape laws and the proposed changes to the law, which still do not address the society's sexism and women-hating. Many of the women providing rape services have begun to develop tactics that they consider more revolutionary in effecting change in our society. But the path to revolution is a controversial one. Debates continue about the extent to which help from the state in the form of the police, the courts and funding to rape crisis centres will make the streets safer for women.

S EXUAL VIOLENCE IS a logical outcome of sexism. The objectification and sex-role stereotyping that historically and currently pervade society in its media, literature, educational system and mores have created a dehumanized view of women as victims who are asking for rape and who deserve it and want it. Sexual violence has always been an isolating experience: the victim of rape has traditionally internalized the guilt imposed on her by society. This has resulted in the self-hatred, emotional breakdown, ostrasization and suicide of millions of women.

It was not until the reemergence of the feminist movement in the late Sixties and early Seventies that rape was taken up as a political issue. Sexual harassment and assault are now understood to be a mechanism of social control over all women. (See articles by Marlene Kadar and Susan Cole in this anthology.) This new feminist analysis has resulted in the beginnings of a change in the legal attitude toward sexual assault. More productively, there is an active anti-rape movement, which is one of the essential elements of women's liberation activities today.

As elsewhere, the legal system in Canada has served to reinforce stereotypes about sexual assault, both in the criminal code and through the courts. Proposals now before Parliament purport to change some of the more blatantly sexist aspects of the criminal code.

In January 1981, Bill C-53 passed first reading in the House of Commons. This bill is the result of years of study and analysis which began with the Report of the Royal Commission on the Status of Women, more than a decade ago. In 1978, Bill C-52, preliminary legislation on sexual assault, was introduced into Parliament. Also in 1978, the Law Reform Commission of Canada's *Report on Sexual Offences* was tabled. Since that time numerous women's groups and national organizations have had input into the formulation of this new legislation.

The proposed changes seem well-intentioned within the context of the law. But it is important to examine them to determine whether there is any likelihood of real improvement in the laws regarding rape. Three major areas to be considered in these proposals include the naming of offences, spousal immunity and consent.

Under the naming of offences, it is considered that ''rape'' and ''indecent assault'' are too closely linked with sexual stereotypes and moral stigma to be useful legal terms. In the new proposals, the violent nature of the offence is recognized and stressed; the old terms are replaced by "sexual assault" or, in the case of extreme violence, "aggravated sexual assault." While these changes have been made with good intent, on the advice of both women's organizations and legal reform commissions, it is uncertain whether they will have much effect. In the present criminal code, the definition of assault varies little from the definition of rape, yet unlike rape victims, victims of non-sexual assault do not have to prove lack of consent. In any case, it is unlikely that elimination of the term "rape" will change the sexism of the courts.

One of the most outrageous sections in current law is that a woman cannot charge her husband with rape, and yet can be divorced for refusing to consent. Current proposals remove this stipulation. While this is apparently a major change in the orientation of the law, unless there is a general societal change in the economically and emotionally dependent nature of many marriage relationships, most women will still be unable to take advantage of it.

The *Pappajohn* case, a controversial 1980 Supreme Court of Canada decision, committed to legal precedent the widely-held belief that women are always "asking for it" and that any attempt at self-preservation can be seen as "playing hard to get." It dealt with the question of whether an accused rapist's "honest" belief that the victim consented to the assault was grounds for acquittal. Now legislation proposes that the accused's belief not only must be "honest" but also "reasonable," that is, believable within the context of individual circumstances. This change potentially could be very valuable although, once again, the interpretation of what is "reasonable" will be left up to the same courts that produced the *Pappajohn* decision.

The vigorous demands of the women's liberation movement have attracted politicians in the area of reform of rape legislation because easy changes can be made in the law without there being any real societal improvements: men don't stop raping because the laws are changed. The law is not now and will never serve as a deterrent to men who view sex as their just desserts.

Without being excessively cynical about the possibilities for real change in the law, the fact that this legislation, in various forms, has been before Parliament since 1978 without passing into law shows the extent to which society is threatened by the slightest shift in sex role-related power systems. Members of reactionary moral majority and family protection groups have begun a campaign against the elimination of the spousal immunity clause. They view it as contributing to the decline of the family through an increase in divorce due to possible prosecution of husbands by wives.

The basic orientation of the proposed law reform is to improve methods of apprehending rapists. While some of the changes outlined will have the effect of increasing conviction rates and making trial situations more bearable for victims of sexual assault, the changes are essentially semantic. As in the past, interpretation of the law will be left up to the courts, which will continue to be controlled by conservative, sexist lawyers and judges.

The reform proposals do not consider or challenge the pervasive system of violence and power that exists in society. As feminists we cannot realistically expect from a legal system that is designed to provide protection of private property, changes that would upset the existing balance of power by eliminating an essential means of social control over women.

Police attitudes toward all levels of women's response to sexual assault continue to be a major problem. Consider the recent statement made by the police chief of Halifax in a letter to a citizen concerned about a rape in the community:

> It is not the Policy of the Department to unnecessarily cause citizens to become overly alarmed about certain crimes in their community. There are some citizens who would like to know what is happening in their community; there are just as many who do not want publicity for a variety of reasons. Here are a few: (a) causes real estate sales to drop (b) causes a poor image in the area (c) citizens become afraid to go on the streets (d) other citizens criticize those living in such an area (e) school children suffer (f) attracts other criminals.

> Police Chief Fitzgerald Fry of Halifax

Policy statements reflecting a private property priority are generally not as clearly and blatantly articulated as in Policy Chief Fry's remarks. However, his views do accurately express the position of most police departments.

Pressure from feminist organizations has resulted in some police forces going through sessions designed to change their attitudes towards victims of sexual assault. Some forces ensure that a female officer is available to women who have been assaulted. Unfortunately, however benevolent the intent, an isolated consciousness-raising session is not capable of changing ingrained sexism – one Halifax officer who had taken a course spoke of rape being a physical problem for the rapist because once he has become sexually excited, it hurts him to stop!

The police are also openly hostile to what they view as women's intrusion into their territory of law enforcement: for example, they see self-defence courses as misleading women into a false sense of power and security. Police presentations to women's groups tend to emphasize passive wariness and place the responsibility for avoiding rape on women, telling them not to exercise their rights – that is, don't walk alone at night. The fact that a majority of women are raped by men whom they are acquainted with is inadequately dealt with. In addition, large-scale public organizing against rape is not supported by the police: reclaim the night marches are viewed with suspicion and often forced onto sidewalks.

An attempt at reform on the part of the police will make a number of rape reporting and prosecution situations more tolerable for a limited number of individual women. However, feminists must be cynical of moves on the part of an organization whose aim is essentially to uphold and protect a capitalist/patriarchal system.

Currently, the various media regard the issue of sexual assault as a newsworthy one. In the past two or three years, brief items on rape have been in vogue on news and information programs, and these are often scheduled side by side with shows and movies that promote and glorify violence against women. While interviewers are either unwilling or unable to take responsibility for the inconsistent policy-making that allows such contradictory programming, it is useful to challenge them within the interview, if only to make the audience more aware of the scope of the problem.

Almost invariably, journalists direct the interview toward a pat and reformist answer to the question, "What will satisfy you women?" – the response they expect being, "a rape crisis centre." Clearly, the answer, ''an end to rape and all violence against women,'' requires a complex discussion that will not fit within the minutes allocated to the issue.

Women's groups, having been burned and/or ignored by the media, have tended to view this interest on behalf of liberal editors and program directors with cynicism. Feminists have come to fear the manipulation and misrepresentation of these important problems by media that view abuse of women as a catchy story instead of a political issue of vital importance. However, if our aim is to change society's view of violence against women, we must learn to take advantage of even this occasional access to a mass audience. We must develop the skills to get across a non-distorted message and not be intimidated by the aura of the media and aggressive interview techniques. A little well-planned opportunism can be very helpful in getting our message across.

A recent development is the formation of groups of men against violence against women. While this movement is far from widespread, it has a potential for becoming a valuable political force. There has always been a great deal of controversy over what action men can take in support of women's struggles against sexual violence, and this is especially true now of the question of men's role in reclaim the night demonstrations. Debates rage about whether the exclusion of men from the public marches alienates more women than it attracts. These debates have often disintegrated into extremely divisive personal battles that subvert energy away from the issue of how to stop rape. The formation of men's groups can help to remove some of this pressure and provide an outlet for well-meaning, concerned men, but men must develop a self-motivated organization that is willing to take a political stance without diverting attention from women's organizing.

The most exciting and constructive rape relief work is being carried out through the varied activities of a wide range of feminist organizations. During the Seventies, the main focus of activity was obtaining state funding for service-oriented rape crisis centres. It was only after years of work that federal and provincial recognition became concrete and a number of centres were established across the country. The Canadian Association of Sexual Assault Centres was set up to provide a formalized sense of continuity and communication in a movement where individuals and groups have often been isolated. The association's newsletter and wide use of its film, *This Film is About Rape* have gone a long way in uniting the movement.

Generally centres that were set up with government money had at least one paid coordinator working with unpaid volunteers. In following this state-sanctioned model, centres have not always challenged traditional, hierarchical organizational structures which end up dividing women. A service orientation, in which a "professional" sexual assault counsellor advises a victim, may sometimes obscure the fact that all women suffer the violence of sexism in this society, and helps to reinforce stereotypes about "helpless victims" of rape. Especially recently, as state funding for liberal social service programs is being withdrawn and pressure from reactionary organizations is more and more vocal, sexual assault centres give support to related issues such as abortion at the risk of loss of monies. The state prefers to view rape as a current crisis that can be managed and controlled by bandaid mechanisms such as service centres and law change, rather than as a basic control over women in sexist society; therefore it does not support a more broad-based, long-term approach to the problem. While we should not ignore the tremendous amount of hard work and support that has been provided by women in rape relief centres, we must also be aware of the possibility of cooption that comes with this reliance on the state.

Although most of the groups working against sexual assault describe their long-term goal as the elimination of all violence against women, the structure and activities of many organizations cannot encompass this broad approach. Currently, especially in the more underdeveloped and chronically underfunded regions such as Quebec and the Atlantic provinces, alternatives to the state-supported model are being considered.

Alternatives rely on broad-based community education and support. One such proposal is the green light method used in parts of Britain and the United States. This approach, which is similar to Block Parents, allows women who are either in a crisis situation or wanting community support, to go to open homes, indicated by a green light. Widespread acceptance of this arrangement would encourage non-hierarchical, political treatment of the larger issue and would generate wider support for other actions, such as reclaim the night marches, protests of violent films and sit-ins at sexist pubs, restaurants and workplaces.

With the continuing decline of capitalism internationally, the current increasing levels of high unemployment, cutbacks and a general atmosphere of demoralization, we can expect to see an up- swing in the trend of generalized violence, and violence against women, in particular. Men will increasingly take out their frustrations on those who have less power within the system than they do. Women will be scapegoated for the economic problems of the world. Already as we move into the Eighties, reported statistics (which only minimally represent abuse of women), show increases in the physical and sexual abuse of women and children, growth of the pornography industry and sexual harassment on the job, as well as other forms of assault and violence. Connections must be made clearly and concretely with issues like reproductive freedom, the battering of women, pornography and cutbacks in all social services. The elimination of violence against women will not be possible in a society that dehumanizes us all. Our goals must be broad-based and revolutionary. We must aim to stop rape and all violence against women, not merely improve state mechanisms for catching rapists.

F U R T H E R   R E A D I N G

Clark, Lorenne and Debra Lewis. *Rape: The Price of Coercive Sexuality.* Toronto: Women's Press, 1977.

Once More With Feeling

HETEROSEXUALITY AND FEMINIST CONSCIOUSNESS

BY JOANNE KATES

A decade ago feminists talked about sex and sexuality (among other topics) in consciousness-raising groups. Aided by the work of Masters and Johnson on the nature of the female orgasm, we redefined our sexuality and talked of ways to more pleasurable sex. Then the communication lines went blank and CR groups became a thing of the past. In part, this happened because as women's consciousness was raised, it needed to be translated into action. And these "personal" issues didn't readily translate into political demands. Joanne Kates breaks the silence for heterosexual women. She speaks of the complexity of combining a conscious angry feminism with love for a particular man, of how sexism has damaged heterosexual relationships so that the love and hate that is woven into such relationships emerges in bed and out. While written in the first person, this article is a composite of the experience of a number of heterosexual feminists who feel that the price of their autonomy is pain and anger in their intimate relationships with men.

I suggest you walk
into my pain as into the breaking
waves of an ocean of blood, and either
we will both drown or we will
climb out together and walk away.

FROM "INTIMACY" BY MARGE PIERCY[1]

I LIVE WITH A MAN and I love him dearly. Do you know how much he enrages me, this person who struggles daily to eradicate his sexism? Do you know how much you can hate someone you love? Do you know how much I hate myself sometimes for the way I am with him? It is in our love-bed that the hatred surfaces most acutely.

We start to make love and he does some small thing that *seems* innocuous: he touches my breast. I freeze. The image that flashes on my mental screen is like a hall of mirrors, multiplying thousandfold the sight of men grabbing women's breasts. I want to forget it all when he touches me, but I've seen those mirror images too many times; I've been grabbed too many times to forget; I've been incestuously molested too many times to forget; I've had to look at pornographic images too many times to forget. Sex times are the most intimate times, the moments for being most open and vulnerable, and hence the moments when I feel most endangered by this beloved person – who has the shape, the size, the salary and the socialization of The Man.

He is not my enemy: my twin enemies, capitalism and the patriarchy, sometimes use him as their lieutenant, but this man (like other men committed to women's liberation) is struggling with all his heart, because he knows that his own liberation cannot happen without mine. As much as I've suffered from not being allowed to be powerful and independent, he has suffered from being cut off from his feelings and his vulnerability. He, too, wants to make love with an equal.

A decade of feminism has substantially changed my relationships with men. In the first place, I am free to *feel* the anger and the horror that used to be hidden under the make-up and the politeness of the nice girl who didn't want to be a ball-buster and drive men away. In the second place, I am far more powerful in those relationships than I was ten years ago. I do not live with this man because I need his money or because I will be damned as an old maid otherwise. I do not fear that he will leave me if he finds out how strong I really am, because I didn't make myself weaker in order to attract him. There was none of that crap about being afraid to beat him at tennis; in fact, this relationship is built as much on my power as it is on his – thanks to the women's liberation movement, which taught me to love my womanpower, and to quit trying to hide it.

What is a feminist relationship with a man? My lust is as powerful as his. I am as aggressive as he is, if not more so (the shrinks call this over-compensation). We keep our money separate, at my insistence, because I remember too well how our mothers and our grandmothers suffered through being financially dependent on their husbands. He does a little more than half of the cooking, the cleaning and the shopping. And we struggle for power.

I fight more with the man I love, precisely because he's the safest one to fight with. Out there in the world, fighting is dangerous. If I tell a man to fuck off when he makes a rude comment as I walk by on the street, he might beat me up. If I refuse to accept the light-hearted sexual harassment at the office, I might get fired. But at home, with my lover who is committed to feminism, it's safe to fight. He has demonstrated his rare and precious willingness to listen to my fury, and his reward for that is to get a lot of it.

So why is it then that I am ashamed of him? Why is my voice so defensive when I write and speak about my life companion? When there's a women's concert or a feminist band is playing for a dance, I don't want him to come, even though I hate to reject him. When I go to a women's meeting or a women's dinner party, I always stay late, as if to pretend to myself and the other women there that I'm not going home to a man. I call this "feminist shame" and I'm not the only heterosexual in the women's movement who suffers from it. There has been a subtle (and at times not so subtle) message in the women's movement that the only real feminists are lesbian feminists and that if we poor, misguided hets would only bite the bullet and give up the privileges we get by sucking up to Big Daddy, we'd find our true lesbian selves. The implication is that if you go home to sleep with a man you don't really love women and therefore you don't really love yourself, and therefore you're not really a feminist. A part of me buys this untruth, because I know that he and I are not composed completely of the people we want to be but also of the gender stereotyped people we were raised to be. At the moments when I buy the untruth that calls feminism and men oil and water, I take it out on him. In fact, my hostility index often reaches the boiling point when I come home after a women's evening. I think this is because we live in a misogynist culture and being in the exclusive company of women is such a relief that it's hard to make the transition back to male company. And sometimes we forget to mention what we love about our men.

Not long ago, at a women's dinner party, I plucked up my courage and told a story that illustrated some positive, indeed "feminist" qualities of the man I live with. A lesbian friend across the table laughed wryly: "Right," she said, "every heterosexual woman I know has one of those – the exceptions." Her point is that all of us heterosexual feminists *think* we've got that precious male exception salted away at home, because to realize the actual depth of our oppression would be too painful – and that crystallizes the whole issue of feminists loving men. I'm sure she's partly right; oppression is part of what I hate him for, in the interstices of our love. And I'm also sure that she's wise enough to know that the men we feminists consort with *are* the exceptions. The contradiction is that liberation and oppression exist side by side.

I often wonder why I continue to sleep with men. Why, after all, when all my friends are women, when I do my politics with women and my socializing with women, do I keep on falling for men? Part of it is training, part of it is Oedipal, part of it is habit, and part of it is that I love their trim, hard bodies. Men are Other, and as such they are fascinating creatures. It is interesting and sexually arousing to be around a person who was not raised to hide his light under a bushel, but rather to shine it on the whole landscape. Part of what I learn from men is how to do that myself.

Being around male confidence is a turn-on, literally and figuratively. We're on the highway and a tire goes. I'm scared. How do you change a tire? He knows how to do it and believes he can. I want that know-how and that confidence, and I'm getting it. It does rub off, if you try hard enough. I have learned how to change tires, hammer nails, clean fish, be the one on top, build fires, chop wood, construct arguments, yell when I'm angry, and a lot of it I have learned from the men I have loved. The ones who try to do it all for you are not worth much. They need to be reeducated, but I don't have the time, and they're not the ones I'm talking about.

So in that same bed where I feel the terror of The Man, I also have power that I couldn't have imagined a decade ago. First I have the power to say no. Having learned that we can survive without men, we are less afraid of provoking their ire or their rejection by refusing to have sex. This ability to say no changes how it is when we say yes; in fact it changes the very terms of our agreement to have sex with them. Part of this new agreement is the *idea of women's rights to sexual pleasure* – one of the victories of the women's liberation movement. We now have social permission to initiate sex, based on that idea. Ten years ago I waited for men to ask me out, waited for men to ask me to bed, waited (usually in vain) for men to pleasure me sexually. The constant passivity sent my sexual power and drive into hiding, but the women's liberation movement has let them out. I no longer wait for men; I ask men out. I ask men to bed. I ask men to pleasure me. And this active role is the basic building block of our new sexual power. Breaking out of the old passivity liberates lust. A powerful woman is a sexual woman. Our new power is the power to demand our pleasure, to say: "I want. . .", to say: "Touch me here. . .", to say: "Not like that." Those are words I never uttered ten years ago and now, in this bed of struggle, I say them often. And it is the power vested in those words that is awakening my sexuality.

Ten years ago I had an inchoate sense that the way men made love to me (it was not *with* me) was not working, but I couldn't put words to it. I knew only that the pleasure I gave myself in bed alone was more exciting than what we did together, and that even after the longest fucking sessions I was frustrated, angry and lonely. I'd been well trained that telling them what I wanted was against all the rules, so I just kept letting them do it to me, and then went home to masturbate afterwards. Ten years ago I was still waiting to "mature" (à la Papa Freud) and have my orgasms vaginally. The women's liberation movement, with excellent scientific support from Masters and Johnson and the other sexologists of the Seventies, has contested the myth of the vaginal orgasm, and the fruit of that struggle is direct clitoral stimulation.

Sex is getting to be more fun. The old way – faked orgasms and waiting for the man to finish – has gone the way of bridal showers and pre-marital virginity. But it's not all hearts, flowers and orgasms for us. I remember a lovely man who turned me down sexually. Within a month he had begun an affair with a woman who was younger, skinnier and less intellectually powerful than I. This is a story I hear from other feminists too. I know from the growing body of scared-man literature that it is a widespread phenomenon. Men were raised to derive their sexual confidence from our weakness, and even the nicest men are scared to death of powerful, demanding women. A lot of them like uppity women as colleagues and friends, but the ones they get it up for aren't as threatening. All of the men we relate to have to struggle with that, and therefore so do we. The man I love has gotten past that particular emotional block, but there are others, and whenever he slips and acts in ways that the culture has trained him to be, I get furious.

Anger is a constant companion in a feminist bed. Why? Because of the consciousness of oppression, both the shadows of the old and reality of the new. Because he has been socialized too well to drop his sexist habits just because he wants to. A feminist has two choices: she can repress that fury and fake it, like our mothers and grandmothers were forced to do, or she can let the anger roar out, time after time after time. In this bed of struggle many lovemakings are aborted this way. I am constantly furious, out loud, for hours. It is the only way for me to be a woman of honour. As Adrienne Rich says: "Lying is done with words, and also with silence."[2] I am finished lying with silence in bed and in love, and I am willing to pay the price of daily anger at the man I love.

I often get submerged by the anger and forget about the love; I often give my anger free rein and keep the softer emotions in check because I am terrified of my vulnerability – and that is not a neurotic fear, but rather the legacy of centuries of women's oppression, of our enforced vulnerability. Knowing that doesn't make the struggle smoother though, and this man I love has a lot of anger to put up with. He stands in for the archetypal Man who has oppressed women down through the ages, he stands in for all men who have ever kept women down, and it is to his immense credit that he accepts all that anger and doesn't go away. It takes really special men to accept feminist anger; but then they get something out of it too.

The other side of the coin called rage is the passion, and the free expression of the anger liberates the passion. I experience this often with my lover: something will make me (or him) angry and we will struggle for an hour or two, letting the rage fly freely. It inevitably results that after the angry feelings are vented the erotic ones surface, and we are able to make love with our whole selves. This is a victory over despair, the despair that says women and men can never work it out, that women ought to stay bound by silence because our anger is fruitless. Our struggles that end in love are struggles that thumb their noses at that despair, that say yes, we can work it out with men who really want to fight sexism. And not only that, but freeing the anger frees the passion that has been buried under politeness for so long. The other fruit of the struggle, of course, is that more of our humanity is involved in the relationship than in the bad old days. The freeing of my power and my anger and my strength gives him the support to liberate his weakness and his vulnerability and hence his feelings. We're both much more attractive with more of our whole selves showing.

Sometimes he shows me things I'd rather not see. For instance: he insists that he no longer cares whether penetration occurs as a part of loving, but sometimes I know he's lying, out of guilt, out of the self-repressive voice inside him that says: "Don't be sexist and demand penetration." Deep down we both know that try as he might to be the perfect egalitarian, he gets it up best when he's on top, and deep down we both hate that part of him. We discuss *Not a Love Story,* the controversial feminist film that depicts pornography, and he confesses unhappily that he was sexually aroused by the pornographic images. It couldn't have been the woman with a gun in her mouth or the woman in a meat grinder. Was it just the polite soft porn, the standard black garter belt stuff? I'm too scared to ask, because I don't want the answer. This person whom I love very deeply is making me sick.

I would like to tell you that he's the one with the problem, that he's still sexist, that I am the perfect feminist and therefore possessed of a perfectly liberated sexuality. But, the truth is, that I too was aroused by some of the images in *Not A Love Story* (though I sure kept it quiet at the time). A renegade part of me is stuck in the sexual past too; he's not the only one. It's a part I have being trying strenuously to disown since a decade ago when I became a feminist and decided that masochistic sexual fantasies were indications of a submissive habit that I hated.

But it's a part that wouldn't go away, no matter how hard I tried to lecture it, ignore it and analyze it. So what does a feminist do when her sexual fantasies are – to her rational self – repugnant? Like the fantasy of being sexually dominated, taken? For a number of years I have been using the mind over matter approach. (And since other heterosexual feminists don't ever mention these things, I assume that they are too – or else they're more liberated than I and they've gotten over them.) The mind over matter approach consists of gritting my teeth and refusing to give the fantasies any air space, either in my head or in the light of day. Good old repression – a technique similar to that used by the Victorians to repress people's sexuality, or the Catholics to repress "impure thoughts."

The problem with this method is that it starts to shut down one's sexuality. Fantasies (whether you act on them or not) are an important part of sexual life, and if you don't allow yourself your sexual fantasies, then your sexuality begins to fade. But surely women's liberation is not about shutting down our sexuality?

It's not easy to be a feminist and to be sexual in this culture. Because sex is so often confused with violence, with money and with power, the imagery around it is debased. The question is what to do about it. I don't mean to suggest that feminists ought to start asking their men friends to tie them down (or whatever). Rather, it's time we removed the veil of silence from this conflict.

We've been labouring under an unwritten but powerful feminist sexual code that outlaws some of the ways we "get off"; the feminist sexual catechism calls some sex (and sexual fantasies) correct and some incorrect. Being active is correct. Being passive is incorrect. Having powerful fantasies is correct. Having submissive fantasies is incorrect. But to restrict sexual behaviour to certain role prescriptions, even feminist ones, is sexually repressive. Selling out our sexuality because mainstream culture has debased female sexuality is like throwing out the baby with the bathwater.[3] We're strong enough now to take a look at this apparent conflict between Eros and feminism.

Nobody is going to push us back into being the little woman. We've gone too far for that.

N O T E S

1. Marge Piercy, "Intimacy," *The Moon is Always Female* (New York: Alfred A. Knopf, 1980), Pp. 38-39.
2. Adrienne Rich, *Women and Honor: Some Notes on Lying* (Pittsburgh: Motheroot Publications, 1977), p. 2.
3. In an interview in the May/June 1982 issue of *Fuse* magazine, Varda Burstyn said about this issue: "Heterosexual women need to feel safe from the feminist superego. The whole notion that if you like to make love on your back, in a missionary position, over 50 per cent of the time, then you aren't really a feminist has got to go – or at the very least get put on hold."

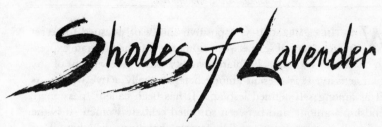

Shades of Lavender

LESBIAN SEX AND SEXUALITY

BY EVE ZAREMBA

Like all women, lesbians have been silenced about sex and sexuality. But in addition, lesbians have had to deal with the hostility, anger and fear that have been the world's responses to an increasing lesbian visibility. Until recently, lesbians themselves have sometimes had as little "appreciation" as the straight world of the variability of lesbian sexual experience. This article is written at a time when discussion articles and literature on lesbian sexuality are just beginning to be printed. Eve Zaremba looks at some of the myths of lesbian sex and particularly at the way that feminist orthodoxy has contributed to those myths.

W HETHER EMBRACED AS a positive choice or pursued in secret shame, genital sex between women is but the ultimate expression of lesbian sexuality. Lesbian sexuality exists independent of any sexual activity. It is present among heterosexually active women as well as among self-defined lesbians. It has been called "passionate friendship" among and between so-called celibate women. It is the emotional underpinning of all female bonding, whether it is acknowledged or not. Lesbian sexuality has a reality beyond all these categories and labels, and therein lies its strength and its subversive potential.

Yet its very existence is clothed in silence. Lesbian sexuality remains to this day undescribed, under-documented and misunderstood. Hunting through books or encyclopedias for information on the fascinating and forbidden subject of lesbian sexuality, especially lesbian sex, inevitably meets with little success.

Where to look? Where to start to fill an abyss of ignorance? The list of sources is not long. First there are the pop "sexperts" like Kinsey, Masters and Johnson and Hite. They mention lesbian sex tentatively and pompously, like magicians producing an unlikely animal out of a hat. More recently, we've been the subject of a few sex manuals, dedicated to answering the question "What do lesbians *do*?" Like all such how-to books about sex they are cutely mystifing when not downright boring. And "lesbianporn," aimed at men, is ever with us: it bears as much relationship to reality as any porn. Lesbian pulp novels, mostly from the 1950s and 1960s, are still around. These are period pieces that can be a turn-on but are not much use to the uninitiated. With few exceptions, lesbian pulp novels are moralistic and didactic, tending to types like alcoholic bull-dykes and sad, misguided young things who come to a bad end unless saved by "the love of a good man."

In our so-called sexually liberated times lesbian sex scenes increasingly appear in "serious" straight novels. Now that everything else has been done in print, writers – men and straight women – rush to prove that they can cope with lesbian experience without fear, favour or first-hand knowledge. Not to be outdone in creative writing, writers who are lesbians (a necessary distinction from lesbian writers) sneak in a little tasteful lesbian lovemaking among scenes of torrid heterosexual sex.

Hand in hand with the women's liberation movement a new era of lesbian writing has dawned. There are some dozen lesbian presses in the United States: they publish periodicals, novels, poetry, short stories, commentary and polemics. There are no lesbian presses in Canada. In our part of the continent Quebec produces the best, most exciting lesbian writing.

In English, lesbian writing runs the usual gamut from very good to bloody awful. As becomes a young, self-conscious literature, much of it is prone to impossible earnestness. Coming-out stories, a favoured genre, tend to naiveté (pleasant or exasperating depending on viewpoint) in matters sexual.

Hard on the heels of all this wishy-washy sex come advocates of lesbian s/m, proclaiming theirs to be the Real Thing, a claim which might carry more conviction were it combined with real erotic imagination. As it is, the sexual activities of proponents of consensual s/m (at least those who write about it) tend to copy gay male sex games, appropriating their conventions along with commercially available "gear." The vocal presence of this group of lesbians disturbs many feminists, especially by its claim to political superiority on the grounds of "sexual liberation." Nevertheless, by putting the relationship between sex, pain and fantasy on the agenda, it has been a salutary antidote to the over-sentimentalization of lesbian sex.

In whatever form or quality, lesbian literature, including the sexually explicit, is now a growth industry. Soon we can look to the day when LesLit will be discovered by critics and taken up by academics as an esoteric area of study. While it is doubtful whether such mainstream "validation" is desirable, all this activity, in bed and at typewriter, should certainly add to our understanding of female sexuality and therefore lesbian sex.

Lesbian sexuality lurks somewhere between gush and gutter, sentimentality and brutality. It is buffeted by naive expectations, influenced by male practices, pressured by politics both feminist and anti-feminist. Politicization of lesbian lives has been a mixed blessing as far as sexual expression is concerned. Politics that attempts to enforce standards of correctness in bed has a sneaky way of taking the fun out of sex, while pandering to guilt and sexual insecurity. On the other hand, those who view sex and access to sexual freedom as the sum total of progressive politics deny that life has any content outside of sex. Both kinds of politics cannot cope with ambiguity and mistrust diversity: prime prerequisites for good sex. Their views of lesbian liberation are limited indeed.

Because lesbian sex is so little understood and so little discussed even by its most avid practitioners, it is particularly vulnerable to bowdlerization and over-politicization. Baby dykes of all ages have to struggle through preconceptions, unspoken orthodoxies and sheer ignorance, in addition to their personal, everyday doubts and insecurities. I do not know what the success rate is in overcoming these obstacles, but I suspect it is quite high – and I know it is worth the trouble.

Definitions of lesbian sexuality are hard to come by. One friend, a witty, recently divorced, sexually active lesbian, found the concept of lesbian sexuality so difficult to put into words that she compared it to defining "class struggle." When pressed, she ventured the opinion that lesbian sexuality is unknown because female sexuality is an unknown, and that the modifier "lesbian" denotes a social category, not a description of sexuality as such. It would seem that for some there is only one female sexuality, regardless how and with whom it is expressed. Another friend, a life-long dyke, was convinced that I was complicating matters unnecessarily. Her definition of lesbian sexuality was a model of succinctness: "Lesbian sexuality is when women turn you on." And who can disagree? She had been conscious since adolescence that only women attracted her. For this friend and women like her there is no sexuality except the lesbian kind.

Much depends on the extent to which lesbianism is perceived as a matter of choice. The crucial distinction is between one's feelings and acts, on the one hand, and one's identity, on the other – what one does and feels versus what one *is*. This can best be understood in terms of three related concepts: *lesbian sex,* which is overt sexual activity between women, *being a lesbian* (or living as a lesbian), and finally, *lesbian sexuality,* understood as the more generalized sexual energy and attraction between women, women who may not necessarily be lesbians or have sex together.

Starting from the top with lesbian sex, it still is and always has been more prevalent than living as a lesbian. Women can be turned on by women and may have sex together without acknowledging it, without even knowing words for it. Women with female lovers can and do sometimes deny that either of them is a lesbian. Lesbian identity can be vehemently rejected. For living as a lesbian clearly involves a conscious social choice. Those who make the choice are doing more than expressing their individual preference for women as sexual partners: they are showing their personal identification with a despised social group. Certainly there is no social encouragement for living as a lesbian. The social, economic and political advantages of heterosexual identity are enormous. Lesbianism remains actively repressed everywhere. (It is the refusal to accept the social identity of lesbians that is at the root of many of the problems between straight people and their lesbian friends and relatives. The former may be quite ready to accept the "sexual preference" – who you go to bed with is your business – but will not cope with the social consequences. It is this syndrome more than any other that renders lesbians "invisible.")

However, choosing to live as a lesbian is more "possible" in some societies than in others. Only where women can be economically independent of individual men is it a real option. In spite of considerable barriers, the opportunity is available in our society, at least to some women. Only a few take the risk of leaving the security and approval of straight life to find out what lesbianism can mean for them, but more and more women are freely choosing to live as lesbians. It is absurd to suppose that women would do so unless there were some uniquely positive qualities about that way of living.

—

What are some of these qualities as they relate to lesbian sexuality and sex? First of all, there is the energy released in experiencing sex and in building a context where the male writ does not run (at least directly). The difference this liberation makes to the self-perception and sexual dynamism of women is immense. In this respect, the importance to all women and to feminism of lesbian sexual expression cannot be exaggerated. Only by exploring our own sexual potential together, without taking account of male desires, can we learn anything about our common female sexuality. As with so many other areas of life and society, human and male sexuality have been equated, and women's sexuality is viewed simply as a service to men. Perceptions of human sexuality are penis-fixated to the extent that people have difficulty accepting as genuine any sex that does not involve that organ. Females have been declared passive and incapable of sex drive independent of males. Since a penis is a necessary referent, lesbian sex is rendered inauthentic. (For the record, most lesbians have not so much as seen a dildo.) This is an important distinction between lesbians and gay men, whose sex drive and performance are not questioned, only condemned.

The notion that sex between women is unnatural and/or unreal is, of course, contradicted by the actual experience of millions. Some may find it surprising how quickly and easily women, with and without previous heterosexual experience, discover just how natural and real it is. Women are fortunate in possessing clitorises; unambiguous evidence that non-reproductive sex is "natural" – at least for women! The clitoris is unique in that it has no function other than orgasmic and pleasure-giving; neglecting it would be very, very foolish indeed. On the other hand, exclusive concentration on the clitoris can become the lesbian equivalent of the "missionary position" of heterosexual intercourse. Orthodoxy is the bugbear of sexual expression. Lesbian sexuality, like any other, grows with energy, freedom and imagination. Female sexuality, as experienced by women with women, is characterized by diversity. Lesbian lovemaking can be immensely varied and different from partner to partner, occasion to occasion, mood to mood and fantasy to fantasy.

This is not to elevate lesbian sex to any impossible level of perfection. Sex between women can be just as so-so, just as dull, unfulfilling and routine as any other. Instances of the earth moving remain uncommon. Lesbian lovemaking is not some ethereal experience, sex-sans-sweat, as some would like to believe. Lesbian sex is real and can be highly satisfying, yet it is not made in heaven by angels, but with our own bodies, here on earth.

Human beings reproduce sexually. Always have (as far as we know) and probably always will. There is no need to fear that we shall fail to propagate the species unless heterosexuality is compulsory. There is no biological or cultural imperative to mandate heterosexuality for all of us, all the time. Human sexual possibilities are too diverse, too complex to be confined within the narrow, rigid bounds of reproductive sex and institutional heterosexuality.

◆

Lesbian sexuality lies in the realm of what Adrienne Rich calls the *unspeakable:*

> Whatever is unnamed, undepicted in images, whatever is omitted from biography, censored in collections of letters, whatever is buried in memory by collapse of meaning under an inadequate or lying language – this will become, not merely unspoken but *unspeakable.* [1]

It is Rich who has put words to the unspeakable. Her concept of the "primary intensity between women" is the fullest evocation of lesbian sexuality that I can offer. As Rich affirms, it is this "intensity which in the world at large was trivialized, caricatured, or invested with evil." [2]

This hostile reaction on the part of the "world at large" is not surprising. Society correctly judges that any primary intensity between women must be contained or else the sexual status quo is jeopardized and with it, the whole system of male domination. Lesbian sexuality is dangerous to institutional heterosexuality and thus to every variety of patriarchy. It is basic and essential to women's liberation and vice versa. Its importance to the movement in Canada and elsewhere cannot be overestimated (see Amy Gottlieb's article in this book). The impact of the movement on our sexuality in all its diverse expressions has been no less profound.

The women's movement demands that we confront hitherto taboo feelings in ourselves – pre-eminently feelings towards other women, including sexual feelings. No one escapes from this issue no matter how it is approached; angrily, with fear; eagerly, with joy; or timidly, with reluctance. No matter how well resolved by each individual, the fact of lesbian attraction, the possibility of lesbian sex and the option of living as a lesbian have become palpable realities.

To accept the reality of lesbian sexuality is not synonomous with doing anything positive about it, much less becoming lesbian.

Negative ideas on lesbian sexuality and fear of lesbianism, both personal and political, persist even within the women's movement. On the other hand, there are lesbians who vehemently deny feminism and its profound impact on their lives and ideas about themselves. Nevertheless, for all lesbians, new or experienced, feminist or not, the existence of the women's movement has transformed the world.

Like ice splitting seemingly solid rock, feminist influence has created fissures within our liberal, pluralistic societies, fissures in which lesbians can find living space. The fact of a feminist movement has enormously enlarged the economic, social, personal, emotional and creative possibilities for lesbians and thus for women generally.

Yes, Virginia there have always been women loving women. But now there is an aggressive, bickering, creative, deceptive, energetic, rambunctious, raunchy, self-involved, supportive, uppity and vocal phenomenon loosely defined as the Lesbian Community. It owes its existence and growth to feminism. It draws its strength from lesbian sexuality.

N O T E S

I want to thank Maureen FitzGerald for her help with this article. However, the research and conclusions are my own.

1. Adrienne Rich, "It is the Lesbian in Us," *On Lies, Secrets and Silence: Selected Prose 1966-1978* (New York: W.W. Norton and Co., 1979), p. 199.

2. Ibid., p. 200.

F U R T H E R   R E A D I N G S

Califia, Pat. *Sapphistry: The Book of Lesbian Sexuality.* Tallahassee, Fl.: The Naiad Press, 1980.

Providing Services

THE FEMINIST WAY

BY JILLIAN RIDINGTON

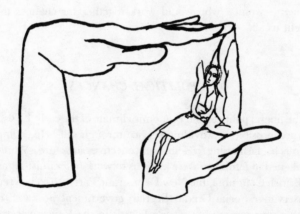

Numerous social services have been set up for women as a result of the energy and initiatives of the women's liberation movement. In them we have attempted to integrate theory and practice, the personal and the political. It isn't enough simply to provide an efficient service. We want to be feminist in structure (non-hierarchical, collective and supportive of our needs) and provide the political basis for building our movement. Most of us have found this a tall order. In this article, Jillian Ridington looks at how three Vancouver organizations have responded to the goals of providing service, feminist structure and political outreach.

T HE WOMEN'S HEALTH COLLECTIVE, Vancouver Transition House and Rape Relief, all in Vancouver, grew out of university-based "women's liberation" groups which, like similar groups throughout North America, were organized in reaction to the male-dominated student left of the late 1960s. In these groups, women began to share their experience, to understand the political implications of that experience and to realize that education gained through self-help was valid and valuable.

We started by identifying our own unmet needs; then we widened our understandings to include the unmet needs of all women. Our insights, inspired by early "new feminist" theory, were evident in the organizations we developed. They were non-hierarchical, organized as collectives. They were set up to provide self-help service, giving women the information and resources necessary for them to regain control of their bodies and their lives. They aimed to strengthen the women's movement by creating bases for communication between like-minded women – women who would work together for changes that would benefit us all.

POLITICAL CHANGES

In the liberal political and economic climate of the early 1970s, anything seemed possible – providing service through self-help, doing political outreach, fashioning a feminist collective structure. Women newly awakened to feminism were anxious to work in feminist organizations. In British Columbia, the New Democratic Party (NDP) had replaced the conservative Social Credit (Socred) government in late 1972. It was establishing community service boards in the Vancouver area, which were to become united under the Vancouver Resources Board. New social service projects were finding access to funding more easily than ever before.

By the middle of the decade, government funding began to dry up. The Socred government took power again in 1975. Funding for rape crisis centres, and for those transition houses not an integral part of the service delivery system, was jeopardized early in 1976, during the purge of services and resources initiated under the NDP. A large demonstration and a great deal of public support brought restitution of funding until early 1982, when the Coalition of B.C. Rape Crisis Centres, of which Vancouver Rape Relief is a part, lost its funding.

Funding has been a source of frustration and instability, and has profoundly affected the decisions made by these three collectives. Each year, complicated forms must be completed, support letters gathered, attacks from opponents withstood. When funds are limited, painful decisions must be made. One decision concerns the use of volunteers. Feminist principles demand the recognition of the value of the work women do. Yet the use of volunteers creates an imbalance between paid and unpaid workers that may undermine a collective structure. On the other hand, underpaying workers, or attempting to survive with too little staff, creates "burnout" and high staff turnover. It means that time for collective work, in the form of staff meetings, support and "constructive criticism" sessions, is non-existent or very limited.

Funding also affects outreach. Feminist outreach in the form of demonstrations, "speakouts" and other overt political work may bring censure from funding bodies. Conversely, stable funding may limit the staff's ability to attack institutions and work for radical social change. It may also mean that women more interested in financial security than in feminism are attracted to employment in women's organizations. Yet stable funding may enable an agency to reach women who might otherwise never know about, much less contact, women's services.

Feminists may consider "self-help" and "service" to be complementary, if not synonymous, but government agencies may disagree, recognizing service as valid only when it is professionally dispensed. Similarly, bureaucrats may refuse to recognize collective structures and insist on interacting with one authority figure, someone they can label as "responsible." Therefore insistence on feminist methods and structures may undermine a group's financial security.

CHANGES IN OURSELVES

Just as the political climate has changed, so have we. Ten years of trying to change things, of providing services on a shoestring and coming to realize that they are only bandaids, have left us frustrated and cynical. Our analysis has become more sophisticated. Now we know all too well that violence against women in all its forms – mandatory motherhood and other health-connected abuses, as well as physical assaults – is a fundamental part of our social system. We know we have only created alternatives, and not the fundamental changes we once thought possible.

There is a chasm now between the women we have become and the women who need feminist services. They come from a perspective that was once our own, but which our vision now tells us is obscured – we can no longer see the world as non-feminist women still see it. Their needs are those of our more innocent selves: support, a chance to exchange experiences with other women; information, which may lead to insights and autonomy. They must begin from their current pain and come to their own understandings.

Yet the urge to press our own politics is strong. The provision of services is political, but the politicization process is gradual. It must proceed at the pace of the women needing our support, a pace too slow to satisfy us now. Political activism at a level that fits our analysis and our need for radical and rapid change may conflict with the needs of women to whom our outreach is extended.

Each of the three collectives has come up with a different equation to balance these political and personal changes. Each has sacrificed at least one of its initial aims, or its funding, in order to preserve the goals it considers most essential.

THE HEALTH COLLECTIVE

The Health Collective has often been described within the Vancouver women's movement as "the best collective around," "the only collective that really works." It is dedicated to eliminating the mystification and hoarding of knowledge, and therefore of power. There are no formal leaders. All members have an equal right to speak for the organization and to take part in decision-making. Two factors that make absolute equality difficult within the collective are that there are both paid and unpaid workers, and that members vary greatly in the length of their membership and the depth of their knowledge. Both of these problems are connected to funding.

The Women's Health Collective began at the University of British Columbia (UBC) and was a full-fledged, functioning collective before it sought funding. Nancy Kleiber and Linda Light, who did extensive research with the collective in the mid-Seventies, saw this as a major reason why the group has effectively resisted cooption by funding agencies.[1] The collective's first funding came in 1972, under the federal Opportunities for Youth program. Federal Company of Young Canadians grants followed, continuing until 1974. These grants were separate from the organization in both geographical and supervisory terms; the funding was minimal and divided among a maximum of workers.

After three years of short-term grants, the collective received a large grant from the federal Department of Health and Welfare. Since 1976, it has received funding from the provincial Ministry of Health that enabled women who previously could not afford to work at the collective to participate. Integration of all knowledge and responsibility, and thus power and leadership, became more diffused. The differential between founding members and "intermediates" – experienced women who still felt less powerful than the founders – was lessened as the more recent workers were able to spend more time doing collective work. The worst effect of grants, according to collective members, was that the salaries occasionally attracted women whose main interest was not in feminism, but in the salary. The election of staff from volunteers already in the collective helped to alleviate this problem.

Self-help is implicit in the fundamental principle by which the Women's Health Collective operates – that women have a right to control their bodies. Kleiber and Light note the relationship of self-help to philosophy:

> Women who are knowledgeable about their bodies and their care are less easily mystified or intimidated by professionals who attempt to

monopolize information and power. Health Collective members encourage each other, and all women with whom they have contact, to take back their power from the medical establishment, by believing in their own sources of information. These sources include their own knowledge of their bodies and information shared by other women. One of the principles central to self-help is that the more that is done for people, the less they do for themselves.[2]

The Health Collective not only affords an alternative to traditional health care, it seeks to change the nature of medical practice and to educate the public "at large" about alternatives to establishment health care. Collective members do "speaks" on women's health and on the health industry. A research group gathers information on health issues affecting women and operates and facilitates skill-sharing clinics on specific topics. The collective also offers information and referrals to women wanting abortions; for women uncertain about continuing a pregnancy, the collective offers support in making a decision. This last is less clearly "self-help" than are the rest; it seems evident that the more critical the situation for which a woman seeks information or assistance, the less workable the "self-help" approach is. A woman having conflicts about a pregnancy may not be able to resolve her problem with resource materials alone. In such cases, the meaning of "self-help" must be expanded to include careful presentation of available options, combined with the empathic counselling required to enable a woman to make an informed decision.

The Health Collective admits, and is concerned about, its lack of outreach to women who may have the most desperate need for their services – women who are isolated by geography, responsibility or lack of language and cultural skills. The majority of women who come to the collective are white, middle-class and well educated. But this is less true of pregnancy counselling than it is of the collective's other services. As the right to choice becomes a more critical issue, this outreach may increase – so long as funding remains secure, and so long as the Health Collective women are able to relate to women whose cares, concerns and experience are very different from their own.

VANCOUVER TRANSITION HOUSE

In 1971 there were no transition houses in Canada. The idea for a shelter for battered women was born that year in Women's Place, an early Seventies storefront drop-in centre that developed from the first UBC women's group. The drop-in centre was to provide a shelter for women in crisis. An attic with a couple of beds, it soon showed itself to be woefully inadequate: the centre received far more calls from women battered by men, or by the system, than it could handle.

In the Women in Transition Society that was subsequently formed, emphasis was placed on the need for secure and adequate funding. The organizers recognized that wife battering was a societal problem, not an individual crisis. They were determined that the house be a 24-hour service, staffed collectively and by paid workers only. They opposed hierarchical structures and believed that the value of the work women do must be recognized – and that the recognition must come in the form of a paycheque. They rejected volunteerism, knowing that many "middle-class" women were left at the end of their marriages with nothing to show for years of family and community service. They were uncompromising; their project was expensive and they sought funding only from governments. It was not until late 1973, more than two years after the project was initiated, that the house received funding from the Children's Aid Society of Vancouver.

When the Vancouver Resources Board (VRB) took over all social services in the Vancouver area in early 1974, it resisted incorporating Vancouver Transition House. By that time, other transition houses were operating in the Fraser Valley and in Victoria, at far less cost to the government. They were run by societies on a "per diem" basis, according to the number of beds filled each day. Their grants were small and did not permit 24-hour staffing. Transition House workers insisted on secure funding, and were ultimately incorporated into the Vancouver Resources Board.

Based in very early and very personal feminist understandings, Transition House was founded at a time when feminist theory was new and feminist networks limited. In retrospect, it appears that its founding principles might have foreordained the evolution of Vancouver Transition House from a feminist outreach program to part of a service delivery system, where the idea of self-help was secondary. Little opportunity for skill-sharing or specific "on-the-job training" has ever existed in Vancouver Transition House. Such collectivist techniques as constructive criticism have never been used by Transition House workers, and the collective at its best has never functioned as well as the Health Collective.

During its time under the VRB, decisions were made by majority vote rather than by consensus. Staff meeting time was limited and heavy agendas generally precluded doing the work necessary for consensus. No concerted attempts to reduce inequalities and interpersonal conflicts were made. Yet, in the early years, it seemed the Vancouver Transition House had achieved an ideal. From its incorporation into the VRB in 1974, until early 1978, the house was operated by its staff collective, with secure funding and very little interference. However, when the Socred government replaced the NDP, it announced plans to take over the VRB and exert more control over social services. Transition House became vulnerable to loss of funding – or to cooption.

During the planning for abolition of the VRB, the new administration made an effort to push Transition House into an independent society. At the urging of the collective, feminists throughout the province wrote to the government asking them to take Transition House into the Ministry of Human Resources (MHR) system. In winning their fight to become a provincial government service, staff members may have lost their last chance to retain the Transition House as a facility based in the collective movement and in feminism.

The new regime soon made changes. Members lost their membership in the Service, Office and Retail Workers Union of Canada (SORWUC), a feminist union for which they were the first certification, and were made members of the large and male-dominated B.C. Government Employees Union (BCGEU). A "resident supervisor" was placed in charge, at a salary much higher than that of the other workers; since then, pay differentials between senior and less experienced staff have also been instituted. In effect, the government reduced the autonomy of the workers' collective.

The positive aspect of the affiliation of Transition House with the bureaucracy is that unlike Rape Relief and the Women's Health Collective, it is guaranteed referrals by workers in the social service and justice systems. Women who would never take the initiative to phone Rape Relief or go to the Women's Health Collective are brought to the Transition House by workers in many other Ministry of Human Resources offices and agencies, as well as by police. Transition House workers are therefore able to demonstrate to women who would never otherwise be in contact with women's groups that women can be knowledgeable, competent and in control of their lives, their bodies and their work. In terms of outreach to immigrant women, native women and women who have been isolated in their homes for many years, Transition House is the most successful of the three groups.

RAPE RELIEF

Rape Relief started up around the same time as the other two groups and first received funding from the provincial government in 1973, under the NDP. Since 1981, its funding comes from three provincial ministries (Health, Attorney-General and Human Resources) and is shared with three other members of the B.C. Coalition of Rape Crisis Centres. Federal funding, in a lesser amount, also comes to Rape Relief via grants given to the Canadian Coalition of Rape Crisis Centres.

Until 1980, Rape Relief workers accompanied women to court on a regular basis. In 1978-1979, one worker was employed by Rape Relief on a grant from the Law Reform Commission and was active in preparing position papers on proposed changes on rape offences. But, by April 1981, as Lee Lakeman, a long-time staff member put it, Rape Relief workers "dealt with institutions only to change them."[3]

The changes in policy at Rape Relief began with internal restructuring and resulted in new ways of dealing with external structures. In an interview in the spring of 1981, Lakeman outlined the process of change:

> There was a constant struggle within the collective about power. . .about the difference between staff and volunteers. If you were on salary you could afford to be here all the time, and therefore, you knew more, and. . .you had more ability, you were seen to be more important.[4]

Like the Health Collective when it made similar observations, the Rape Relief collective first tried electing staff. Their experience contradicts that of the Health Collective. They found that electing the staff worsened the problem. As Lakeman explained, "Now you've got the people that everyone decides are the best people on pay and having more power." To redress the imbalance, the collective broke into committees, each concerned with one major area of work, and each assigned one staff member, in an attempt to spread skills and diffuse power. In a reexamination of priorities it was found that "Most of our energy was not going to organize women, it was going to talk to professionals who were in jobs which were designed not to change society." And finally, the changes that began with analysis of the power relationships between paid and unpaid staff members culminated in the decision that *no* staff members would be paid: "Feminism is not a career. . . it is organized resistance and creation."[5]

A job-finding committee was established in early 1981. Six women took jobs in factories. They shared their paycheques with other collective members and were still considered involved on a full-time basis. This implication that providing feminist services is not real work is bound to be disagreed with by many women. However, Rape Relief's most critical decision was to start an alternate transition house, without government funding. The downpayment for the house was raised by donations, and it will be paid off and maintained on funds raised by the Rape Relief collective and its "allies." It is intended to house rape victims, battered women and victims of incest.

Convinced that it was better to choose the men they wanted to work with, than to work with male bureaucrats and lawyers, Rape Relief workers selected a group of men they knew to be supportive of their policies and asked them to help in the financing of the house. A funding committee was formed and it successfully raised a downpayment of over $50,000. The house opened its doors in October 1981.

Since 1980, Rape Relief workers have run support groups for women. Women who call the centre

> either because they have been raped or abused or because they want to help rape victims, or because they are mad and want to do something right now, are responded to in the same way. They are seen once or twice to see to their specific needs and then introduced to one of Rape Relief's Support/Education/Action groups.[6]

The fact that all women who call Rape Relief are treated in a similar way is consistent with the collective's philosophy.

We don't think of the women who come here as victims, separate from all of us being victims. We think of all women as victims of sexist violence, and that we get access, through a rape crisis centre, to women at one point at which they're victimized.[7]

This last statement is understandable, coming as it does from a woman who has worked with victims of abuse for a very long time. It may not, however, reflect the needs of women to whom rape is a very personal and critical event. The groups deal with women at "a point where they are victimized"; they should reflect the victim's needs, not the analysis of those from whom she sought support. Until 1979, Rape Relief required collective members to leave the centre after two years, to prevent "burnout." The fact that it no longer does this may be a cause, as well as an effect, of Rape Relief's new strategies – and its current problem.

Although women now state that they lost trust in Rape Relief some years ago, the "Rape Relief debate" only became "public" in late 1979, when an article by ex-Rape Relief member Ellen Baragon appeared in *Kinesis* (the newspaper published by Vancouver Status of Women). Baragon stated that Rape Relief was making "not to court" an official policy and that women were being encouraged to confront their rapist with a supporting group of women. In part, the article said:

The rape victim. . . will be given literature to read on the negative aspects of the prison system, with grim descriptions of what her attacker will face inside. . . she will be told about the unpleasantness of being a witness in a rape trial.[8]

Rape Relief confrontations have caused great controversy. Some critics point out the dangers of erroneous identification or the traumatic effect on a man's family. Other women state that it is "him or her," and that Rape Relief's work with men was making them more concerned for the offender than they were for the victim. Prosecuting rapists, on the other hand, and keeping them off the streets, benefits all women, as well as validating the victim's experience to herself and her community. Critics argue too that rapes that are "resolved" by confrontation will not be recorded, and a major problem that all women face will be seen to have gone away, although it remains prevalent.

Other criticisms followed. Among them were accusations that Rape Relief was being moralistic and doctrinaire; that it was not communicating its new policies or decisions to other feminists, that its male "allies" were influencing its "unfeminist" new policies. Critics also pointed out that Rape Relief had not consulted with Vancouver Transition House staff before developing their own plans for an alternative house. Therefore Rape Relief did not take into consideration that the needs of women who had been abused by those who shared their homes and their children, were in many ways different from those of women violated by a stranger or chance acquaintance.

The debate continued during a series of "in-movement" meetings held in the fall of 1980. The meetings were attended by large numbers of women; there was limited time for varying viewpoints to be heard and a great deal of confusion arose as to whether accountability of groups to the women's movement or the specific policies of Rape Relief were at issue. No clear resolution was made. Rape Relief refused to attend any more such meetings, although it continued to write articles delineating its position in *Kinesis.*

In early 1982, the B.C. government presented the Coalition of Rape Crisis Centres with an evaluation proposal focused on "determining the goals and services" of the centres, and assessing whether the activities specified in their contracts with the government were being performed. The proposal would have required a great deal of time on the part of both Rape Relief workers and government evaluators. Vancouver Rape Relief refused to participate in the evaluation. In January 1982, funding to all B.C. rape crisis centres was withdrawn.

Although letters of support were sent from many feminists and feminist organizations, and some rallies were held, the outrage that would have occurred had any other feminist service been cut off funding did not take place. Then, in March, a letter from the Women's Research Centre was circulated to women's groups. It stated:

the primary consideration must be rape victims' need for and right to appropriate services. . . . It is essential that a community based women's organization, with demonstrated ability to provide such services, be supported in developing a new rape crisis centre in Vancouver and in obtaining funding. . . . Such a centre should offer to rape victims the support,

accompaniment, information, and advocacy services. . . that have traditionally been recognized as critical by the women who initiated and ran
rape crisis centres across Canada.[9]

By May, a group of ex-Rape Relief workers were proposing such
an alternative service. A statement withdrawing support from Rape
Relief, signed by former workers and a total of 81 Vancouver feminists,
appeared in *Kinesis*. The new group, known as Women Against
Violence Against Women/Rape Crisis (WAVAW/RC) received funding in
mid-July 1982. Undoubtedly the issues raised in the debate are ones that
will involve Canadian feminists through our second decade.

LEARNING FROM OUR PAST

In a feminist utopia or a truly egalitarian society, there would be no
need for rape relief centres or for shelters for battered wives, and the
information now available only through women's health collectives
would be common knowledge. In the real world, all these services are
vital, and their continued existence must be a first priority for the
women's movement.

The experience of the three collectives, Rape Relief, Transition
House and Women's Health Collective, shows us that continued
existence requires compromise. The model of securely funded, self-help
services, run by feminist collectives tightly connected to the women's
movement and drawing new women into a feminist community, has
proven difficult. Compromises have been necessary. Priorities have
been reassessed, choices have been made. We can criticize those decisions; more importantly, we can learn from them.

Very early in our first decade, we discovered and celebrated the
value of women's experience, of the lessons learned from our own
lives. Collective lives are also illuminating. The lessons to be learned
from the failures and successes of these three collectives include the
importance of political awareness and communication in building a
strong women's movement and the importance of recognizing that our
experience can obscure as well as enlighten.

Our politics and our service were once entwined. But our politics
have gone beyond the ability of feminist services to encompass them.

In the conservative 1980s, it is imperative that our services be inherently political, and that a strong relationship between services and activism be maintained. Service should inform politics, and politics must inform services. But to continue to treat the two as symbiotic is to endanger both. Some women may be able to do both service and political work, choosing their arenas and contexts. But most women must choose to work on one side or the other, crossing over when their needs, or the needs of the women seeking service, impel them to.

Transition House workers now provide service only; overt political work to relieve the oppression of violated women is done by others and/or elsewhere. The Health Collective provides service and does political work, but the effect of their work on the lives of most women is limited. Rape Relief has seen political work and service as inseparable, and lost its financial support and the trust of many feminists as a result.

Our political awareness must be comprehensive. We must understand not only our own history and our own movement, but the larger political context in which we work, in order that we can foresee and assess the long-term effects of our current decisions.

N O T E S

1. Nancy Kleiber and Linda Light, *Caring for Ourselves: An Alternative Structure for Health Care* (Vancouver: University of British Columbia School of Nursing, 1980), p. 144-45.

2. Ibid.

3. Interview with Lee Lakeman, April 1981.

4. Ibid.

5. Ibid.

6. Vancouver Rape Relief, "Making It Happen," *The National Newsletter* of the Canadian Coalition of Rape Crisis Centres, March 1981, p. 51.

7. Ibid.

8. Ellen Baragon, "To Court or Not to Court," *Kinesis,* November 1979, p. 9.

9. Jan Barnsley, Letter from Women's Research Centre to the Women's Movement, March 18, 1982.

Into the Work Force

WOMEN HAVE ALWAYS WORKED. Today, our traditional job maintaining a household is for increasing numbers of women supplemented by paid work outside the home. The double day, now more than ever before, defines the content and structure of our daily lives. The kind of work we do, how it's done and the conditions under which jobs are performed influence the quality of women's existence. With so much at stake, it is no wonder that the issue of women and work has become a primary concern for feminists.

Traditions of the home and family have been a long-time target of the women's movement. Resistance to change, however, remains great. By arguing that work in the home is not necessarily just women's work, feminists undermine entrenched views of masculinity. Aprons, diapers, stoves and laundry play little part in man's image of himself. "Real" men don't wash floors, bake cakes or tend to children's needs. And today, few men suffer the burden of the double day. They accept the necessity of their wives' paid work, but in the main still refuse to share in the work at home. For feminists, the challenge is to transform the household into a shared domain of responsibility while finding alternative and more humane means of discharging the tasks necessary to maintain it.

Defying traditions of paid work and women's role in the labour force has met with equal resistance. The economic crisis now confronting Canadians has compounded the struggle, yet has also made it more critical. With interest rates and inflation both soaring, women have no choice but to work. Women on their own and those supporting children need jobs, and two incomes are essential for sustaining most families. With the necessity for paid work so immediate, we couldn't wait for slow attitudinal change. Opposition has been brutal – the pin money myth is thrown at us; our femininity is attacked. Demand for day care brings guilting – we are damaging our children's lives and destroying the family. Increasing unemployment has intensified the assault – we're depriving men, the "real" breadwinners, of their jobs.

This section examines the struggle over work. The chapters are ordered to reflect the increasing scope of women's work, focusing first on the home and ending with an analysis of the inroads into non-traditional job areas. Intermediate articles explore the necessity for day care; women organizing in and out of unions; and those concerns that influence the quality of women's paid work – sexual harassment, health and safety, and equal pay for work of equal value. This is far different from the image touted by the media. Focusing as it does on a few middle- and upper-class women who have made it up the professional and corporate ladder, the media presents a reality that includes a profusion of executives sporting Yves St. Laurent designs, who successfully balance the demands of home and career, with energy left for theatre-going and dancing till dawn. Advancing such a vision grossly distorts the true situation, as well as the objectives of the struggle. It suggests that work is no longer an issue, that women are "doing great," in well-paying, satisfying jobs, when in fact, most of us are still struggling to survive. At the same time, it implies that our goal is to merely replace men as bank presidents and corporation heads.

The women's liberation movement has consistently been critical of hierarchical work structures. We are not interested in becoming bosses of sweatshops or owners of assembly-line plants. Instead, we want to free the workplace from the domination and exploitation that characterizes it today.

The Home

A CONTESTED TERRAIN

BY MEG LUXTON

The women's liberation movement has often been accused of attacking women who stay at home to take care of household and family. However, feminist analysis has helped us recognize the importance of the work that women do in the home. The significance of the study of ''domestic labour'' is that it has highlighted the contribution that women make to the economy either in our role as full-time housewives or as part of a double day for those women who work for wages as well. Following on this analysis, feminists have sought to have our work recognized in property settlements in the courts. This analysis also enables us to see that what welfare mothers demand is their legitimate right, not a government handout. In this article, Meg Luxton moves beyond the analysis of women's work in the home to focus on the politicizing potential of that work. The Right is determined to consolidate women's traditional role in the family and the home. Unless we recognize all housewives as potential feminist activists, their activity may be organized by the Right to continue to trap women in their stereotyped family roles. Luxton thus strongly encourages the women's movement to take up the struggles that all women confront in the home.

T ALKING ABOUT THE problems associated with housework and child
care, a full-time housewife commented to me:

Sometimes I feel like I'm caught in the middle of a war. On one side are
women's lib people pulling me one way; on the other side are the tradi-
tionalists, like my church or the Right to Lifers, pulling me the other way.
Both sides want me on their side. And then sometimes I feel that I'm not
just wanted as troops for either side but that I myself, my body, is the
battleground itself.[1]

She's right. The family is a contested zone. It is at the centre of the
struggle for women's liberation and it is the place where the right wing
has staked out, preparing for battle. Winning housewives to feminism is
one of the challenges still facing the women's liberation movement. We
have to convince them that feminist concerns are their concerns.

A major victory of the women's liberation movement is that it has,
in effect, "blown the cover off" the family, by showing that the ideal
family does not correspond to the reality of family life, especially as it is
experienced by women. This has come about through the gradual
realization of the compelling interconnections between the personal and
the political and then through the slow process of "problematizing"
issues that had previously been taken for granted. The sexual division of
labour and the social relations between men and women that this division generates have become central concerns. Thanks to the women's
liberation movement there is a growing recognition that women's role in
the family is not "natural" – the occupation of housewife is a job, not
the logical extension of an innate feminine characteristic.

Feminists have clearly shown that in doing domestic labour,
women work for their husbands, their children and themselves –
sustaining life in as tolerable, or as pleasant a way as possible. A part of
this work is the reproduction of human life. As a result, in industrial
capitalist societies, the work women do in the home has the necessary,
though indirect result of producing workers – their husbands and
themselves in the present, their children for the future. By caring for the
individuals who will exchange their ability to work for the money to buy
food, shelter and other necessities and pleasures of life, women are
ensuring that those workers will be physically and emotionally able, and
relatively willing, to staff the factories and offices of the capitalist
economy. In this way, although domestic labour is not under the direct

control of capitalist production, it is profoundly linked to the economic system. Far from being a separate, private family activity, isolated from capitalist production, domestic labour lies at the heart of the system and women's work in the home is central to keeping the whole economy going.[2]

This analysis was important for helping to cut through the privacy of the family household, showing that it too is an arena for political struggle. It allowed us to see that when women in the home act to improve the situation of women, their activities are fundamentally feminist. And, with the understanding of the specifically feminist character of housewives' efforts, the potential for links between housewives and other feminist groups has become much clearer.

THE RIGHT TO SAFE WORKING CONDITIONS

THE RIGHT TO A CLEAN AND SAFE ENVIRONMENT

Like other workers, housewives have always tried to find ways to improve their immediate working conditions. In the last few years women in the home have begun to apply the lessons learned in the occupational health and safety movement to their own households. A fifteen-year study of Oregon women in the U.S.A. has suggested that those who listed their occupation as "house-wife" died of cancer at a rate 54 percent higher than women who worked outside the home. The authors of this study argue that these high cancer rates are probably caused by a combination of unsafe workplace hazards. Many ingredients in common household products are highly toxic and no tests have been done to show what their combined effects might be. In addition, most households have at least one machine (television, micro-wave oven) that gives off low level radiation.[3]

The U.S. Women's Occupational Health Resource Center has responded to such concerns by investigating the hazards entailed in handling typical household cleansers. They have organized a campaign aimed at both housewives and paid domestic workers in an effort to improve household working conditions. Such campaigns not only alert women to the hazards of their work, but they lay the basis for housewives to link up with other workers engaged in health and safety campaigns.[4]

Housewives in a number of cities in Canada have realized that members of their households have become ill because of unsafe environmental pollutants. In Stouffville, Ontario, women have campaigned against radiation poisoning caused by the dumping of radioactive wastes near their homes. In Toronto, certain neighbourhoods run the risk of lead poisoning from nearby paint factories. Although housewives initiate actions against these dangerous conditions because they are concerned for the health of their families, these campaigns often lead to more sustained political fights over larger questions such as industrial pollution and nuclear power.[5]

STOP VIOLENCE AGAINST WOMEN

In recent years the women's liberation movement has shown that the family is not a haven of love and security but is instead, for many women, a dangerous and violent place. It is estimated that one out of every ten women in Canada is so badly beaten by her husband that she requires hospital care. It is also estimated that one out of every four women is sexually assaulted by the age of eighteen. In the vast majority of cases these girls are molested by their fathers or brothers.[6]

By identifying these issues as crimes against women, the women's liberation movement has helped to break the silence that trapped abused women inside their own pain and shame. Feminists have established hostels and crisis centres to provide emergency shelter and assistance to women in crisis. Counselling, therapy and retraining programs have helped women to come to terms with their experiences and have enabled them to overcome the dependency on the family that allows these horrors to go on. While these services are too few in number and are chronically underfunded, they have nevertheless provided essential help for some women and have created a public awareness of just how unsafe the family can be. Most significantly, the women's liberation movement has made links between these issues and related ones, which occur outside the family – for example, rape and sexual harassment on the streets and at the workplace.

THE RIGHT TO ECONOMIC SECURITY

ECONOMIC SECURITY WITHIN MARRIAGE

At the heart of women's oppression in the family is the economic dependence of the married woman on her husband. Given the types of jobs and the levels of pay available to the majority of women, there is an economic compulsion towards marriage, especially for women who want to have children. Within marriage, even if the woman has a paid job, her husband typically earns considerably more than she does. This gives him breadwinner power – an economic basis for male dominance and female subordination within marriage.

Different currents within the women's liberation movement have proposed a number of strategies designed to meet the immediate problems of women trapped by this economic dependency. Some women have organized around the demand for ''wages for housework.'' These women argue that women's economic dependency in the family can be broken if women's valuable domestic labour is given a wage, like other work. Critics of this position point out that wages for housework, if put into practice, would in all likelihood be paid for out of higher taxes. They argue that these wages would tend to increase state interference in the family and, in short, to reinforce the existing assumption that only women can do domestic labour.[7]

Other groups have attempted to maximize women's economic security within marriage by organizing political campaigns either to decrease household expenses or to increase the household income. Housewives have extended their normal activities of comparison shopping by forming price watch committees. Groups like Women Against Rising Prices (WARP) monitor costs of essential goods and attempt to prevent price increases through boycotts or supermarket occupations. In similar activities, women have campaigned for decent housing, for rent controls and sometimes they have organized rent strikes, asserting their right to adequate living and working conditions.[8]

A variety of cooperative efforts that enable women to do their domestic labour more easily and in a more socialized and collective manner have been set up by other groups. Babysitting exchanges, cooperative child care centres, food purchasing cooperatives and other skills exchanges all bring people out of their private labour into a group effort.

In a similar vein, housewives in communities such as Cape Breton, Joliette, Sudbury, Hamilton and Flin Flon have taken to the streets and joined the picket lines of their striking husbands. These women understand that their domestic labour is tied to the wage labour of their husbands. They know that their husbands' struggles for higher pay, shorter hours and better benefits directly affect their own work and their families' lives. They have also demanded that the men, and the male-dominated unions, take women's concerns into account during negotiations.[9]

ECONOMIC SECURITY WHEN MARRIAGE ENDS

While economic dependency has serious effects on the power relations of the family on a day-to-day basis, it emerges most starkly at the end of a marriage. Based on the feminist insistence that women's work in the home is socially necessary and a real contribution to the economy of the family household, women have won a number of significant changes in family law, the division of property and in pension funding – all reforms that have improved the situation of housewives.

The federal and most provincial legislatures have been forced to acknowledge that housewives make an economic contribution to their households. While the courts are still interpreting family law very conservatively, the legal system has begun to establish certain safeguards for women. In Quebec, for example, the family house cannot be sold without the woman's permission. In Ontario, housewives are now entitled to a share in the family assets if the marriage breaks up.

Women who work in family businesses such as farms or corner stores are now entitled to earn wages and thus can both claim unemployment insurance if they lose their jobs and draw pensions when they retire. Canadian law now even makes provision for giving women half of their husbands' pensions. Critics have pointed out, of course, that such changes in property disposition really only benefit middle-and upper-class women. They do nothing at all to help the majority of women, many of whom live, with their children, well below the government-defined poverty line.[10]

EQUAL WORK AND EQUAL PAY

The ultimate solution to economic dependency is for women to hold paid jobs. Older women who have been full-time housewives for many years experience great difficulties when they try to reenter the paid labour force. Various feminist organizations have been set up to help women deal with this problem. Displaced homemakers' centres provide material and emotional support for middle-aged women who, because their marriages have ended through death or divorce, find themselves "unemployed housewives." These centres also provide special retraining programs to help women find paid work.[11]

Increasingly, younger women are not leaving the paid labour force, even when they have very small children. As women with young children juggle domestic labour and paid labour simultaneously, they push for changes that will make it easier for them to cope with their double shift. And these women, moving from their household base into struggles at the paid workplace, have begun to challenge the very existence of the sexual division of labour.

In the household, the married women who work at both paid labour and domestic responsibilities are increasingly insisting that domestic labour be shared among all household members. A few recent studies suggest that individual women are starting to get men and children to take over some of the domestic labour. While the amount men and children are doing is still very small – domestic labour is still primarily women's responsibility – this represents a small victory in challenging the existing division of labour.[12]

As working-class women in the paid labour force have taken up feminist concerns, the unions have slowly begun to recognize their demands. Issues such as access to all jobs, equal pay, paid maternity and paternity leave, a shorter work week and quality child care have in recent years become recognized parts of union contract demands.

In Quebec the Confédération des Syndicales Nationales (CSN) adopted in 1976 a women's resolution, which represents a full women's liberation program. It calls for an end to the sexual division of labour, for the socialization of domestic labour and for twenty-four-hour child care under community control.[13] While they have not yet won their full program, the fact that the unions have begun to raise these feminist issues makes the situation for women, both in the home and in the paid labour force, that much easier.

The changes that have been won to date make things better for some women but they are ultimately very limited gains. Real change depends on eliminating the economic dependency within marriage and finally on abolishing the sexual division of labour. Here the struggles of women in the home are linked directly with the struggles of women in the paid labour force who are demanding equal pay and equal access to jobs. As long as men make more money than women, the economic imperative to marriage will continue to operate. Only when such inequality no longer exists will women be able to choose, freely, whether or not they want to associate intimately with a particular man.

THE FUNDAMENTAL CHALLENGE

The sexual division of labour in the household touches on the way people organize their personal, emotional, sexual and domestic lives. The family, particularly women's role in the family; how sex gets regulated; how children are conceived, born and raised – all these lie at the heart of patriarchal relations. In trying to alter the family and domestic labour, feminists are challenging long established gender relations. We have the whole weight of tradition resisting our efforts.

There has always been a strong current of scorn and contempt for housewives. It is part of the generalized women-hating so prevalent in modern society. It is also related to the absence of a wage payment for the work housewives do that contributes to the notion that they "don't work." As the women's liberation movement identified this woman-hating, we became associated with it. Just as the ancient Greek rulers used to kill the messengers who brought bad news, so certain anti-feminist forces have tried to kill women's liberation by claiming that we are not just the bearers of bad news, but bad news itself! Many conservatives and right-wingers, for example, have argued that it is the women's liberation movement that is to blame for the unhappiness, discontent and restlessness of many women. The media have gone out of their way to portray feminists as "anti-housewife."[14] This is part of an attempt to defuse the power of the women's liberation movement by creating hostility to feminists on the part of other women.

In addition, in the last few years, an opposition movement of the right wing has emerged to specifically challenge all the issues feminists have raised. As a result, women's role in the family, especially women's responsibility for domestic labour, has become a central arena of political struggle.

In her analysis of the so-called Right to Life movement, Deirdre English points out that many of the more committed activists of these anti-abortion, anti-women, anti-life groups are working-class and lower middle-class housewives. She suggests that housewives may be attracted to them because it allows them to get out of the family household and become active in the community without denying their traditional housewife role. The leaders of these anti-feminist movements often urge women to join by arguing that women's liberation has no use for housewives. They further argue that if the demands of the women's liberation movement were won, all the things most cherished by these women would be destroyed. To a large extent, the strength of these right-wing movements lies in their ability to tap the very real and deep-seated fears that many women have.[15]

So, while the women's liberation movement has made some vitally significant gains in the past decade, there are still major gaps between what the majority of housewives believe about feminism and what the women's liberation movement actually says about the family and domestic labour. Central to feminism is a critique of the family and of the way people are currently able to organize their personal lives. Many women, particularly those who consider their domestic commitments a major priority, find it hard to imagine giving up the kind of family they have now. They cannot think where else they could get even a modicum of sustained affection, emotional security and love. Some are genuinely afraid that their children will be hurt if they do not grow up in "normal families." Such fears are real and often make women resistant to feminism and vulnerable to right-wing appeals.

The women's liberation movement is slowly and often painfully evolving a vision of a better way of life. The basis for such a vision exists in the experiences that women are having every day. A Toronto woman, for example, when her husband left her, had to arrange day care for her child because she had to get a paid job. The first day she left her child at the centre she was in tears. She felt guilty and considered the day care centre nothing more than a necessary evil. Over the next year as she watched her child thrive, she became a keen advocate of day care:

> Now that I've experienced day care, I've seen how wonderful it is for my child and I realize that what I used to think was just wrong. There is a better way of caring for children. . .

In Sudbury, after a protracted strike against Inco, a housewife who had been active in the Wives Supporting the Strike committee observed:

> I'll never be quite the same again. Now I have a vision of another way. I guess I learned that ordinary women like me can fight a big multinational company like Inco, and win. . . . I learned that there are other ways of organizing our daily lives, ways of living as a community together, ways of being husbands and wives that I never imagined before.[16]

Such concrete experiences demonstrate to women that other ways *are* possible and that a critique of the family does not mean an end to loving, intimate relationships. As we expand and develop our vision of what human relations could be like across the generations, between the sexes and between people of the same sex, more and more women will come to identify with feminism.

N O T E S

1. The interviews quoted in this article were all conducted with housewives in Ontario during the summer of 1981.

2. See Bonnie Fox, ed., *Hidden in the Household: Women's Domestic Labour Under Capitalism* (Toronto: Women's Press, 1980) and Meg Luxton, *More Than a Labour of Love: Three Generations of Women's Work in the Home* (Toronto: Women's Press, 1980).

3. *Northern Women's Journal,* Vol. 7, No. 2 (1982), p. 12.

4. Harriet Rosenberg, "The Home is the Workplace," in Wendy Chavkin, ed., *Report from the Front Lines* (New York: Monthly Review Press, forthcoming).

5. Zuhair Kashmeri, "Fear Was Weapon in Dump Battle," Toronto *Globe and Mail,* April 30, 1982.

6. Linda MacLeod, *Wife Battering in Canada: The Vicious Circle* (Ottawa: Canadian Advisory Council on the Status of Women, 1980); Elizabeth Janeway, "Incest: A Rational Look at the Oldest Taboo," *Ms*, November 1981, p. 61.

7. For both sides of this debate see Ellen Malos, ed., *The Politics of Housework* (London: Allison and Busby, 1980), especially the Introduction by Ellen Malos, pp. 7-43.

8. Helen Austerberry and Sophie Watson, "A Woman's Place: A Feminist Approach to Housing in Britain," *Feminist Review*, No. 8 (Summer 1981), pp. 49-62.

9. Meg Luxton, *More Than a Labour of Love*, pp. 229-31 and "From Ladies' Auxilliary to Women's Committee: The Role of Wives in their Husband's Unions" in Linda Briskin and Lynda Yanz, eds., *Rising Up Strong: Women and Unions in Canada* (Toronto: Women's Press, forthcoming).

10. Kevin Collins, *Women and Pensions* (Ottawa: Canadian Council on Social Development, 1978); Canadian Advisory Council on the Status of Women, *Pension Reform For Women* (Ottawa: CACSW, 1981).

11. Rae Andre, *Homemakers: The Forgotten Workers* (Chicago: University of Chicago Press, 1981).

12. Meg Luxton, "Changing Patterns in the Division of Labour in the Family Household" (Paper presented at the annual meetings of the Canadian Sociology and Anthropology Association, Ottawa, June 1982).

13. Heather Jon Maroney, "The Impact of Working Class Feminism on the Canadian Women's Movement," in P. Resnick, ed., *The Left in the Eighties* (Toronto: University of Toronto Press, forthcoming).

14. Maxine Sidran, "Feminist Myths Trap Many Women," *Toronto Star*, February 1, 1982.

15. Deirdre English, "The War Against Choice, Inside the Antiabortion Movement," *Mother Jones*, February/March, 1981.

16. Meg Luxton, *More Than a Labour of Love*, p. 231.

F U R T H E R   R E A D I N G S

Fox, Bonnie, ed. *Hidden in the Household: Women's Domestic Labour Under Capitalism.*

Luxton, Meg. *More Than a Labour of Love: Three Generations of Women's Work in the Home.* Toronto: Women's Press, 1980.

Minding the Children

BY PAT SCHULZ

Our society takes for granted a universal free educational system for children over five. What is the reason for not supplying a universal free child care system for children up to that age? The expense is not so formidable as the fact that it is not a government priority. But why aren't more women, who are increasingly part of the paid labour force, demanding government-funded day care? Part of the answer is in the feeling (that we've been socialized to have) that day care means abandoning our children to institutional and therefore inadequate care. But more importantly, the kind of caring, beneficial and educative day care environment we would like to see for our children is hard to find and is too expensive for most working people. As a result, many women opt for less expensive but often inadequate home care. In this article, Pat Schulz envisions a neighbourhood-based, mutually supporting set of diverse child care facilities. She also looks at the changes that have occurred in organizing strategy to obtain day care over the last decade.

T HERE CAN BE no equality for women until we have equality in the home. As long as women have the primary responsibility for maintenance of the home and for child care, we will be less able than men to pursue job opportunities and our domestic commitments will be used to justify discriminatory employment practices. Free universal quality day care is an essential element for equality of women in the labour force and for women's liberation in general.

Women lose a portion of their income when they become pregnant and must return to work after 16 weeks of leave or lose their jobs, benefits and seniority. They used to lose their jobs – period! Women searching for employment often restrict their search to work close to home and with hours that facilitate child care. Travel and overtime are difficult, if not impossible, and out-of-town programs and promotions are usually out of the question.

Employers utilize and exaggerate these problems to justify restricting women to low-paying job ghettos. The myth of a higher incidence of time lost through sickness and of the likelihood of women quitting a job due to pregnancy are frequently cited.

Problems with alternative child care are made more troublesome by the fact that they extend over a number of years. Yet it is not difficult to envisage a child care system that would be beneficial to children and alleviate the stresses on the family, and particularly on the mother. The Ontario Coalition for Better Day Care describes such a system:

> A wide range of options is essential if parents and children are to choose the method of childcare that best suits their needs. . . . Day care ought to be available in the vicinity of each family so that children need not be transported long distances and so that they can play with their daycare friends when they are at home. . . . In each neighbourhood centre the following services would be offered: all-day group care, supervised private home care. . . overnight care for children of shiftworkers, perhaps in the child's own home, half-day nursery school, parent and child drop-in centre, and facilities for parent education. A public health nurse should also be located in the neighbourhood childcare centre with facilities for early diagnosis of physical, mental or emotional difficulties. The [neighbourhood centres] would provide resources for the private home care providers including relief staff, a toy lending service, training and advice. The children in private home care could periodically participate in some aspects of the group program.[1]

This day care service ought to be free – that is, publicly funded, without user charges. Universal access to facilities for healthy physical, mental and emotional development should be the right of all children under the age of six, as it is for children over that age. To foster a closer liaison between the elementary school system and early childhood education, and because the school system is free and universally accessible, day care should be licensed and funded through the education system rather than through social services. It is important, however, that certain aspects of the day care system be retained or improved: low child-staff ratios, specific training in the care of *young* children with a developmental approach and control of the centres by parents, staff and community members. Only the provision of this kind and range of services will enable women to participate fully in the work force, secure in the knowledge that their children are receiving the best of care.

Now contrast that with what is presently available. Women are confronted by waiting lists for group day care and supervised private home care spaces. Subsidized care is available for only a small percentage of very low-income families. Nationally, 75 percent of day care costs are paid by parents. The cost of quality care, which may be as high as $400 per month for infants, is prohibitive for most families. These factors force most parents to use the unsupervised, unlicensed care provided by untrained women in their own homes. In fact, only 12 percent of children are cared for in licensed, supervised settings. And even here, the reluctance to charge high fees to parents results in pressures that keep the quality of care down. In particular, day care workers' wages are very low, and the consequent high turnover of staff reduces the quality of care. One study of informal arrangements (used by the remaining 88 percent of parents) concluded that care ranged from superb to abusive, with most of it being mediocre, involving little outdoor play, poor nutrition and a great deal of television watching.

Emergency child care for sick children or sick parents and 24-hour care for the children of shift workers are almost non-existent. The lack of day care services causes stresses which are compounded by employers' unwillingness to make any allowances for parenting responsibilities. These problems now affect 50 percent of mothers of children under 10.

This crisis in day care is rooted in its history. The first centres, opened in the 1850s, were a response to the needs of mothers who had to work outside the home because they had no other means of support. The service was initially a charitable one; as the government's role in funding all social services grew, day care too received government funding, but only for those "in need." In this respect the route taken by free public education was totally different.

The government's attitude and role changed during World War II. Instead of being a charity, day care became a necessity. An expanded day care program was promoted by the federal government because they needed mothers in the work force to solve a severe labour shortage. Ontario and Quebec participated in the program, which provided care primarily for women working in essential industries. However, after the war, the federal government withdrew its support, the Quebec government closed its centres in spite of long waiting lists and the Ontario government was prevented from doing the same only by a large protest movement.

The post-war period was characterized by a growth in the rate of women's participation in the work force. Federal and provincial government support for day care was minimal or non-existent until 1967, when the federal government became involved in funding through the Canada Assistance Plan. This method of funding again reinforced the welfare connotations around day care. Only those "in need" were to receive government assistance. In the next decade provinces adopted legislation that enabled them to take advantage of these funds, and considerable expansion occurred.

The problems inherent in the welfare framework then became apparent. Day care was available only to those very poor who could find subsidized spaces and the rich, who could afford to pay fees. The whole middle-income group and the low-income parents who could not find a subsidized space were excluded from the system. They turned to informal arrangements, which studies showed to be totally inadequate.

The expansion of the early Seventies was curtailed later in the decade by the deteriorating economic situation and consequent social service cutbacks. The philosophy that justified expansion of day care services in World War II was now used to justify restriction of services.

Since women are perceived to be an optional portion of the labour force, available when needed but able to be pushed back into the home when unemployment rises, government social policy, particularly around day care, reflects this perception. Social service cutbacks hit day care at an extremely bad time. While some social services, like education, are experiencing a decline in demand, day care is in the opposite position.

A more fundamental problem confronting the movement is the attitude of the general public to day care service. Despite studies which prove this isn't so, it is still widely argued that home rearing is superior to day care. This follows from the traditional notion of the father as provider and the mother as housekeeper and nurturer. Those who believe that women belong in the home raising children do not realize that women have no options. Women's incomes are not secondary – they are necessary to keep up with the rate of inflation. The real choice society must make is not between children in day care and children staying at home with the mother, but between custodial care and quality care.

A second argument against subsidized care is that parents chose to have children and should therefore take the whole responsibility for them. Advocates of that position do not object to free public education, nor do they acknowledge the responsibilities that remain to parents even when their children are in day care.

These attitudes are changing, however, and have done so dramatically over the past decade. In part the change is due to people's personal experiences. Everyone now seems to know someone who needs or uses day care. The women's movement has done an excellent job of helping to legitimize both women's work outside the home and the use of a day care service. An emerging day care movement has also played an important role in educating and publicizing the issue. One sees evidence of this change in attitude in the support that exists for expansion of the service and the demand for free universal care.

Ten years ago, a small core of day care activists and feminists fought to set up new centres and maintain existing services in campaigns that didn't reach beyond those immediately involved in the service. Today, active support exists in the trade union movement, the NDP, the teachers' federations and the social service sector. Many but not all of these groups support free universal care; all support expansion and a massive increase in government funding. Furthermore, this change has taken place on a national basis. The B.C. Federation of Labour has given some support to day care. There is a strong and aggressive day care movement in Quebec where in 1970 there was no legislation and scarcely any centres. The Canadian Labour Congress and the federal NDP are active around the issue. In Ontario a broad coalition has been formed that includes the Ontario Federation of Labour, the teachers' federations, the day care workers' professional association, social service groups and Action Day Care. But how did these changes occur?

In the 1970s, the day care movement, which included parents, day care owners, administrators, workers and social workers, was able to defend the quality and importance of the service but it was unable to shift its focus and mobilize the day care community to fight offensively to gain more spaces for children.[2] In part, this was because the users and providers are not easy groups to organize. The users – the parents – who combine the responsibilities of a job with those of a family, have little time to become heavily involved. Day care workers are often still upgrading their education at night and frequently are exhausted and discouraged by their working conditions.

To make significant gains, the day care movement would have had to mobilize parents, the consumers of the service, through their workplace or their political organizations. Lobbying within political parties had already proved effective – day care facilities had been expanded after the NDP were elected in B.C. and after the Parti Québécois came to power in Quebec. Unfortunately, the movement in Ontario had no clear strategy for approaching the parties, and consequently valuable time was lost by lobbying individuals and establishing advisory committees.

It wasn't until 1980 that the situation began to change in Ontario. Statistics were made public that revealed the alarming need for day care: "58 percent of working mothers now had children of pre-school age needing care; 1400 parents per month were being turned away from Metro Toronto day care centres;"[3] and projections that the female labour force would increase dramatically by 1990 demonstrated that more and more women *needed* to work.

Action Day Care, an organization formed in 1979, and composed of parents, day care workers, representatives from women's groups and a few rank and file trade unionists, stepped in at this time and pushed the day care movement to another stage of development. It came up with a series of demands and activities that were more concrete and less far-reaching than the aim of free universal day care, which was maintained as Action Day Care's ultimate long-term goal.

Action Day Care launched campaigns to organize day care workers, to get additional funding from the government in the form of a direct grant of $5 per day per child to all non-profit day care centres regardless of the financial positions of the parents, and for the addition of 10,000 more subsidized spaces. Meanwhile changes were taking place within the labour movement. As the concerns of feminists percolated through society, working women were standing up at conventions urging fellow unionists to defend women's right to work, to support demands for equal pay for work of equal value, affirmative action programs and, of course, for child care.

The Women's Committee of the Ontario Federation of Labour was instrumental in pushing day care as a critical issue not only for trade union women, but for the entire union movement. In October 1980, they organized the conference, "Sharing the Caring." Concluding statements from the conference merged Action Day Care's demands with specific trade union concerns. The OFL proved its concern by calling for day care at union functions and insisting on contract negotiations for family-related provisions, such as job-sharing and part-time work with the same benefits and pay, flexible work hours, allowances to cover day care costs and the limitation of voluntary overtime. It voted to organize public educationals throughout the province and called for all provincial political candidates to support universal day care in their election campaigns.[4]

The support by the OFL was significant in that it was the first major institution to recognize day care as a central concern of all working people. It gave the issue "the force that is required to make day care a potential reality rather than a mere ideological goal."[5]

Since that time, the OFL has been the key group, along with Action Day Care and the teachers' federations , keeping the coalition operating. The British Columbia Federation of Labour is involved in a similar coalition. In Quebec the Confédération des syndicats nationaux is actively involved in negotiating for workplace day care. Labour's support has given a whole new impetus to day care organizing.

The development of a day care program and strategy is further complicated by the confusing role of governments at the federal, provincial and municipal levels. While the jurisdiction is primarily a provincial one, the federal government provides up to 50 percent of the funding in some provinces. Furthermore, the form of federal funding considerably shapes the funding of the other levels of government and the way in which the service is delivered. At present, the federal government contributes just under a hundred million dollars per year – partially through the Canada Assistance Plan, which assists very low-income families, and partly through income taxes lost because of deductions for child care. Since it is an income tax deduction and not a credit, only people who pay income tax benefit at all. Furthermore those with a higher income receive greater benefits because they are taxed at an increased rate. The provisions of the Canada Assistance Plan, which restrict federal cost sharing to assistance for very low-income groups, are used by the provinces to justify similar policies. This means that the majority of parents must pay the full cost of day care themselves with the consequences I have already mentioned.

Changing the method of federal funding is one of the most important challenges facing the day care community, particularly considering there is no national day care organization. A national day care conference scheduled for the fall of 1982 will, we hope, consolidate the energies of day care activists throughout Canada.

The constantly rising demand for day care and the impact of the women's movement on such groups as unions means that the day care movement is much broader in its base and more far-reaching in its demands than ever before. The fact that this occurs in a period of economic recession and social service restraints and cutbacks means that the conflict will not easily be settled. A prerequisite for free universal day care is a profound change in Canada's political climate.

N O T E S

1. Ontario Coalition for Better Day Care, "Day Care Deadline 1900," a brief presented to the Ontario Cabinet, Fall 1981.
2. This is Sue Colley's argument in "Day Care and the Trade Union Movement in Ontario," *Resources for Feminist Research, Women and Trade Unions,* Lynda Yanz and Linda Briskin, eds., Vol. X, No. 2 (July 1981), pp. 29-31. A revised version of this article will appear in Briskin and Yanz, eds. *Rising Up Strong: Women and Trade Unions in Canada,* which will be published by the Women's Press in Spring 1983.
3. Ibid., p. 30.
4. Ibid., p. 31.
5. Ibid., p. 30.

F U R T H E R   R E A D I N G S

Johnson, Laura C. and Janice Dineen. *The Kin Trade: The Day Care Crisis in Canada.* Scarborough, Ont.: McGraw-Hill Ryerson, 1981.

Ross, Kathleen Gallagher, ed. *Good Day Care: Getting It, Keeping It, Fighting For It.* Toronto: Women's Press, 1978.

GETTING ORGANIZED

...in the Feminist Unions

JACKIE AINSWORTH, ANN HUTCHISON,
SUSAN MARGARET, MICHELE PUJOL,
SHEILA PERRET, MARY JEAN RANDS,
STAR ROSENTHAL

Rather than fight in the women's committees and caucuses of male-dominated unions, some
women in the west of Canada have sought a different strategy – the organization of feminist
unions. The Service, Office and Retail Workers Union of Canada (SORWUC) and the
Association of University and College Employees (AUCE), organized primarily by women
around feminist principles, have fought for their lives over the last decade. They maintain that
only a women-centred union can effectively organize and fight for the large numbers of
unorganized women in the service sector of the economy. SORWUC developed a high profile in
the Seventies as the small gutsy union that took on the banks. Both SORWUC and AUCE have
considered joining the CLC. But the terms for their admission to this trade union central have
always been the dissolution of the union and the merger of various segments into other unions.
This article, written by women from both unions, demonstrates the significance of feminist
unions and explains why AUCE and SORWUC continue to fight for the right to be independent
trade unions.

T HE MESSAGE OF the women's movement has always been that "no-body can do it for us"; that women have the skills, competence and ability to organize to fight our oppression. The Association of University and College Employees (AUCE) and the Service, Office and Retail Workers Union of Canada (SORWUC), both independent feminist unions, are concrete examples of this struggle.

As clerical workers, our employers may look awesome and all-powerful, and we sometimes see ourselves as "just tellers," "just typists" and "just women." But we are not inherently less valuable or less skilled or even less powerful than other workers. When clerical workers have the courage to organize and to strike, we have the power to win.

AUCE and SORWUC have records second to none in fighting for women workers in unorganized industry. Before clerical workers at the University of British Columbia (UBC) formed AUCE, they had already tried to organize through the Office and Professional Employees International Union (OPEIU) and through the Canadian Union of Public Employees (CUPE). When organizing with OPEIU/OTEU in 1971-72 (in B.C., OPEIU is called the Office and Technical Employees Union, OTEU) they found that the professional union leaders assigned to UBC were a hindrance rather than a help. UBC clerical workers wrote leaflets about their pay and conditions and the need for a union at UBC, handed them to the OTEU business agents for distribution and never saw them again. The OTEU refused to give the UBC organizers a copy of the union constitution. When they finally got hold of the constitution, they were shocked at the powers of the international president and the provisions that allowed the international to replace elected local officers with appointed "trustees."

---

*This article was originally published in **Kinesis** (September/October, 1980) as a defence of Association of University and College Employees (AUCE) and Service, Office and Retail Workers Union of Canada (SORWUC) as democratic unions of working women. As feminists and clerical workers, we were responding to an article advocating that AUCE should be absorbed by the Canadian Union of Public Employees (CUPE). (Since then, the AUCE membership voted in referendum in favour of AUCE and against joining another union.) This article was updated and submitted for this book because we feel that the debate about strategy for organizing women as workers is important to the women's movement as a whole.*

When the OTEU campaign failed, the organizers looked at CUPE as an alternative. But CUPE's constitution is almost as undemocratic as OTEU's (in CUPE the national executive can replace local officers with a trusteeship) and its record at UBC in representing its own women members was poor. The wage gap between men and women who were covered by the CUPE contract was even greater than between unorganized men and women support staff!

UBC clerical workers concluded that our only hope for success was to organize our own independent union. We didn't want a union where power could fall to an elite few, where the majority of members are women but the appointed officials are men.

AUCE succeeded where CUPE and OTEU had failed. Beginning with UBC in 1972, AUCE went on to organize Notre Dame University, Simon Fraser University, Capilano College, College of New Caledonia and the teaching assistants at SFU. We won some of the best clerical workers' contracts in the country. We spent our time building our union without having to fight to convince conservative union business agents or a male-dominated union executive in Ottawa or New York.

SORWUC was also formed in 1972 and has enthusiastically organized small units of day care workers, social service workers and clerical workers. In the restaurant industry, SORWUC has taken on viciously anti-union employers. At Muckamuck Restaurant in Vancouver, SORWUC maintained an effective picket line for over two years and paid strike pay the whole time. The union successfully fought injunctions, unfair labour practices, decertification attempts and an application for certification by a company union. In an industry where unions are often defeated by decertification or by loss of a strike vote, the strength and determination of the Muckamuck strikers is inspiring. In spite of the wealth and intransigence of Doug Chrismas (the owner), the restaurant has been shut down since November 1980.

The conditions that led to the formation of AUCE and SORWUC still exist: most women workers are unorganized. Nearly all the growth in union membership among women is a result of public employee organizations achieving union status. The increase in the number of women union members has had no effect on the fact that the average woman earns just over half of the average man's wage; the wage gap between men and women is actually widening.

In 1981, clerical workers in CUPE made equal pay for clerical workers the main issue in the civic workers' strike in the Lower Mainland. The Vancouver Municipal and Regional Employees Union (VMREU), an independent union of inside (office) workers, played an important part in mobilizing support and counteracting the reluctance of CUPE staff to push the equal pay demand. The media, union members and thousands of office workers discussed whether it was possible and just for clerical workers to win "one base rate" to apply to labourers and clerical workers. In the end, the CUPE staff convinced one of their locals to accept a contract which *increased* the differential between the starting rate for outside labourers and the starting rate for clerical workers. This contract formed the basis of the settlement with the municipalities negotiating through the Greater Vancouver Regional District. The final settlement was a disappointment, but this strike and the campaign around equal pay were effective in popularizing the legitimate complaints of clerical workers. The civic workers' campaign, carried out in spite of the CUPE staff, convinced many clerical workers that they were entitled to compare their wages to wages outside our job ghetto. And many saw for the first time a possibility of fighting for our rights through union organization.

Clerical workers will join unions that challenge the wage differential between male and female workers. The hundreds of thousands of women workers in the job ghettos of the private sector have the power to do it, but it is a difficult battle. Some of the most powerful corporations in this country depend on the cheap labour of women for their profits. It is estimated that in 1974 women workers in Canada lost about $7 billion in potential wage and salary income due to male-female inequalities. Our employers won't give up those profits without a fight.

The Canadian Labour Congress (CLC) can't organize working women because the people who run the CLC don't want to challenge that wage differential. They have no respect for our skills as clerical workers, and no respect for our right to run our own organizations. Democratic organizations of women workers are a threat to the stability of the organizations these bureaucrats administer. Often they actually oppose equal pay. For example, a CUPE business agent giving a stewards' seminar said that to demand that clerical wages be brought up to the base rate for general labourers would be an insult to general labourers.

This attitude is reflected in CUPE agreements. In the CUPE agreement with the District of Surrey which expired in 1980, mostly male outside workers got a second-year increase of 7.5 percent while the lower-paid clerical workers got only 7 percent.

The CLC's Union of Bank Employees in its organizing meetings and in its negotiations for bank workers takes the position that wages are not an issue in the banking industry. They say it makes sense to sign poor contracts to get "a foot in the door" or "a base to build from." But in fact, their contracts are used as an anti-union argument by management in unorganized bank branches. SORWUC was criticized for refusing to sign such contracts and for withdrawing from negotiations in 1978 when there were not enough bank worker members to win anything better. But the last three years have showed that SORWUC was right to say that contracts that provide for no wage increase could not be organizing tools or a base to build from. There are now only about 80 certified bank branches in the whole country (including those organized by the CSN in Quebec) and the CLC's Union of Bank Employees is not growing. As long as bank workers see that union branches get the same wages as non-union branches, they will not join a union in large numbers.

The total bargaining power of clerical workers would be substantially reduced if AUCE and SORWUC were to disappear. The idea that somehow we would all be stronger if we were all "united" in CUPE is the opposite of the truth. The fact that VMREU is an independent union made it possible for women inside CUPE to carry on a campaign for fair pay for clerical workers. If VMREU had not existed outside CUPE, that campaign would not have happened. If the bank workers' local of SORWUC had joined the CLC in 1978, under the terms specified by the CLC, we would be in no position now to revive aggressive organizing in the finance industry.

Those who opt for AUCE joining the CLC confuse the argument by using words like "merger" and "joining forces." They imply that AUCE will continue to exist as an independent democratic union, when in fact they propose that it cease to exist and be replaced by CUPE. The same kind of argument was used against the bank workers' local of SORWUC in 1977. Even though the CLC made it clear that SORWUC would cease to exist and be divided up among affiliates, people criticized SORWUC for not "affiliating" with the CLC.

SCHOOL OF
Graduate Studies

Dissertation on the Lake

Overnight writing retreat on the shores
of Elbow Lake

Goal Setting • Productivity • Self-Management • Motivation • Overcoming Procrastination

Dissertation on the Lake: **Monday, August 29-Friday, September 2**
Cost: **$75.00** Includes all food, transportation and accommodations.
Registration **opens July 5.**

To register: **queensu.ca/sgs/retreat**

SCHOOL OF
Graduate Studies

Dissertation Boot Camp

Achieve the momentum you need to write your thesis

Goal Setting • Productivity • Self-Management • Motivation • Overcoming Procrastination

Pre-boot: Orientation Breakfast/Writing Session **Friday, June 3**
Dissertation Boot Camp: **Monday, June 6-Friday, June 10**
Registration for this free event is **now open**.

To register: **queensu.ca/sgs/dissertation-bootcamp**

Queen's
UNIVERSITY

Rather than attacking AUCE and SORWUC for being outside the "House of Labour," CLC supporters should criticize the CLC for excluding our unions. We should not have to give up our democratic constitutions and traditions, our feminist goals and our control of our own collective bargaining objectives — to meekly "merge" into another union like CUPE — in order to gain admission. This is the condition the CLC has put on our joining it. SORWUC should not be forced to divide itself among the affiliates designated by the CLC executive (restaurant workers to the Hotel and Restaurant Employees International Union; day care workers to CUPE; clerical workers to OTEU/OPEIU; agency homemakers to CUPE). Feminists who support the CLC should demand that they allow AUCE and SORWUC to affiliate as AUCE and SORWUC.

The argument against the independent feminist unions is one that has been traditionally used against the women's movement and its right to exist. Whenever we demand our own organizations we are accused of splitting the working class. It is a critical question for feminists: is it necessary for us to have our own organizations, our own independent power base, or can we win by influencing and infiltrating established male-dominated organizations?

While we support the struggle of women within the CLC, our immediate tasks are different. Our goals in AUCE and SORWUC are not the establishment of women's committees and caucuses within our unions. These are important and necessary in institutions like CUPE that are male-dominated, where women must struggle to have their voices heard, but they are not the final goal of feminists. Our objective is to build unions of working women controlled by working women, whereas the advocates of "merger" are prepared to destroy one such union in the interest of being able to participate in women's caucuses, committees and conferences within male-dominated unions.

Advocates of AUCE joining CUPE deplore the fact that debate on this issue has become increasingly heated. They patronizingly admonish us to "be sure we understand where and why we disagree." As women who have been on the left, the women's movement and the trade union movement for many years, we have all heard this "now, now, let's be reasonable" kind of argument before. Well, we are full of rage. We see our struggle for fair wage rates as clerical workers, for benefits when we get pregnant, our very livelihoods, getting lost in an uncaring bureaucracy. We see control over our lives being handed to a male power elite. We see losing hard-won gains and starting our struggle over again at the bottom. We see standing up in union meetings to speak and being harassed by wolf-whistles from men union members. This is not just an intellectual or abstract debate to us, but a fundamental and gut issue.

The only way we can organize clerical workers into a force strong enough to win the contracts that we need and deserve is to organize and build unions that clerical workers control. We have had and will continue to have more impact on the labour movement and on our wages and working conditions as a women's union than as part of a CUPE women's committee. The reason for the creation of AUCE and SORWUC is the same as the reason for the creation of the present women's movement — we learned that in the trade union movement, as in the male-dominated left and in society at large, our concerns are treated as secondary.

One of the more seductive arguments of those who think AUCE should "dissolve" into CUPE is the question of "whether we have the resources to defend ourselves." They go on to attack what they call the AUCE tradition of volunteering, and state that this "excludes the involvement of working mothers." In fact, AUCE locals encourage membership participation by holding union meetings during working hours, rather than in the evening, and (in Local 6), by providing child care during union meetings.

Rather than proposing ways to make it easier for working mothers to participate effectively in decision-making in the union, the advocates of CUPE propose that we throw up our hands in despair and turn over the decision-making to experts appointed by the national office. There is no reason to believe that the use of highly-paid "professionals" to do the work of the union will encourage membership participation. One of the reasons that so many people distrust and dislike unions, and see them as corporate concerns, very much like "big business," is that union members have little or no say in the running of things. Members become alienated and cynical when they realize that their input is actually discouraged by the paid officials who have the "expertise."

This is hardly a situation that encourages the involvement of working mothers.

AUCE's union representatives are elected by and from the membership and paid at the same rate as their regular job, or at a rate in the collective agreement. In contrast, CUPE, which is held up to us as an example of democracy, hires its business agents through its national headquarters in Ottawa. The members of the local have no say in the hiring process. While being in CUPE may not necessarily mean more paid union staff, it does mean losing membership control over the paid union staff. For all 136 B.C. CUPE locals, there are only 17 staff reps, and of these 17, only 2 are women. In Canada, CUPE has 160 staff reps, of whom only 9 are women and 151 are men. AUCE, on the other hand, has 8 paid union reps, 7 of whom are women.

As examples of gains made by women workers, the advocates of CUPE point to the motions and resolutions passed at CLC, B.C. Federation of Labour and CUPE conventions calling for the inclusion of women's rights clauses in union contracts. Instead of going to conventions to fight for resolutions, AUCE and SORWUC feminists have been able to spend our time organizing our workplaces and fighting our employers for these rights on the job.

AUCE and SORWUC have won contract clauses giving women full pay for the period of unemployment insurance maternity leave (the employer is required to pay the difference between UIC benefits and the woman's regular salary). This clause was challenged by UIC and AUCE fought it through to the Federal Court of Appeal and won. AUCE Local Six, Teaching Support Staff Union at SFU, signed a first contract that includes compassionate leave for the death of a worker's "homosexual companion" and a clause giving members the right to fight sexual harassment through the grievance procedure. AUCE and SORWUC have won the right to have union meetings during working hours with no reduction in pay, in recognition that most of our members have two jobs — one for wages and the other at home — which make evening meetings impossible to attend and make membership involvement difficult. SORWUC has won clauses providing employer contribution to employees' day care costs, and clauses allowing for paid leave for children's illness and paid paternity leave. Most important, both AUCE and SORWUC have always seen women's wages as a feminist issue and have fought hard for equal pay.

Those advocating that AUCE join CUPE will tell you that it is worth it to trade off control for "access to greater resources." It is dangerously naive to assume that because these resources (strike funds, professional staff, etc.) exist, they will be used in the interest of the local union membership. When the highly-paid male business agent who has never done clerical work in his life negotiates a contract for low-paid female clerical workers, is it likely that he will effectively represent their concerns, or even understand them? Is it likely, if they reject the deal he has negotiated, that he will recommend to the regional and national union executives (also well-paid, mostly male professionals) that strike funds be released to those workers? It is no wonder that AUCE's contracts are better than CUPE's. It is no wonder that CLC reps say bank workers' wages aren't an issue, and it is no wonder that with their multi-million dollar resources, they have failed to organize in the finance industry. Ultimately, the best and only effective resource that a trade union has is the unity and militancy of its members. The biggest strike fund in the world will not help if the members are not willing to fight, or if their union representatives sign sellout agreements behind their backs.

Women workers with the right to strike have the power to win some of the demands of the women's movement regarding child care, maternity benefits, economic independence, sexual harassment and discrimination against lesbians and gays. But the overwhelming majority of women are unorganized, and most of the minority who are union members are in bureaucratic unions dominated by men who discourage the fight for women's rights. In order to exercise our power, working women must build organizations that we control ourselves.

F U R T H E R   R E A D I N G S

The Bank Book Collective. *An Account to Settle: The Story of the United Bankworkers (SORWUC).* Vancouver: Press Gang Publishers, 1979.

GETTING ORGANIZED

...in the CCU

BY SUE VOHANKA

The Confederation of Canadian Unions was formed as a trade union central which would offer an alternative to the Canadian Labour Congress and the domination in the CLC of the large international unions whose head offices were far from the action in Canada. Sue Vohanka argues that the reason the CCU has put women workers in the forefront and fought for them is because the unions of the CCU are rank and file controlled unions. She details the issues that the CCU has fought around – most notably the fight for equal pay for work of equal value that CAIMAW workers (both men and women) fought for in the Kenworth plant in Vancouver – in its continuing struggle for equality in the workplace.

◄ 141 ►

T HE CONFEDERATION OF Canadian Unions is a national labour central with 20 affiliated unions representing more than 40,000 workers across the country, in every sector of the economy. The CCU is dedicated to building a democratic and sovereign labour movement in Canada, where rank and file workers control their own Canadian unions. Since its founding in 1969, the CCU has demonstrated its strong commitment to fighting for the rights of working women, and has had an impact considerably greater than its numbers may suggest.

A great many changes must take place before working women will gain equality in the workplace. Women are still grossly underpaid, earning on the average only 58 cents for every dollar that men earn. Women are still concentrated in low-paid job ghettos. And a much larger percentage of women than of men remain without union protection.

Trade unions are the most effective vehicle for women to achieve change in their workplaces. The CCU also believes, however, that the unions which are able – and willing – to fight effectively for workplace equality or any other issue are democratic Canadian unions, responsive to and controlled by their rank and file membership.

The CCU's view of the importance of rank and file control is rooted in experience. The initial impetus for the CCU was the building of independent, democratically structured unions that responded to their membership. It came from workers who did not accept that the decisions they made at the local level – about contract settlements, strikes and control over dues money – could be overruled by union officials in the United States. But the constitutions of their unions vested final decision-making power in the U.S., and when local union members tried to change or challenge them, they were disciplined, arbitrarily removed from elected positions, barred from holding union office. They were left with no choice but to build their own unions. The struggle for control is far from over. Although the percentage is declining, nearly half of Canadian trade unionists still belong to the so-called international unions, which are in reality American unions with headquarters in the United States and branches in Canada.

The issue of union control is especially important for working women. For example, when negotiations begin for a new contract, there are many cases where demands of particular importance to women members start off on the bargaining table. However, as bargaining

moves closer to a conclusion, these demands are all too frequently trad-
ed off or forgotten by committees or officials who are not responsive or
accountable to the women membership. Women must be able to control
their unions if they are to ensure that their unions persist in fighting for
the issues that are important to them. In sectors of the economy where
women predominate, the labour movement must encourage women to
build their own unions. The CCU and its affiliates encourage and support women to take leadership positions, and place a special focus on
addressing the needs of immigrant women.

EQUAL PAY FOR WORK OF EQUAL VALUE

In the CCU's view, the fight to win equal pay for work of equal value is
the cornerstone of the struggle to gain equality for women in the
workplace. Equal pay for work of equal value addresses the root of
economic discrimination against working women, by comparing
dissimilar jobs in order to raise the pay within the female job ghettos to
the level of pay of male-dominated work. While programs aimed at
gaining affirmative action and encouraging women to work at non-
traditional jobs help some women move out of the job ghettos, neither
approach addresses the situation of those women – most working
women – who are in job ghettos now and who will remain there. The
resistance by governments and employers to the equal pay concept con-
firms how crucial it is: while they are willing to discuss affirmative action
and non-traditional job training programs, they stubbornly oppose
equal pay for work of equal value on the grounds that it would be too
complicated – and too expensive – to implement. Certainly, it will be expensive. A fundamental redistribution of money will be necessary to
upgrade pay for women whose work has long been undervalued and
underpaid simply because women perform it.

The CCU's struggle for equal pay for work of equal value takes
place on two fronts – fighting for legislative changes, and negotiating
improvements in collective agreements – and must be backed up by
day-to-day enforcement to ensure that gains actually result in the
establishment of fair practices.

The first Canadian labour central to endorse the principle of equal pay for work of equal value, the CCU also led the fight to have the equal value concept incorporated into federal human rights legislation. The organization continues to actively campaign for equal value laws to be enacted at the provincial level, and at the federal level is opposing new exemptions to existing equal value laws, as well as working to ensure that the federal law results in good settlements.

The CCU is also firmly committed to fighting wage controls, and pointing out that their emphasis on percentage increases is a factor which retards the struggle of women to win equal pay.

On the collective bargaining front, the CCU encourages affiliates to fight for across-the-board wage increases rather than percentage increases. Because percentage increases provide larger dollar amounts to workers at the top end of the wage scale, they actually widen the gap in pay between high-paid jobs which men tend to hold and the lower-paid jobs where women are usually ghettoized. At the same time, the CCU emphasizes upgrading lower wage classifications, which are frequently the jobs women perform.

There is a strong commitment to this method of fighting for improvements, and it does produce results. One precedent-setting example is the seven-month strike fought by the Canadian Association of Industrial, Mechanical and Allied Workers (CAIMAW) against Canadian Kenworth in Burnaby, B.C. One of the major issues in the dispute was the wage discrimination against women workers in Kenworth's data processing operation. The seven women joined the union during the term of the previous contract. They earned a base rate of $6.97 an hour, compared to a base rate of $7.83 hourly in the plant. The wage discrepancy meant that an unskilled, inexperienced student working in the plant for the summer would start off earning $1.10 an hour more than the data processors.

As soon as the women joined the union, CAIMAW took the issue to arbitration, but the case did not succeed. When the contract expired, the company's offer for a new agreement would have put all data process operators well behind the plant base rate – by as much as $1.52 an hour.

In late May 1980, the Kenworth workers – the vast majority of them men – voted to strike to back up their demands for a good contract settlement. It took seven months, but when workers ratified the settlement in late December, they had won a decisive victory.

They won a general wage increase averaging 45 percent over the three-year contract term, considerably more than the 23 percent over two years the company had offered before the strike. Over the three-year term, data process wages increased between 61 percent and 72 percent, putting data process operators either within a few cents of the plant base rate or well above it. The senior operators received $1.07 an hour above the plant base rate.

The strike clearly illustrated that unions can win equal pay for work of equal value when the membership is committed to fighting for the principle. The victory at Kenworth inspired other unions to take up the equal value issue in their own contract bargaining, and equal pay for work of equal value became a key issue in subsequent strikes, such as the 1981 fight by the municipal workers' unions in the Greater Vancouver area (see Pat Davitt's article in this anthology).

SPECIFIC WOMEN'S STRUGGLES

Determination and persistence in fighting on key issues are perhaps the most important elements in winning victories that set precedents for all working women. In pursuing legislative changes which recognize women's right to equality in the workplace, the CCU is prepared to do battle with any government. The CCU believes that unions must avoid the kind of uncritical support for a single political party that hinders unions from publicly criticizing governments when they adopt policies that are detrimental to working women. And, in attempting to implement equality in the workplace, the CCU fights through every possible avenue. In collective bargaining, affiliates push hard for contract language that will guarantee the rights of working women, as well as for wage adjustments and increases that will provide equal pay for work of equal value. These demands are backed up – by strikes when necessary – to win improvements. Once affiliated unions have won these rights for their members, they ensure that they are enforced on a day-to-day basis, by fighting grievances and arbitration cases against employers that try to violate or ignore agreements. Where appropriate, cases are taken to human rights commissions and pursued.

Two specific examples of struggles waged by CCU affiliates highlight why persistence is necessary, and also the successes that can be achieved as a result of it.

THE PURETEX SPY CAMERAS

This three-year battle for civil rights and human dignity at the workplace resulted in a precedent-setting victory. The 220 workers at Puretex Knitting Company in Toronto, most of them immigrant women, won their long and difficult struggle to have closed-circuit television cameras removed from all production areas of the plant.

The workers, members of the Canadian Textile and Chemical Union, had filed two grievances over the cameras, before the union went to the Ontario Human Rights Commission with a complaint that the company was using the cameras in a discriminatory fashion against the women in the plant. One of the cameras was actually pointed at the entrance to the women's washroom. After the complaint was made in 1976, there were two years of proceedings before the commission abdicated its responsibility and dismissed the case.

In November 1978, the workers went on strike to get rid of the cameras and to win better wages and seniority rights. The union won broad support for its fight against the surveillance cameras and its call for laws to prohibit electronic spying against workers on the job. Members of both the Liberal and New Democratic parties tabled bills in the Ontario legislature which aimed to outlaw television surveillance on the job – both were defeated by the Conservative government.

After a three-month strike, the workers ratified a settlement which provided that the company would immediately take down the camera that was beamed at the women's washroom door. The settlement also called for interest arbitration, which is much stronger than grievance arbitration, to decide whether the eight remaining cameras would be removed. In late May 1979, arbitrator S.R. Ellis ordered the company to remove the remaining cameras in the plant's production areas. His decision described the cameras as "seriously offensive in human terms" and said that "the use of the cameras in the production areas of the plant cannot be justified."

The victory has helped other unions, such as the Canadian Union of Postal Workers, in their own collective bargaining efforts to protect their members from employer attempts to spy on them. The CCU is continuing the struggle to win legislation that would ban electronic surveillance of workers.

THE COFFEE GRIEVANCE

This landmark arbitration decision was an important gain in the struggle by women workers against performing work of a personal nature for their bosses. In the autumn of 1978, the 1,000 members of the York University Staff Association (YUSA) – 85 percent of whom are women – went on strike for 16 days to win a new contract. One victory was a contract clause saying that employees would not have to "perform any duties of a personal nature not connected with the approved operations of the university." The union negotiated the clause because a number of its members didn't want to have to make coffee, balance personal chequebooks or walk dogs for their bosses.

However, soon after union members went back to work, one woman filed a grievance because her supervisor insisted that she continue to make coffee for him. The union took the grievance through several internal steps before going to arbitration. At each internal step, the university claimed that any order given by a supervisor was an "approved operation" of the university.

The arbitration decision in October 1979 said that while serving coffee at business meetings might be considered an operation of the university, fetching it for a supervisor was not. The arbitrator ruled that the supervisor was attempting to have his secretary perform work of a personal nature.

The arbitration case, the first of its kind in Canada, demonstrates that it is possible to begin to break down sex stereotyping of working women. The victory was possible because the union had negotiated contract language covering this issue. Few union contracts contain such language: YUSA won the clause because it stood firm during negotiations on an issue important to its women members. The precedent set an example which other unions are now fighting to achieve.

THE CONTINUING STRUGGLE FOR WORKPLACE EQUALITY

A commitment to equality, determination and the willingness to fight does result in victories. However, a great many more of them are necessary before equality in the workplace will become a reality for all working women. The CCU and its affiliates are continuing the struggle on the legislative front as well as at the bargaining table.

Education and support work are also important. Delegates at conventions of the CCU and of its affiliated unions decide policies, which are communicated to the membership through our own publications, and beyond, through public speaking appearances by CCU representatives in schools and before other groups. Labour schools for CCU members include workshops on issues of particular concern to working women, such as how they can improve rights clauses in their contract bargaining. As well, affiliates such as the Pulp, Paper and Woodworkers of Canada have held conferences where their women members examine the role of working women and the changes needed to achieve equality in the workplace. The CCU and its members also actively support other unions and groups which are fighting for women. This support, which takes various forms, has included picket line support for unions like the Canadian Union of Postal Workers during their 1981 strike on the issue of parental rights. Another form it has taken is active participation in the National Action Committee on the Status of Women: as a member organization, the CCU plays a leading role in developing NAC policies on issues which affect working women, and ensuring that these policies are pursued.

All of these approaches are useful in the continuing struggle for equality in the workplace. This struggle involved a number of issues in addition to equal pay for work of equal value. While the list is long, it is an important one. If we are to achieve equality in the workplace, unions must keep up the fight for:

- **Parental rights.** The CCU is fighting for both legislation and union contracts which provide paid parental leave comparable to that won by Quebec public service workers in their 1979 contract settlement. Other major demands are the right to an additional two years unpaid parental leave with accumulated seniority, provisions for paternity and adoptive leave, and no employer-forced early leave.

- **An end to discriminatory Unemployment Insurance Act provisions.** Provisions which discriminate against women on the basis of pregnancy must be removed, as must penalties on re-entrants and new entrants. The CCU also opposes the department's continued interest in the two-tier system of benefits, those "with dependents" and those "without dependents."

- **Improved occupational health and safety legislation and stronger enforcement of the laws.** The laws must be able to meet the new dangers of our society, such as video display terminals. A much larger range of industrial diseases must be recognized as such so that workers have access to compensation benefits. Workplace health and safety laws must also be changed so they are oriented to the needs of women as well as men.

- **Better conditions for part-time workers.** The large majority of part-time workers are women. They have a right to the same benefits that full-time workers enjoy, such as holidays, sick benefits and pensions. They should be entitled to union protection. The inclusion of part-time workers in a bargaining unit should not be subject to an employer veto.

- **Child care.** A greatly-expanded and community-based child care system is necessary. It must be accessible, inexpensive and available to people who are in the work force or want to enter the work force.

- **No discrimination.** Working women need stronger federal and provincial human rights codes with enforcement procedures that guarantee full legal and practical equality for Canadian women. In collective bargaining, CCU affiliates work toward this goal, by negotiating strong "no-discrimination" clauses which can be used to protect women from sexual harassment and clauses which protect union members from having to perform work of a personal nature.

- **New organizing.** A large percentage of unorganized workers are women. Legislative changes should be made to better protect the right of workers to unionize and to speed up the unionization process. CCU affiliates also try to facilitate the participation of women in organizing campaigns by, for example, choosing meeting times that suit working women.

- **Improved minimum labour standards.** Because many women work in low-paid job ghettos and are unorganized, they are disproportionately affected by minimum standards legislation, including minimum wage standards.

- **An end to homework.** The homework system, which mainly affects women workers, must be outlawed, especially in the face of the growing development of microtechnology and the increased number of homeworkers it threatens to introduce.

- **Equal opportunities in training and upgrading programs.** Discrimination in these programs is one factor which helps keep women in traditional, stereotyped jobs. Discriminatory practices must be removed, both through collective bargaining and legislative change. Governments must refuse subsidies to companies which discriminate against women in their training programs. In collective bargaining, unions must fight to achieve plant-wide or office-wide seniority. Bargaining unit-wide seniority helps women in their struggle for the right to retrain for non-traditional jobs – and for promotion to more highly-paid jobs which are usually performed by men – according to the length of time they have worked in the plant, not just within a particular department. Plant-wide seniority rights are especially crucial for women workers during a time of high unemployment and widespread layoffs.

- **Fighting the piecework system.** Unions must fight the spread of this exploitative system, which predominates in the textile industry.

- **Pensions and benefits.** The Canada Pension Plan should cover all workers in Canada, and be expanded to provide decent livable pensions fully indexed to the cost of living. Workers who temporarily leave the work force to bear children and/or to care for them, should accumulate credits.

- **Rights for domestic workers.** Domestic workers must be fully covered under provincial minimum standards legislation.
- **English classes.** The CCU supports more public funding for accessible English classes, especially for immigrant women, who face double discrimination in the workplace. In order to maintain independence in developing course curriculum, the classes need to be located near, but not in, the factories themselves.
- **Jobs for women.** The CCU opposes cutbacks in social services and in the public sector. The CCU is also fighting for job protection and legislation requiring employers to give a minimum notice of six months for plant relocation, closure or technological change affecting employment. Plant closures and layoffs, as well as changes due to the increasing spread of microchip technology, more frequently affect women workers.

The CCU has also taken an active role in making recommendations for the self-reliant development of labour intensive industries, such as textiles and clothing, to keep jobs in Canada. Features of this kind of development would include mandatory global quotas, price controls to protect consumers, and priority for Canadian production of basic, non-luxury goods at affordable prices.

The movement for a democratic Canadian labour movement is growing. As part of this movement, the CCU and its affiliated unions have won a number of important, precedent-setting victories in the struggle for equal rights for working women. They have been won because of the strong commitment and willingness to fight for the rights of working women. That determination and commitment, as well as the struggle for equality, continues.

F U R T H E R   R E A D I N G S

Cornish, Mary and Laurell Ritchie. *Getting Organized: Building a Union.* Toronto: Women's Press, 1980.

Salutin, Rick. *The Organizer: A Canadian Union Life.* Toronto: James Lorimer, 1980.

The Equal Pay Coalition, "Equal Pay for Work of Equal Value." (Copies of this booklet available from The Equal Pay Coalition, c/o 521 Parkside Drive, Toronto, Ontario M6R 2Z9 or c/o 113 Spandina Road, Toronto, Ontario M5R 2T1.

GETTING ORGANIZED

... in the CLC

BY DEIRDRE GALLAGHER

The sexual division of labour results in different interests for men and women workers. Because most unions represent men's interests, it is important to struggle within the unions for the particular needs of women workers. This article by a feminist who has an equally long history as a trade unionist sets out the gains that have been made for women in the larger unions that make up the Canadian Labour Congress, the largest trade union central in Canada. As we head into an economic depression, there is an urgency to increasing women's participation in unions. Yet the problems continue for women in joining and participating fully in unions. Deirdre Gallagher argues that the fight be intensified in the women's committees and caucuses of the large powerful unions. Implicit in this argument is the need for strong and supportive connections between feminists who are inside and those who are outside of the unions.

FIRST AND LAST

W OMEN IN THE Canadian labour movement are proud of the many victories we have won in the last ten years. There are so many firsts it is difficult to count them all. The first women pilots, miners, the first women working on the green chain in the B.C. logging industry, the first women to climb telephone poles on line crews, the first women to work on the coke ovens at the Steel Co. of Canada – and, since the Second World War, the first woman electrician, carpenter, and tool and die maker. Individuals or small groups of women are crossing the occupational borders between the sexes.

There are other firsts – paid maternity leave, winning equal pay for work of equal value for thousands of low-paid service workers in the employ of the federal government, protection against sexual harassment in union contracts and the winning of union rights for part-time workers at the post office.

These achievements are reflected in the developing power of women within the labour movement. Women's numbers in the organized trade union movement have increased at double the rate of men's. There are growing numbers of women's committees and caucuses and more women are represented in union leadership bodies. And most of these successes are a direct consequence of women's activism. However, breakthroughs for women workers, while symbolically of exceptional importance, do not reflect the actual state of most working women's lives.

The vast and challenging entry of women into paid labour in the last decade initially provided an increased standard of living for working-class families; but today, with high inflation and an escalating cost of living, families are barely holding their own. Moreover, women's entry into the paid work force has not been matched by increased social services, especially in the area of child care, nor by a greater sharing of domestic responsibilities by men – women work harder than ever before. And, as a group, women still stand last economically in our society.

GETTING ORGANIZED

As 29 percent of union members, women are a minority of organized workers. One of the most serious weaknesses of the Canadian labour movement is the absence of organizing breakthroughs in the sales and service area, where women predominate. The growth in women's union membership has largely come from the transformation of public service associations into real unions, which are now affiliated with the Canadian Labour Congress (CLC). But in other areas, the news is not so good. The CLC's much publicized campaign to organize bank workers has floundered against terrific opposition from the banks. Hardly a dent has been made in the vast numbers of unorganized women workers in the new technology industries. Most of the major department store chains in this country are also without unions. And it is an uphill battle to win union rights for workers in the food producing, textile and garment industries and the low-wage industrial ghettos.

The reasons for the low rate of successful unionization are many and complex. Two dominant factors are fierce employer opposition and poor legislative protection of the right to join a union. Women are frightened to unionize, fearing the loss of even the meagre income they have. Women's double responsibilities for work and the home also leave little leisure for union activity. In addition, within the labour movement, there is difficulty turning a traditionally male-dominated institution toward a style of organizing that speaks in the language of working women.

THE ROLE OF MEN

Trade unions, like all political institutions in our society, are dominated by men. As such they tend to reflect men's interests, represent men's needs and operate according to the standard of male social behaviour. It is true that where men's and women's interests coincide, the labour movement defends the needs of working women. As workers, people of both sexes face high inflation, unemployment and government policies that favour the privileged in our society. Men and women are allies in a common struggle for a decent standard of living and a life of dignity.

It is also true, as a measure of women's success in the labour movement over the last ten years, that many men have supported the fight for women's equality. They earn the right to be called union brothers when they support the inclusion of maternity leave in contracts and then take it one step further and ask for leave for fathers to spend time caring for their young children.

Some men fight against sexual harassment from supervisors and co-workers, not out of a paternalistic attitude, but because they understand such treatment degrades all workers. Others express their solidarity with women by fighting for across-the-board increases rather than percentage wage hikes even though men tend to be at the top end of the pay scale and gain more by percentage increases.

Some men have stood in support of women who are fighting to gain entry into non-traditional jobs or training programs and have shown support for their union sisters by voting and campaigning for them at union election time. Some men have even joined women's committees in local unions because they believe that the fight for women's equality concerns all trade unionists.

Women have been gratified by the support of men and have been exhilarated to see the changes in their attitudes and behaviour these last years. Women do not want to fight with men: we want to fight together against the real injustices we live with every day of our lives. Not only does this strengthen the women's cause but it creates a more powerful labour movement.

WOMEN'S LEADERSHIP

In spite of the growing support of men, women must direct our own battles and act as leaders representing both men and women in the trade union movement. Many unions remain untouched by the developing awareness and needs of their women members, and it is virtually unheard of for a union to examine the position of women within its own structure, and begin to do something about it.

According to a recent paper on affirmative action prepared by the Ontario Federation of Labour's Women's Committee,

> If we are advocating mandatory affirmative action programs within the workplace, we must be aware of the implications of such a demand on our own structures. . . . It is no longer acceptable to say that the women simply aren't there, or they're not qualified, as both labour and management have been saying. The women are there. What we must do is ensure the necessary supports are also there so that women can become involved, and that the methods we use to hire and promote, the education and training, are as open to women as to men.

Let us examine some of the statistics. In 1978, statistics show that while women comprise 29% of union membership, just 17.5% of all union executive board members are women. In 1982, the CLC, which represents 75% of all union members in Canada, has one of its four national officers a woman and three out of 26 on the executive council (13%). In the OFL, one out of sixteen executive board members is a woman (6%).

CUPE, at 44%, was the national union with the highest number of female members in 1980, but just 7 of the 18 national executive officers were women (38%), 5 of the provincial officers (27%) and only 20 of the 170 staff representatives were women (11%). In the Public Service Alliance, with a 43% female membership, in 1982, none of the national executive officers is a woman and 3 of the other 19 members of the national board of directors is a woman (6%). In OPSEU , with a 50% female membership, 4 out of 28 executive board members are women (14%).

Female involvement is more representative at intermediate and local leadership levels . . . . But even at this level women are under-represented with OPSEU, for example, having 25% of local presidents as women and 36% of local executive members women in 1981 compared to an overall female membership of 50%. When you look at the statistics, it is apparent that the person who usually makes it to the top more often than not is a man. Somewhere our democratic structures are failing.

BARRIERS TO WOMEN'S INVOLVEMENT

Why are women inadequately represented in leadership positions and what can be done about it? There are four major barriers – women's disadvantaged position in the work force and its effect on women's union involvement; the double day of work for women; prejudice and discrimination; and the negative aspects of power politics in the labour movement.

WOMEN'S WORK

The conditions of women's work and their lower standard of living is the most important factor undermining women's participation in the labour movement. For many women, life is a constant struggle just to make ends meet. If one works piece rate in the garment industry, on incentive in a factory, or at video display terminals eight hours a day, at average wage levels half of men's, there is precious little left over either in energy, time or money. It costs money to be a union activist, to come downtown for meetings, to pay for dinners away from home, to go to the pub where a lot of union politicking goes on after a meeting, or to pay for a babysitter. All the things we fight for in the labour movement – equal pay, maternity leave, freedom from sexual harassment and for unionization – contribute to the advancement of women's equality within our own ranks, because they provide a better standard of living and conditions at work, more leisure and peace of mind.

An example of this can be found in the Canadian Union of Postal Workers (CUPW). At a recent conference on the workplace and the family, Jean-Claude Parrot, the head of the postal workers, described his union's efforts to improve women's position on the job and its effect on their participation in the union. Over several sets of contract negotiations, the union fought to include part-time workers in the bargaining unit, to ensure they received pro-rated benefits and wages and were protected by seniority. The vast majority of part-time workers were women whose inferior wages and conditions were being used to undercut those of the full-time workers, the majority of whom were men.

Achieving this allowed part-timers to use seniority to become full-time workers if they wished and many did. As well, part-time workers were given full union rights. This increased the percentage of women in the union and provided the incentive to include maternity leave in the last set of negotiations. Fighting for this put women's concerns front and centre in union negotiations and winning it means women don't have to drop out when they have children.

Women's involvement in CUPW has also increased considerably and Mr. Parrot pointed to the election of a woman as full-time president of one of the largest locals in the country in Toronto. Improving the conditions of work helps to support women's position within the union and organizing more women into unions increases our overall political weight.

THE DOUBLE DAY

Another major obstacle to women's participation in the union movement is the fact that we continue to shoulder the major responsibilities for home life. Active women unionists not only handle our jobs and union responsibilities like men do but we also go home to another job. And recent statistics show little change in the amount of housework and caring for children done by men. If we were to examine it, we would find that in the past the few women who did make it into union leadership positions were single or childless or became active after their children were grown, or, in a few remarkable cases, may have had husbands who shared family responsibilities. Today's union woman wants to participate fully even if she is a parent. Parenthood has never been an impediment for men.

Some unions have taken a number of actions to facilitate women's involvement. The scheduling of union meetings at times convenient to women workers is one. Making child care or child care subsidies available for local union meetings and conferences also encourages women's involvement and is increasingly seen as a right.

Much more remains to be done. For union staff, adequate maternity leave and reasonable hours of work are necessary. And union education programs must encourage men to carry their share of home duties to free up women for union activity.

PREJUDICE

Many people claim that the prejudice women face when they run for union office is a problem of attitudes, which change slowly – and that it is a question of time. However, there are concrete things we can and must do to overcome the prejudice. In any union, the first step has to be the adoption of union policies which ensure the fair representation of women, and which encourage and find the means to set up structures like women's or equal opportunity committees. Secondly, the union must undertake an active educational campaign to promote an understanding of equality issues.

In the Steelworkers, as in a number of other major unions, educational programs have changed in the last few years to include a greater emphasis on equality for women. There are courses on women's rights that also encourage the participation of men, and an integration of these concerns throughout the whole education program in union leadership and stewards' training courses, health and safety, and collective bargaining. Special scholarships have been set aside for the specific use of women as an affirmative action measure to encourage their participation in union schools.

Most Steelworkers' courses are taught by rank and file local union people who are trained as instructors by the union. One-third of a group of new instructors in Ontario are women. That didn't happen by accident; women were mostly overlooked before; now they are being actively sought out. Clearly, putting women up front as leaders and giving them the opportunity to meet each other and work together is crucial for the development of women's leadership.

At the level of union leadership, structural changes are needed to guarantee the representation of women. Only one of 17 executive officers of the Ontario Federation of Labour (OFL) is a woman, for example. The OFL women's committee is recommending a number of approaches to ensure a 30 percent representation of women, reflecting our numbers in union ranks.

It is also important for union organizations to hire full-time staff responsible for equal opportunity programs. Now, only the Canadian

Union of Public Employees (CUPE) and the Ontario Public Service Employees Union (OPSEU) have such staff. Without union time and resources being devoted to women's programs, new policies aren't worth the paper they are written on.

HUMANIZING THE POLITICAL WORLD

Until recently, men have been free to participate in union life with the support of a woman at home taking care of their family responsibilities. Men, because of women's work at home, have had time to be involved. Because few women participated, the political world has been dominated by men who are socialized to be highly competitive and ambitious. Women are ambivalent about exercising power in their own right because of the negative stereotypes associated with ambition in women, and because they lack confidence. On top of that women often have to work twice as hard to receive the same recognition men come by more easily.

Men are socialized to aggression and the hiding of feelings; women to passivity and emotional expression. Women feel conflict very intensely. We have also been trained to mediate conflict. But women are forced to operate by the standards of male political behaviour that were set before we arrived. It is true that in the process we have learned a lot that is positive: to be assertive, to speak out, to fight for what we believe in and to lead with greater confidence. Many women, however, resent the idea that they have to become "one of the boys" to make it in union leadership. For one thing, power politics and intense competition don't appear to be all that healthy.

Many women in male-dominated work environments succumb to male standards. But many others have tried to assert that what we know and see as women has value for men. Women acknowledge having learned a lot from men but more and more we are confident enough to realize they have much to learn from us. New roles for men and women and new standards of political behaviour are a necessity for the labour movement.

OUR FAIR SHARE

The importance of these issues was underlined at a recent union equality school. In a film on microelectronics a woman shop steward spoke about how tech change was hurting women workers, in particular. She was concerned that as the number of jobs are reduced, men and women are forced to compete with each other for work. She wasn't confident that men unionists would stand by women's right to work and thought they might fall victim to the idea that women should go back to the kitchens where we supposedly belong.

The discussion after the film revealed that everyone shared this woman's fears, especially considering the recession. To a person, including the two men in the class, they agreed that women might not be able to count on union men when push comes to shove over jobs.

Many men do support us. We have allies. But it is the force of numbers and the examples of our struggles that have won us respect and recognition. Winning support from men is important but everyone agreed that it is even more crucial that women become powerful in our unions in our own right, because that is the only way our needs will be represented.

When we demand of employers and government our fair share of the economic pie in good times or bad, union women have to put our political muscle behind guaranteeing our rights in the union movement too. That's why it is a major goal of women union activists to elect women to negotiating committees and union executives and to see to it that women are hired as union staff in proportionate numbers. That's why we will continue, more than ever, to organize through women's committees and caucuses.

If the promise of the last ten years for union women is to be kept, it will require an intensification of the fight on all fronts, for equality within the labour movement, to organize the unorganized and a concerted push by the unions and the women's movement for women's right to work.

The 1982 CLC convention, where the labour movement declared its opposition to wage concessions, also heard women call for no concessions on the principle of women's equality. Women do not want to fight men for jobs. We want social and economic policies that guarantee full and equal employment for all. But it is an obligation and a necessity that we organize to defend and extend our right to a job.

This is the crunch. It is a time of testing the labour movement's commitment to women's equality. It is a time of testing women's power.

GETTING ORGANIZED

... in Saskatchewan
Working Women

BY DENISE KOURI

The existence of organizations such as Saskatchewan Working Women, Organized Working Women in Ontario and Union Sisters in Vancouver testifies to the fact that more is needed than women's committees and caucuses in the unions. These organizations provide working women with the opportunity to make links and fight together to achieve their common goals. Some of these organizations have been restricted to unionized women, but one of the problems of women workers is that large numbers of us are as yet unorganized. SWW recognizes that the best way to be a powerful presence within the labour movement and yet maintain some autonomy from it is to include women who are not in unions. Denise Kouri outlines how SWW has combined feminist and trade union concerns in its strike support for women workers and its struggles around issues like day care and organizing the unorganized.

S ASKATCHEWAN WORKING WOMEN (SWW) embodies an important strategy for class-conscious feminists: it is an autonomous women's organization, linked to the labour movement but not controlled by it. SWW acts as an educational and support group for women workers, representing their concerns to employers and governments as well as to the union movement itself. SWW does not choose between feminism on the one hand and trade unionism on the other; rather, it poses problems and their solutions within an analysis that addresses both together.

SWW was formally founded in September 1979, after the idea for it was introduced at a Saskatchewan Federation of Labour (SFL) Women's Conference in the spring of 1978. Never a formal part of the SFL structure, SWW is open to all women who agree with its principles, whether they are unionized or not, or employed or not. Remaining within the SFL would have limited us to having union women only as members and to dealing exclusively with union-related issues. An open organization was thus a step toward a broader direction.

SWW tries to function as democratically as possible and encourages all members to be active. There are no paid positions. While SWW holds educationals and discussions and formulates policy on particular issues, we are concerned to be public, outward-reaching and militant.

The theme of the SWW Founding Convention in 1979 was "cutbacks." Still reeling from the federal government's "restraint" policies of 1976-77, SWW members discussed how cutbacks affect working women: as paid workers, as consumers of public services and as workers in the home. When cutbacks occur in health care services, for example, they affect nurses, nursing assistants and other support staff; they affect patients; and they affect mothers and housewives, who have to carry more of the burden within the home. SWW took the position that for everyone, but especially for women, what happens on the job cannot be separated from what happens in the family. At that convention, members also encouraged the labour movement to take an outreach approach, and address itself to the community in its struggle against public sector cutbacks.

The 1970s have often been called the decade of the public sector union and SWW's activities certainly confirm this. Members carried out support work in strikes against the three levels of government in Saskatchewan. In 1979, the Saskatchewan Government Employees Association (SGEA), with 11,000 members across the province, the majority of whom were women, went on strike for the five-four work schedule for clerical staff, better seniority clauses and better pay. In December 1980, SWW assisted the SGEA Liquor Board workers. This group had a minority of women, but an important issue was upgrading the bottom of the pay scale, which, of course, affected mainly women. In the spring of 1981, SWW supported the CUPE Local 59 workers in their strike against Saskatoon City Hall. The issues in this case were the five-five-four work schedule, an across-the-board wage increase to boost the clerical workers' pay scale and parity for public health nurses. In all these strikes, SWW support work involved more than just a presence on the picket lines. Part of the job involved informing the membership and the public at large about the issues involved, and why they were important for working women. Media coverage and mailings were used: in the Liquor Board strike, there was a special picketing of boycotted restaurants, and in the case of the Saskatoon Civic Workers, SWW presented a brief to City Council.

SWW also acts as an organizational advocate for working women. In 1980, we presented a brief to the Saskatchewan Human Rights Commission (SHRC), urging freedom of sexual orientation, no discrimination against people with children, critical support of the SHRC Affirmative Action program and more active enforcement of human rights provisions in general. In March 1981, SWW presented to the SFL, in conjunction with two CUPE locals, a brief suggesting improvements in the Trade Union Act. Among other points, the brief stressed the problems the current Act has with respect to organizing drives, obviously an issue for working women today.

SWW has also been refining its position on affirmative action. While SWW supports affirmative action in principle as a tool for helping to overcome discrimination, it acknowledges that all forms of affirmative action are not equally worthy of support. SWW is working on positive proposals for use by unions in formulating and pressuring for affirmative action programs.

From this description it is clear that SWW does not see the problems of working women as being strictly job-related, but that we place them in the context of women's position in the family and society as a whole. Some people have the misconception that SWW is strictly union-related. We do devote a lot of time to union work, because we cannot see major changes in women's position in the work force unless there are major changes in the unions, which represent an important collective weapon for workers. To this end, SWW is active in promoting rank and file involvement in unions and in pressing unions to be more active around women's issues.

The child care issue, for example, is one of our main priorities. And our educationals have concerned themselves with every aspect of women's lives – from occupational health to nuclear power to reproductive freedom. We have also cooperated with other groups on various related issues. For example, we supported a transition house's fight for funds, the Nicaraguan Women's Health Brigades and the Carleton university women's struggle against sexual harassment.

In SWW two social movements have come together. On the one hand, SWW is one more aspect of the struggle for women's rights. The women's liberation movement of the 1960s was composed of a wide range of political ideologies and strategies. In the 1970s, this broad movement went through the inevitable process of sorting itself out along political lines. SWW is one of the results of this evolution – an organization committed to fighting along class lines in the struggle for women's liberation. On the other hand, SWW is linked to an emerging radicalization within the labour movement. Rising militancy and increasing pressure for democracy and rank and file involvement are growing trends in the labour movement. This trend is crucial to the formation and continuing existence of SWW.

The labour movement has been severely criticized for its failure to respond to the needs and problems of working women. The usual explanation for this has been that unions are mostly led and controlled by men, who tend to ignore "women's issues." While this is no doubt true, this explanation obscures another very significant reason for the labour movement's relative inactivity regarding women's problems – the dominant political character of the labour movement itself. The conservative, reformist-at-best nature of the dominant stream of the union movement in Canada has not welcomed radical non-economistic tendencies of any sort within its ranks.

Organizations like SWW represent a challenge on both fronts, in countering male chauvinism and in representing a radical tendency within the union movement. The two are clearly related. The nature of women's problems on the job, the double burden of job and family: these cannot be addressed within the narrow parameters of traditional business unionism. Confronting these problems necessarily widens the struggle to encompass the whole social structure and consequently the broader political forces in society. Fighting for women's issues inevitably means fighting for rank and file control of unions, because that is where women are, and rank and file control is what is needed to change trade union policy. These factors have not endeared groups like SWW to the current trade union leadership.

In Saskatchewan this tension has involved the particular problem of the New Democratic Party (NDP). The CLC policy of supporting the NDP resulted in total SFL acquiescence to the Saskatchewan NDP government's policies. This allowed the government to implement anti-labour policies that would never have been tolerated from other governments. For example, the NDP's April 1981 amendment to the Trade Union Act impedes strike action by workers, such as hospital workers, who bargain on a voluntary provincial basis. The amendment went unopposed by the SFL. The struggle for a militant, progressive labour movement in Saskatchewan is inextricably tied to labour's independence from the NDP. Although the initial reason SWW was formed autonomously from the SFL had to do with membership criteria, political differences – such as SWW's criticism of the NDP and SWW's general approach to trade unionism – are perpetual sources of tension.

SWW nevertheless maintains itself as a strong organization, with support from individual unions and rank and filers. The priorities of the organization continue to be education and solidarity among working women. Technological change and child care will be major concerns, as will be the involvement of unorganized and rural women in SWW activities. Within the labour movement, SWW will continue to agitate and educate around women's issues and to fight for a more progressive direction for labour. The eventual success of SWW's efforts is strongly linked to the growing struggle for progressive unionism, of which SWW is itself a part. Fundamental change for working women cannot be achieved without struggle in the labour movement – but just as important, the struggle waged by women workers will help to transform the labour movement itself.

Sexual Harassment

AS A FORM OF SOCIAL CONTROL

BY MARLENE KADAR

As women we have been traditionally trained to regard a sexual comment either as a compliment or as a silly joke, to ignore obscene gestures and to keep quiet about our feelings about more overt sexual invasions of privacy. Often we have internalized our feelings into guilt that we have done something to warrant this treatment from men. Until we defined it as "sexual harassment" we had to contend individually with these disturbing incidents in our everyday lives. Once these incidents had been labeled it allowed us to focus on our anger – anger at the intrusiveness, and rage that our bodies were violated. When sexual harassment occurs in the midst of our work lives it is a double jeopardy because often the man who is at fault has power over our jobs. Marlene Kadar's article brings us up to date on union contract demands for protection from sexual harassment as well as on how union women are dealing with the problem of co-worker harassment.

S EXUAL HARASSMENT, like other forms of violent sexual assault, strikes right at that part of ourselves we learn we should reserve for intimacy – our sexuality. Is it any wonder that working women from Halifax to Vancouver are forcing this skeleton out of the closet? This is an issue that doesn't just affect the bank account – as it surely does – but it also, and perhaps more importantly, does long-term damage to the self, to our dignity and self-respect.

Sexual harassment is one of the levers those in power use to control those who are not. When society is suffering from economic hardship, it is particularly important to control groups of workers and the most vulnerable group is women. Because we are increasingly vocal, those in power feel a need to grant some measure of equality to us. But there are continuing subtle ways of controlling large masses of human beings who must sell their labour in order to survive. Sexual harassment is one of those ways – and we must become as vocal about it as we are about equal pay or affirmative action.

Sexual harassment is not a new crime, but it is true that we are talking about it more today than ever before. The recent influx of women into the labour force has been so great that sexual harassment has become a problem that is hard to ignore.[1] Sexual harassment is almost expected in job ghetto areas where women represent the service and clerical occupations. Here women are most vulnerable to a supervisor's or a co-worker's explicit or implicit demands.

This is not to say that women in non-traditional jobs, for example, are invulnerable. Though there is still a lot of controversy about the exact nature and degree of sexual harassment in these jobs, it is clear that the problem exists. One thing we can all agree on is that more research is needed. Women participants at the Winnipeg Women in Trades Conference (1982) were especially concerned about the isolation of the lone woman worker. Male co-workers tended to ignore the lone woman, making it difficult for her to sustain the pressure of always being alone and, hence, silent. Other tradeswomen talked about extreme forms of sexual harassment on the site; one welder wrote about her experience with attempted rape. Edmonton writer, Joann Kolmes, has dramatized the experience of a lone construction worker in her play, "Powerplays,"[2] in which a woman is forced to sweep floors while her brothers build buildings. Her credentials are immediately undermined, and she is easy bait for the harassment that follows. In the end she is fired for "causing a disturbance." Yet other tradeswomen have cited better co-worker relations on the site or in the factory than inside the office. One Alberta woman, a machinist, felt that once a tradeswoman had established herself among her male co-workers (by speaking up, for example), she was accepted and protected.

Backhouse and Cohen argue in *Sexual Harassment on the Job* that sexual harassment cuts across class lines, cultures and languages. They call the myth that the higher-status working woman is not sexually harassed the "Archie Bunker theory," and point out that to say working-class women receive more harassment is tantamount to saying working-class men who work with or supervise these women harass more than their upper-class counterparts. *Not true.*[3] Theoretically, at least, there seems to be more potential for less harassment in the non-traditional trades jobs, if only because the relationship of one welder to another, for example, is more equal than that of a clerk to an executive.

SEXUAL HARASSMENT: DEFINITIONS AND SURVEYS

The way we define sexual harassment is indicative of the kind of battle we intend to wage against it, and is therefore extremely important. A definition sets the tone of a complaint or a media interview or a board of inquiry hearing, and, as such, must be written with women's – not the union's, management's, or campus authorities' – interests in mind.

In Alberta, members of the Alliance Against Sexual Harassment (AASH), have come up with a definition of sexual harassment written by women for women – a definition with as wide appeal and as few limiting clauses as possible. Although several definitions of sexual harassment had been in use, they were limited and did not apply to situations of co-worker harassment. As Laura Lee, a member of AASH and the Letter Carriers Union of Canada (LCUC) said: "We wrote the definition with the negotiator's first rule in mind: ask for everything that you want and you may get something you can live with." AASH took this rule seriously because it wanted to work with the grass roots of the union movement in Alberta. Many of its own members are active in their unions and would negotiate clauses into their collective agreements. The definition AASH presented reads in part as follows:

> Sexual harassment is any unwanted sexually based or sexually oriented practice which creates discomfort and/or threatens a woman's personal well-being or functioning (mental, physical or emotional). Sexual harassment includes verbal abuse, jokes, leering, touching or any unnecessary contact, the display of pornographic material, the invasion of personal space, sexual assault and rape, or any threat of retaliation or actual retaliation for any of the above.[4]

Although there are no national surveys on sexual harassment to date, and although the response rate to questionnaires has not always been high, we have more than enough information to ascertain that most women have experienced some form of sexual harassment on the job, on campus or in the streets. A few samples: 83 percent of women responding to a questionnaire put out by the Thunder Bay Committee on Sexual Harassment in 1980 considered sexual harassment to be "a serious problem" and 40 percent of the respondents had suffered serious repercussions from harassment. Ninety-two percent of the women who responded to a 1981 Women in Trades questionnaire felt that they had been sexually harassed. In a survey that I conducted through the Alberta Union of Provincial Employees (AUPE), 80 percent of the women who responded had experienced some form of sexual harassment. And, in a course I taught at the University of Alberta in 1981-82, all of the women, with one exception, responded that they had been harassed. None of the men in the course thought that they had been. The evidence is there: the problem exists.

EFFECTS OF SEXUAL HARASSMENT

There are psychological and physical effects of sexual harassment as well as job-related consequences. As the Thunder Bay Committee has said: "Sexual harassment is women's most dangerous occupational hazard. It threatens our paycheque, it undermines our health and self-image."[5] Women lose their jobs through firings, or they resign because of pressure. We also lose future job opportunities: how many women who have left or lost their jobs would get good references from their supervisors, especially if the supervisors were the harassers?

Backhouse and Cohen have described and given a name to the health condition that results from sexual harassment: "sexual harassment syndrome."[6] In Canada, sexual harassment syndrome hasn't yet got the authority we need to present to our various tribunals as "evidence." Neither doctors nor lawyers talk about it as if it were a serious condition. Yet the stress effects, both physical and psychological, are very serious: ulcers, eating problems, insomnia, depression. Sexual harassment syndrome is perhaps closest to the reaction experienced by a rape victim. There is a sense of guilt and shame and powerlessness. Therapy is often required and this is where support groups can be especially useful. For those women who seek compensation through human rights bodies, who hire a lawyer to sue the harasser, or who file a grievance with their unions, it is to the advantage of their cases to seek the advice of a professional psychologist as soon after the incident as possible.

REMEDIES

There are no real remedies; there are only partial remedies, and some are better than others. Most of them require that the victim of sexual harassment initiate an action and follow it through. Not all women have the psychological or financial resources to initiate an official action such as a union grievance, a complaint to the employer or human rights commission, or a legal battle. Worse, most of the "official" solutions initiate an adversary process requiring, in many instances, the woman to defend herself against the accusations of the harasser. We would be better off to create new ways of seeing this problem, by providing new channels for our protection, and by continually educating ourselves and the public on the issue. In order to be truly effective, women have to retain control over the course of action. As it stands, all victims relinquish a certain amount of control as soon as they approach an official public body. Women, already vulnerable, perhaps jobless, perhaps threatened, experiencing a lot of self-doubt, are easy targets for lawyers and union representatives who choose to defend the harasser. Each case must be carefully assessed before deciding on the route to take, because – and I can't say this often enough – there are many variables to consider, and each case is different.

PERSONAL SOLUTIONS

Under certain circumstances (especially when they feel secure in their jobs), women might want to opt for the personal solutions listed below. In any case, women should keep personal diaries and/or records, as outlined in points 4 and 6.

1. Confront the harasser, and firmly demand an end to his behaviour.
2. Put your statement to the harasser in writing and demand a reply. Duplicate all correspondence.
3. Let your trusted co-workers know; see if there are or have been any other cases of sexual harassment in your workplace.
4. Keep a diary of all events: time, place, how it happened, the conversation that transpired. Look for reliable witnesses to corroborate your story, and note your conversations with them.
5. Try a sympathetic person at personnel, the harasser's supervisor, a union steward, and examine all company and union policy. Follow up meetings with memos, and keep copies for your own files.
6. Keep a record of any changes in your duties or in evaluations of your work (both verbal and written).

OFFICIAL REMEDIES:
THE CIVIL CODE, THE CRIMINAL CODE
AND HUMAN RIGHTS COMMISSIONS

Backhouse and Cohen point out that there are limitations to using the criminal and civil codes, and to consulting human rights bodies. All have their first interest in restoring equilibrium rather than in eradicating the problem of sexual harassment. What a woman chooses to do must depend on the specific conditions of her case, her financial situation and her physical and mental health. These variables must be assessed before a woman can be properly advised either to sue or to file a complaint with a human rights commission.

Criminal actions seem the most obvious route to take, but we must remember that there can be no conviction in criminal actions unless the crown attorney proves the case "beyond a reasonable doubt." The burden of proof is already great – and in sexual harassment cases (as in rape cases) it is especially so, because a woman's credibility hangs in the balance. Moreover, there are not always witnesses in sexual harassment cases, and when there are, they may not feel comfortable coming forward. After all, once they do, their jobs might become insecure.

The probability of conviction increases if the rapist – or the harasser – is a stranger to the victim. In employment situations this is unlikely to be the case. Though an employee may not know her supervisor or co-workers *well,* she does know them. This causes further problems when the prosecuting lawyer tries to establish credibility.

Civil actions have a greater chance of success than criminal actions, but only in criminal actions is the offender punished. Unlike criminal prosecutions, which are state-initiated, with the goal of penalizing "criminals" in order to protect society as a whole, "tort liability" exists to award damages to an injured person by compelling the wrongdoer to pay money to the victim. The victim brings the action to court. Torts are based on actual cases and as such are part of what is known as "common law." Torts do not cover every situation, every unsavoury conduct, or the exact circumstances of every case – there is no such thing as the "tort of sexual harassment." However, "the law of torts. . .should attempt to discourage certain forms of socially undesirable behaviour."[7] (The word "tort" derives from the Latin *tortus,* meaning twisted, as in "tortuous," which I think is apt.) To effectively use torts, one must take the particular case of sexual harassment and twist it enough so that it fits into another case, or into some other kind of tort.

Though civil remedies have rarely been used in sexual harassment cases, Backhouse and Cohen see the potential for "some very fruitful and financially rewarding litigation." They caution women, however, that chances are a woman will lose her job, if she has not already done so.

The goal of human rights bodies is to "conciliate," to reconcile the two parties to a "mutually acceptable resolution." If a complaint to a human rights commission is substantiated, the "court," or the tribunal, may order that "the discriminatory practice cease," or that "compensation be paid" for wages lost or "for damage to the victim's feelings or self-respect." The commission may demand reinstatement of the victim, or a letter of apology. A person must decide how valuable each of these "awards" is before she proceeds with a complaint, because the chances of success are, as with some of the legal remedies, not great. Of the 13 cases that Backhouse and Cohen summarize, for example, nine were found to be "unsubstantiated." In the cases where awards of money were made, the amounts seem small: $250, $300, two weeks' severance pay. That was a few years ago, and things have changed somewhat. (In a recent Alberta case, the woman was awarded $1,500.) However, human rights commissions' emphasis on "settlement and negotiation immediately renders the commissions a less than effective agent."[8] In this way commissions band-aid stresses in the employment system by "restoring equilibrium." Clearly this is true of each of the remedies we have reviewed. The union movement *should* be different, but is it?

UNIONS AND WOMEN'S ORGANIZATIONS

Today in Canada one-quarter of all working women are members of unions, and in the past decade they have entered unions in unprecedented numbers. If you are a member of a union, it makes sense to go to your union for action on the question of sexual harassment. Under the duty of fair representation, unions have the legal obligation to defend all of their members, regardless of sex. More than that, it is in the best interests of unions to take sexual harassment seriously because it can be "a first-rate organizing tool,"[9] especially in public sector unions, where women have a large representation.

However, there is what I will call a "resistance" on the part of unions to actively take up what have unfortunately come to be known as segregated "women's issues." In order to counter this resistance, unions should take responsibility for illustrating how sexual harassment violates women and is no credit to men. It is in the best interests of work, of satisfying work relationships and of fulfilling love relationships for all of us to put an end to sexual harassment.

My own experience in a public sector union attests to this resistance. Even when individual men and women wanted to support a campaign against sexual harassment within the union, others felt the pressure from peers not to break rank, not to diverge from the dominant view or the needs of the brotherhood. Some are just embarrassed by the subject. As the editor of a union magazine, I published an interview with one of the union's members, a woman who had been sexually assaulted by her supervisor. In the weeks after publication of that issue, I understood one thing for sure: sexual harassment gets everybody talking. One woman member, reputed to have been a shop steward, wrote a scathing letter about the article. What she said about her union sister, the woman who had agreed to be interviewed, was worse: "This lady does not need a Union, she needs a psychiatrist!" She did not see her sister's experience as something she or her union could fight for: "If this is a factual article," she says, "the woman you describe can never hope to be considered equal. This woman is 'Victim Material' and does not represent the female work force." The letter writer said she was in agreement with equality, but she seemed to think sexual harassment was not a part of it. The interviewee, or the victim, had a different point of view. She said that even though her co-workers "realize sexual harassment is going on, they are not willing to do anything about it." Those who knew she had made a complaint about sexual harassment treated her differently than they had before. She said, "In some instances I have felt a cool breeze, if you know what I mean, from some of the ladies. Most of the men seem to think that it is funny and absolutely shun the entire matter." These two women reveal the range of responses to sexual harassment inside their union.

Apart from the high profile and very positive influence of the National Union of Provincial Government Employees (NUPGE) on the subject of sexual harassment (largely the work of one person, Susan Attenborough), the unions, despite good intentions, have not held their own in this area. Half of the women who responded to a union questionnaire said that they did not even call the union when they were harassed. Those who did call say they "got no action." Though the responses varied, not one of the callers was encouraged to file a grievance, and, consequently, none of them did. One respondent said that the union rep "laughed" when she called, but that her co-workers supported her so that she wouldn't have to be alone with her boss. Another woman who called was just told to "be extremely cautious." She said that her spirit was broken, and that she had "received a bad exit evaluation." Another woman was told that her case was "too difficult to prove," and therefore nothing could be done. She was a secretary, and she commented that most women were "too embarrassed" to do anything about sexual harassment. "Educating them to react would help tremendously," she said. Another woman, a duplicating equipment operator, interestingly enough thought that at least some of the men would benefit from education. She thought "the older men" were "worse than the young men, who can at least be spoken with and possibly instructed." A few other women reported that when they phoned their union rep they were advised to see the union psychologist.

A difficult problem arises when a co-worker and co-member of the union is guilty of harrassment. As reported by the _Toronto Star_ (December 27, 1981), a worker can be dismissed if he has sexually harassed a co-worker. The union may have to, and will, try to defend the harasser. This puts tremendous pressure on the woman who finds herself allied with management against the union: she will probably be isolated if her union and co-members try to convince her to withdraw her complaint, water down her testimony, tell the arbitration board that "really, he is such a nice guy." They may try guilt: "You're not a real trade unionist;" "He's got a wife and three kids to support!" This kind of problem can be dealt with only in the long term, by forcing discussion and union accountability. It cannot be done by isolated individuals.

It is because of unions' resistance to the issue of sexual harassment and other issues of concern to working women, that women have found it necessary to organize outside of their trade unions in order to raise and defend their interests without being threatened, dismissed, laughed at, or just burnt out.[10] Women in Trades (WIT), Ontario Working Women (OWW), Saskatchewan Working Women (SWW) and the Alliance Against Sexual Harassment (AASH) are prime examples of a response to this need. In these organizations, women retain control over their own struggles, and at the same time, provide the impetus and the information needed to educate the labour movement in general about their concerns.

What can we reasonably accomplish in the name of labour without compromising ourselves, and without giving up?

1. We must continue to support our independent organizations, realizing that alone we can do very little.
2. We must try and work with unions on the very specific needs of women workers around the issue of sexual harassment. Conferences such as WIT can initiate at least two major projects: a survey of the members and their experiences with sexual harassment and a policy

statement on sexual harassment, whose distribution could be coordinated across Canada. This policy statement might address itself to some of the negative effects of the nonetheless pioneering statement put out by the British Columbia Government Employees' Union (1980), which begins defensively: "Although there may be instances of employees who initiate or encourage sexual activities with male supervisors, clients or co-workers, harassment is distinct from 'acceptable' flirting; however, on occasion this line may be difficult to draw." This is essentially an anti-employer statement, and starts out by actually blaming women, which does us more harm than good. We come first; the goal is not "to get" employers – it is to put an end to sexual harassment on the job. The ideal statement explains why sexual harassment is a problem in the workplace, how it should be defined, and why – because people are afraid to talk about it – *we* must take responsibility for it. Then it should present a number of clear proposals for future actions.

3. Our union constitutions should contain a clause which specifies that union members must respect each other's rights, including the right not to be sexually harassed. Then the union can in good conscience take disciplinary action against a member who sexually harasses another member. Complaints could then be resolved within the union structure.

4. The most important thing we can do is to negotiate clauses into our collective agreements which include a) a comprehensive definition of sexual harassment; b) a strong policy statement; c) a specialized grievance procedure. In the better collective agreements that I have seen, the clause has two parts: the first is a no discrimination clause that is free of ambiguity; and the second part is a specific clause prohibiting sexual harassment and providing for express remedies. The best example of this is a collective agreement negotiated by Canadian Union of Public Employees (CUPE) Local 2348 and Klinic Inc. Community Health Centre in Winnipeg. It reads:

Sexual harassment shall be defined as sexually oriented behaviour that undermines an employee's health or job performance, or endangers the employee's employment status or potential through:

a) *Impediment* by obstruction of physical or professional progress;

b) *Intimidation* by following, gesturing obscenely, heckling, or insulting, making rude noises, exposure of genitals/breasts;

c) *Coercion* by threatening withdrawal of professional support or co-operation, or termination of professional relationship unless the person agrees to sexual activity OR by requesting or suggesting

> sexual activity as payment for past or future professional
> assistance or consideration;
>
> d) *Annoyance* by repeated and persistent irritating, sexually sug-
> gestive acts or comments.
>
> A complaint of sexual harassment shall be eligible to be processed as
> a grievance.

Whoever wrote this clause understood all of the sources and all of the
effects of sexual harassment, and all at the same time! The only thing
missing is a specialized grievance procedure that would honour con-
fidentiality and swiftness in processing a complaint.

Women have worked alongside men for centuries. They have
worked as hard as men, as long as men, sometimes instead of men.
They have done "men's work," and they have done "women's work,"
and sometimes they have done both at the same time. They have
worked in our homes, keeping and nourishing our families. Their work
has protected our traditions; through the labour of childbirth they have
connected our generations, one to the other – and our cultures. Women
have even given birth to men, to our employers, to the men who run our
governments and our unions. Women deserve their respect.

N O T E S

1. For facts and figures, see Women's Bureau, Labour Canada, *1978-1979:*
   Women in the Labour Force (Ottawa: Minister of Supply and Services, 1980),
   pp. 32-33. Figures are taken from this source unless otherwise mentioned.

2. Joann Kolmes' "Powerplays" is a collection of unpublished skits first performed at International Women's Day celebrations in Edmonton, March
   1982.

3. Constance Backhouse and Leah Cohen, *Sexual Harassment on the Job: How to*
   Avoid the Working Woman's Nightmare (Englewood Cliffs, N.J.: Prentice-Hall,
   1981), p. 42.

4. This definition was produced at the Women and Legal Reform Conference
   in Edmonton, September 1981, and was then adopted by the Alliance
   Against Sexual Harassment.

5. See Kathy Cram, *Sexual Harassment in the Workplace: An Occupational Health Hazard* (Thunder Bay, Ontario: Thunder Bay Committee on Sexual Harassment, 1980). This was pointed out to me by Thunder Bay member, Monica McNabb.

6. Backhouse and Cohen, pp. 38-39. See also Peggy Crull, "The Stress Effects of Sexual Harassment on the Job" (available through Working Women's Institute, 593 Park Ave., N.Y.), an excellent resource for "expert witnesses" and counsellors in Canada, too.

7. Cecil A. Wright and Allen M. Linden, *The Law of Torts: Cases, Notes and Materials* (Toronto: Butterworth, 1970), p. 54.

8. Backhouse and Cohen, p. 115.

9. See "Trade Union Reactions to Women Workers and their Concerns," *Canadian Journal of Sociology,* Vol. 6, No. 1 (1981).

10. Ibid., p. 22.

F U R T H E R   R E A D I N G S

Backhouse, Constance and Leah Cohen. *The Secret Oppression: The Sexual Harassment of Women.* Toronto: Macmillan, 1979.

IS YOUR JOB

Hazardous to Your Health?

BY MARIANNE LANGTON

With our increased knowledge of environmental hazards, workers have begun to pay particular attention to the issue of health and safety on the job. Rather than focusing on the general problem of health and safety in the workplace, employers have centred on the possibilities of harm to the fetus. As Marianne Langton points out, the fetus is of particular concern to employers because its health and safety is not covered by workers' compensation boards and they are therefore liable to lawsuits. While employers have acted merely to remove women from certain jobs, especially in industry, feminists see that clearly, the solution is to eliminate the hazards, not the workers. Women must become increasingly vocal and aware of the hazards in all of the jobs we do – in offices and labs, as well as in the home.

"**W**HY NOT?" the government ad campaigns asked the country back in International Women's Year. Women can do the same work as men; give them a chance. Rachel Barriault was one of the women reaping the benefits of this tide of equalization. In the summer of 1974, she and a handful of other women were hired by Inco Metals to work in its Sudbury nickel refinery.

Within six months, Rachel was transferred from the packaging and shipping area to a coveted position in the section of the refinery where nickel is treated with carbon monoxide gas. Not only did she earn more money there but the working conditions were more pleasant as well. "It was so clean, you could eat off the floor," she says.

But six months after her transfer, the company had discovered an answer to the question, "Why not?" One day, Rachel reports, she and the shop steward were called into the manager's office. "He told me that the company had instituted a new policy whereby women would not be allowed to work in the unit," she recalled. "The problem was the antidote which had to be administered if someone was exposed to poisonous nickel carbonyl gas. Apparently they thought it would have harmful effects on the fetus if a worker took it when she was pregnant. The manager was really stern. He said, 'I don't even want you to go back to get your lunch box.' "

Rachel estimates that she earned about $2 per hour less after she was transferred. "All I did after that was shovelling," she says. "I wanted to work a forklift but because the job involved picking up loads where I might be exposed to nickel carbonyl, I wasn't allowed to. I was upset because guys with less seniority than me would get transferred into better jobs. I couldn't get any job that demanded responsibility or was exciting."

The substance that kept Rachel locked in a dead-end job was a drug called dithiocarbamate. It is administered in the event that a worker is exposed to nickel carbonyl gas, a byproduct of the refining process. If dithiocarbamate is not given, nickel carbonyl poisoning can prove fatal within six to twelve hours. In 1975, Dr. Ken Hedges, then medical director of Inco's Ontario division, noted that dithiocarbamate had never been tested for teratogenicity (ability to cause birth defects). As a precautionary measure, he therefore instituted a policy forbidding women of childbearing capacity from working where they might be exposed to nickel carbonyl.

Inco has not been alone in excluding women from jobs that may involve hazards to reproduction. This has emerged as a concern in a number of industries across Canada where women have begun to enter jobs formerly held only by men. For example:

- In 1976, General Motors removed six women from its battery plant in Oshawa, on the grounds that exposure to lead could cause reproductive problems.

- Ontario Hydro has excluded women from working as atomic radiation workers because of limits to the permissible radiation dose for women capable of bearing children.

- Diamond Shamrock Alberta Gas, Ltd. has refused to hire women of childbearing capacity in its Port Saskatchewan, Alberta plant due to fears that exposure to vinyl chloride may cause birth defects.

- Flin Flon, Manitoba, Hudson Bay Mining and Smelting has refused to hire fertile women in its smelting operation, citing fear of lead exposure.

Management argues that such exclusionary policies are not intended to be discriminatory – women just happened to have the bad luck to be the vehicles for carrying the future generation. "There is not much evidence that adult females and adult males react differently to toxic chemicals," explains Dr. Ernest Mastromatteo, Inco's director of occupational health. "But the fetus seems to be more susceptible than the adult. . . .I suppose that from the point of view of women's career aspirations it's unfortunate that they have to nurture the fetus. But the biological factor cannot be changed." While Dr. Mastromatteo will admit that the company has an obligation to make the workplace relatively safe for its workers, he does not believe that this responsibility extends to the fetus. "To make the workplace safe for the fetus would be ideal but not practical," he says.

Dr. Mastromatteo's perspective is shared by his counterparts in other industries. At Ontario Hydro, women of childbearing capacity have been barred from work in nuclear plants as operators, mechanical maintenance personnel or control technicians because these jobs involve exposure to radiation at levels higher than those allowed fertile women by the Atomic Energy Control Board (AECB). When asked why Hydro did not reduce the radiation level instead of excluding women from more than 2,000 jobs, Grant Childerhouse, Hydro's manager of radioactivity management and environmental protection explained, "That would require extensive redesign of the whole plant. It would not be practical. It would increase the number of staff and capital costs. We're concerned about what the taxpayers would have to pay."

"Excluding women from these jobs doesn't depend on us," adds Dr. Tom Hamilton, Hydro's manager of health services. "We're just following AECB regulations."

These regulations are part of the federal Atomic Energy Control Act, which sets ceilings on the amount of radiation to which workers may be exposed. The limit for all atomic radiation workers is 5 rems per year but for women of reproductive capacity the Act adds a further restriction limiting the radiation dose to 1.3 rems per quarter and to .2 rems per two weeks. (A rem is a unit of radiation dose related to the amount of biological damage that may be caused to a human being.) In other words, for women workers the radiation dose must be spread out more evenly over the course of the year. The reason for this, explains Dr. Hamilton, is that in the initial phases of pregnancy, the woman probably does not know that she has conceived. These regulations were intended to protect the fetus during this time.

Anne Cecchetto is one woman who has experienced first-hand the impact of Hydro's interpretations of these regulations. A graduate in chemical engineering technology from Sudbury's Cambrian College, Anne applied to Hydro for a job as a research technician in 1979. Along with a number of fellow graduates, she went through extensive application procedures, scoring "excellent" on mechanical and common-sense testing. After promising first interviews, however, Anne and several of her classmates received letters from Hydro informing them that the radiation levels in the jobs for which they were being considered were too high and that women of reproductive capacity would therefore not be eligible.

Employer concern for the children of workers often seems hypocritical to workers who have spent years struggling for improved health and safety measures. Some charge that it is fear of legal action, rather than paternal regard for child welfare, that motivates such protectionist policies. Under the Workmen's Compensation Act, an insured worker forfeits the right to sue an employer for any impairment incurred on the job. But the legal rights of workers' children are not covered by this restriction. If the child of a worker is harmed by some agent to which her parent has been exposed at work, it is possible for the child or an adult acting on her or his behalf to sue the employer for damages. Reporting to the Canadian Centre for Occupational Health and Safety, lawyer Michael Izumi Nash advised that "in the common law of Ontario, it is quite clear that a child who has suffered damage while in utero may sue for those damages after birth through his or her guardians." If a fetus should die as a result of workplace conditions, obviously it would not be able to sue. But, Nash speculates, under Ontario's Family Law Reform Act,

> parents, grandparents, brothers or sisters could maintain an action against an employer where the child was stillborn or later died as a result of injuries caused to the child in utero. The amount of money recoverable might not be very large because of the difficulty of showing the pecuniary loss suffered by the relatives, although this loss may include a sum for loss of companionship at the very least.

Though there have to date been no precedents for a suit based on reproductive damage sustained in the workplace, employers both in Canada and the United States are sensitive to the possibilities. Some have quite deliberately decided that they would rather hazard charges of discrimination than a lawsuit over a birth defect. As an American Exxon official commented, "We would rather face an Equal Employment Opportunity inspector than a deformed baby."

Reg Basken, of the Oil, Chemical and Atomic Workers, has observed that employers are very concerned about birth defects, which are immediately apparent, but they ignore the fact that the same agents may cause cancer or other diseases years after initial exposure. Discussing the removal of women from exposure to vinyl chloride by Diamond Shamrock Alberta Gas, Basken commented to the Toronto *Globe and Mail* that "It seems they are taking precautions [for fetuses] because proof can be given relatively easily. It could be 25 years before it [vinyl chloride] hurts anyone else."

Women who anticipate having children are understandably leery about taking any job that has even a remote chance of causing birth defects. But others who have no immediate plans for a family resent being considered potentially pregnant by employers and the state. They point out that rules affecting all women of childbearing capacity fail to recognize an individual woman's right and responsibility to decide for herself whether she will have children. "I asked the Medical Director at Inco if I could keep my job if I was on the birth control pill," says Rachel Barriault. "But I was told that the only way they would consider it was if I were sterilized."

Canadian women have achieved some success in fighting discriminatory policies through human rights complaints. In 1981, a Saskatoon woman complained of discrimination to the federal Human Rights Commission after being refused work as a mine helper trainee by Eldorado Nuclear. The company's refusal to hire her was based on its lack of equipment needed to monitor radiation dose in compliance with AECB regulations. Since the complaint was filed, the company initiated a monitoring program and hired 14 women to work in the mill and the mine. A complaint against Ontario Hydro was also filed with the Canadian Human Rights Commission by a Parry Sound woman who, like Anne Cecchetto, was denied work as a result of AECB radiation limits.

Following intervention by the Human Rights Commission in response to these complaints, the AECB proposed changes to its radiation limits in September 1981. Under these proposals, the maximum permissible radiation dose would be set at equal levels for both men and women, although lower exposure levels would be retained for pregnant workers. Ontario Hydro subsequently agreed to modify its hiring policy after the AECB changes are put into effect.

There has not, to date, been a similar precedent on the provincial level. In 1976, women transferred out of General Motor's battery plant in Oshawa filed a discrimination complaint with the Ontario Human Rights Commission. The case was dismissed in an ambiguous ruling that did not exactly exonerate GM, but admitted the Commission's inability to judge the medical questions involved. In 1980, a task force of the Ontario Advisory Council on Occupational Health and Occupational Safety was established to examine issues relating to women and occupational health.

For many women, at the heart of the controversy surrounding reproductive hazards in the workplace is the broader issue of women's right to be fully active in society and the work force without being forced to relinquish their right to mother children. The struggle for reproductive safety in the workplace is therefore two-pronged. On the one hand, women have had to fight for full access to all jobs, unobstructed by artificial barriers based on their reproductive roles. At the same time, they have had to strive for the right to working conditions that do not jeopardize their ability to bear healthy children. This right must extend, not just to those jobs in which women have been traditionally under-represented, but to those jobs which comprise the "female job ghetto" as well. Women concerned about both job safety and equality of opportunity have pointed out that attempts to keep women out of reproductively hazardous "non-traditional" jobs reflects a double standard on the part of employers, who have often turned a blind eye to reproductive threats which abound in traditionally "female" jobs.

For example, hospital and health care workers are exposed to a broad range of workplace hazards, such as ionizing radiation, infectious agents and anaesthetic gases, which have been linked to a high incidence of miscarriages and birth defects. Teachers face the danger of exposure to the rubella virus, which causes deformities in the fetus. Hairdressers are exposed to a variety of toxic substances, including hair dyes that have the potential to cause mutations. Women who work in laundries and dry cleaning operations are exposed to solvents that may be associated with birth defects. Similarly, the electronics industry, which employs a high percentage of women, entails exposure to a number of toxic metals and solvents. But where the majority of workers are women, employers have rarely voiced concern about reproductively hazardous substances. "There's no hue and cry about keeping women from working as X-ray technicians or in operating rooms," says Cathi Carr, employment relations officer with the Ontario Nurses' Association (ONA).

The position of organized labour and groups speaking for working women has been that the workplace should be safe enough to assure the reproductive health of all workers. In cases where it is not immediately possible to guarantee reproductive safety, some groups have called for policies that allow a pregnant woman to transfer out of a job that might harm the fetus, without loss of pay, seniority or benefits.

In Canada, precedents for such policies have recently been set in relation to the use of video display terminals (VDTs). Concern over the reproductive effects of VDTs was heightened following reports of a high incidence of birth defects and miscarriages among VDT operators in several Toronto offices. Shortly after these reports, several pregnant employees of Bell Canada exercised their legal right to refuse unsafe work by refusing to work on VDTs during their pregnancies. Following this protest, their union, the Communication Workers of Canada (CWC) negotiated a Memorandum of Agreement with Bell that allowed pregnant VDT operators to choose to take extended leaves of absence for the duration of their pregnancies, or to transfer to other work in the bargaining unit. The B.C. Government Employees Union has negotiated a similar clause in its contract with the Open Learning Institute of Richmond B.C. VDT operators at the Workmen's Compensation Board of Ontario and the Ontario legislative building have also achieved the right to optional transfer to non-VDT work during pregnancy.

Other companies, however, have proved less amenable to accommodating women's concerns about reproductive hazards. When Joanne Clifton, a worker in the blast furnace at Stelco in Hamilton, Ontario, became pregnant, she and her doctor feared that occupational exposure to carbon monoxide might be dangerous to the developing fetus. Stelco, however, refused to grant her request for a transfer to a safer job. Not wanting to risk harming her child, Clifton resigned her job for the duration of her pregnancy. The company denied her sick benefits and refused to assure her that she would be rehired after completing her maternity leave.

Had Clifton been working in Quebec, she might not have had to resign, or might have received worker's compensation benefits during a temporary leave of absence. Quebec's occupational health act has broken new ground in Canada through a provision that allows a pregnant or nursing worker whose doctor attests that workplace hazards might harm her child to transfer to a safer job without loss of pay. If a safer job is not available, the woman may take a leave of absence from work and receive worker's compensation benefits.

Although the Quebec law and the VDT agreements represent improvements in protecting workers from reproductive hazards, labour representatives point out that transferring women from potentially hazardous jobs leaves much to be desired. In terms of industrial hygiene principles, such measures constitute "administrative controls" – the reduction of hazardous exposure through selective personnel policies. A much preferable approach is the adoption of "engineering controls," which reduce the hazard through redesign of processes and equipment.

The agreement negotiated with Bell Canada is less than satisfactory, admits Gary Cwitco, national representative for the CWC. "Certainly we would much prefer to be confident that use of the machines are safe for all employees, through engineering controls that would reduce all radiation emissions to non-measurable levels, a control which I'm convinced is technically feasible."

In workplaces with myriad reproductive hazards and a high proportion of female workers, engineering controls may be the only way to assure safety. Hospitals, for example, entail so many potential reproductive hazards that a requirement that pregnant women be transferred into safe jobs may be impossible. There are, in fact, indications that Quebec hospitals may find the province's occupational health act particularly onerous in its provisions regarding pregnant women. Some hospitals, reports Cathi Carr of ONA, have initiated controls that reduce reproductive hazards, such as scavenging equipment, which removes waste anaesthetic gases from operating rooms. Such actions indicate that where it is not practical to change the nature of the work force, measures can be taken to change working conditions.

Concern about reproductive hazards that focuses exclusively on women fails to take into account the fact that male workers are also susceptible to agents that cause reproductive harm. A wide variety of substances, such as many pesticides and toxic metals, may cause infertility and impotence in men. Others may result in birth defects or miscarriages by causing mutations in sperm. It is also possible that substances to which a prospective father is exposed may harm the fetus his partner is carrying, through contamination of clothes brought home from work, or even from her absorption of toxic substances through his semen.

For many workers and unions, the major issue raised by the exclusion of women from reproductively hazardous jobs is the failure of the employer to provide a safe workplace for all employees. In at least two Canadian plants where workers are exposed to lead, unions have fought employer policies on these grounds. The United Steelworkers have filed a complaint with the federal Human Rights Commission over the exclusion of women from its Flin Flon smelter. And in the winter of 1979, the United Auto Workers (UAW) fought a case before the Ontario Arbitration Board on behalf of workers in Oshawa's GM plant. In both these cases, the union argued that lead is as dangerous to men as it is to women, citing studies that showed that lead impairs male fertility and may lead to the production of abnormal sperm. The company is actually practising reverse discrimination, they say, by protecting women while allowing men to remain in a hazardous work environment.

Toxicologists who support protecting men as well as women note that many companies have failed to make the proper distinction between a teratogen, which can harm a developing fetus, and other substances that can cause reproductive damage to men or women before conception. Lead, for example, is thought to be capable both of damaging sperm and of harming a fetus during development. Evidence to this effect prompted the U.S. Occupational Safety and Health Administration (OSHA) to take the position that "there is no basis in the record for preferential hiring of men over women in the lead industry, nor will [the standard for lead] create a basis for exclusion from work of any person, male or female, who is capable of procreating."

Notwithstanding such arguments, the UAW lost its case before the Ontario Arbitration Board. In defining the issue, the arbitrator maintained that the exclusion of women of childbearing years from excessive exposure to lead was not in itself discriminatory, unless it could be shown that lead affects men and women equally. Despite the union argument that this is in fact the case, the arbitrator acceded to the claims of GM's medical director that "the evidence shows marked difference in the effects of lead on the two groups [men and women] and did not support the necessity to extend the policy to the male group." Nevertheless, the ruling noted that a fertile man may have the right under Ontario's occupational health law to refuse to work where he might be exposed to dangerous levels of lead. Such a case, however, would have to be fought under another grievance. Also yet to be tested is a provision in Ontario's Code for Medical Surveillance for Lead, which differentiates between women of childbearing capacity and other workers in its requirements for removal of workers from exposure to lead. According to this Code, women capable of bearing children must be removed from lead exposure when the concentration of lead in their blood reaches .40 milligrams per litre. For other workers, the level is .70 milligrams per litre.

Workers in Canada and other countries have organized to focus public attention on issues raised by reproductive hazards in the workplace and to press for changes in government and industry approaches to occupational health. In the United States, members of labour and women's organizations have formed the Coalition for Reproductive Rights of Workers (CRROW), committed to ''exposing the corporate policy of eliminating workers rather than hazards'' and seeking an end to ''the unacceptable choice between a job and the right to reproduce.''

Closer to home, women in Vancouver have formed Women's Action on Occupational Health, which has sponsored educationals and published material on workplace hazards faced by women. Windsor Occupational Safety and Health (WOSH), an organization of workers involved in occupational health struggles, has drawn public attention to reproductive hazards encountered by workers in Windsor's pharmaceutical industry. In Toronto, labour organizations have sponsored a number of conferences devoted to examining occupational hazards that affect women.

In a 1980 position paper on reproductive hazards in the workplace, the Canadian Advisory Council on the Status of Women (CACSW) called for a number of changes in federal policy with respect to occupational health. The CACSW advocated amendments to the Canadian Human Rights Act and the Canada Labour Code to outlaw discriminatory practices related to reproductive physiology, and urged that standards governing workplace hazards be set to protect the most susceptible worker of either sex. The position paper also recommended that potential effects on reproduction be taken into account when setting standards and screening new substances for safety.

A 1980 proposal by the U.S. Equal Employment Opportunities Commission (EEOC) offered further policy direction for protecting workers against reproductive hazards without violating their rights. The EEOC's proposed guidelines, which were scrapped by the Reagan administration shortly after it took office, would have set limits to the circumstances in which employers could bar women from jobs because of reproductive hazards. Employers instituting such policies would have been required to offer scientific evidence that the hazard in question does indeed cause birth defects, and that its effects operate through women only. It is interesting to note that where such guidelines adopted here, the action of companies such as Inco would be prohibited. As Ernest Mastromatteo has admitted, dithiocarbamate, the drug responsible for Rachel Barriault's transfer, is not even a known teratogen, but is only *suspected* of causing birth defects. In fact, a recent literature search on reproductive effects of dithiocarbamate revealed no evidence connecting it to reproductive damage in women. It did, however, turn up one study suggesting that the drug might adversely affect sexual potency in male dogs. "On the basis of this evidence," commented one scientist who reviewed this data, "an unbiased observer might be tempted to conclude that males rather than females should be excluded from the nickel refinery work force."

Occupational health policies have often been imprinted with the traditional attitude that women who bear and raise children belong at home, not at work. In setting standards for permissible exposures to workplace hazards, authorities have failed to take into account the harm they may be causing workers' children. As U.S. occupational health expert Vilma Hunt has observed, "When the standards were being set, society had not awakened to the fact that women were working and procreating at the same time."

Concerns that hazardous working conditions might harm the children of working women is not new. Historically, some of the first occupational health legislation passed in Canada and other countries was intended not to protect the worker but to safeguard the health of future generations. The 1884 Ontario Factory Shops Act, for example, was amended in 1901 to limit working hours for women and children for the purpose of protecting against "degeneration of future generations." And the U.S. Supreme Court, when upholding a similar law in 1908, intoned that "the physical well-being of women becomes an object of interest and care in order to preserve the strength and vigor of the race.'' According to such reasoning, women deserve protection from harmful working conditions, not because they are human begins entitled to good health, but only because they are the vehicles that carry the next generation.

Laws and policies based on this rationale have had both positive and negative effects. On one hand they provided excuses and justification for keeping women in second-class positions in the labour force. On the other, however, they could act as levers with which to fight for safer working conditions for all workers. This double-edged quality of protective policies persists today, as workers are forcing society to recognize that the health of future generations can only be preserved by assuring all workers, male and female, an environment free from hazards.

The issue of reproductive hazards in the workplace shares an underlying principle with many other struggles women have waged in the past decade. This is the principle that women have the right to choose multiple roles for themselves – to be mothers, workers and full participants in society, without having to sacrifice one role at the expense of another. Like the struggles for day care, for abortion and for maternity leave, the fight for a workplace free from reproductive hazards is aimed at winning for women the right to integrate the reproductive roles they choose for themselves with the other elements of a fulfilling and satisfying life.

An earlier version of this article appeared in *Healthsharing* magazine in September 1980. Thanks to Wendy King for help researching the original article.

F U R T H E R   R E A D I N G S

Deck, Cecilia, ed. *A Worker's Guide to Health and Safety.* Windsor Occupational Safety and Health Council and the Ontario Public Interest Research Group. Toronto: James Lorimer, 1982.

George, Anne. "Occupational Health Hazards to Women: A Synoptic View." Advisory Council on the Status of Women. Hull, Quebec: Government Printer, 1978.

Stellman, Jeanne M. and Susan M. Daum. *A Handbook of Health Hazards in the Workplace and What You Can Do About Them.* New York: Vintage, 1980.

WHEN ALL THE SECRETARIES DEMAND

What They Are Worth

BY PATRICIA J. DAVITT

The ever increasing wage differential between the average earnings of men and women workers graphically expresses the power imbalance between the sexes in our society. We do not compete as equals in the job market. And perhaps nothing else keeps women so "in our place" as a lack of access to a decent income. It is little wonder then, that equal pay for work of equal value has become a central union demand of women workers. Patricia Davitt advocates that the least we should aim for is an equalization of base rates within a particular employment situation, regardless of the type of job. She also argues against percentage increases in wage settlements because these serve only to increase the wage differential between male and female workers. Davitt's article details the way equal pay was taken up in a strike of civic workers in Vancouver and makes recommendations for future union struggles around this demand.

THE EQUAL PAY RALLY AT CITY HALL, APRIL 6, 1981

Whatever will we do, whatever on this earth
When all the secretaries demand what they are worth?
"THE BOSSES' LAMENT," TERRY DASH

W E STOOD AMID the bulging, stinking remains of a city's domestic life. Black and green plastic tatters no longer enclosed the orange peels, the egg shells and the cat food tins, the garbage deposited at City Hall by irate Vancouverites who wanted to tell the city to settle with its striking workers. Over a thousand of us stood waiting, singing, speaking, listening and chanting as the message was hurled at the high stone walls of Vancouver City Hall. "Equal pay is fair pay." "What do we want? A contract! When do we want it? Now!"

CUPE and VMREU (See B.C. Union ABCs for a list of all the abbreviations used in this article) speakers for the striking workers pointed to the necessity for all workers to enjoy a livable wage: we all have to pay high rents, buy expensive food and run our cars on increasingly costly gasoline. There are no discounts for being female when it comes to the marketplace, until we try to sell our labour. At the rally, we heard what had been accomplished by other unions: maternity benefits and family illness clauses in AUCE contracts; paternity leave in SORWUC contracts. We were told about the CAIMAW Kenworth factory strike, a seven-month conflict that hinged on the demand for equal starting rates for the data processors (female) in the office, a demand which was won in part because the men in the plant supported it and stayed out.

We waited for the three invited guest speakers – Vancouver's three alderwomen – to make their appearances to support our demand to equalize starting rates for female and male municipal employees. They didn't show.

While we waited, we sang: labour songs, strike songs, traditional songs and others written especially for the occasion. And in male/female solidarity, the men of CUPE 1004 marched in with a thirty-foot banner proclaiming their willingness to stand firm for equal pay.

At the end of the rally it could be fairly concluded that the alderwomen would not address their rambunctious employees, and that our unions were on strike for equal pay. But that's not how we started.

B.C. UNION ABCs

AUCE Association of University and College Employees. An independent union (not affiliated to either the B.C. Federation of Labour or to the CLC), which is currently certified at the University of British Columbia, Simon Fraser University and several community colleges across the province.

CAIMAW Canadian Association of Industrial, Mechanical and Allied Workers. Affiliated to the CCU; most noted for its raids on Steel (United Steelworkers of America); important herein for the Kenworth strike.

CCU Confederation of Canadian Unions. An umbrella group of many wholly Canadian unions with no ties to American unions.

CLC Canadian Labour Congress. The umbrella group of many unions in Canada, both Canadian and international (i.e., American) at the national level.

CUPE Canadian Union of Public Employees. The largest public sector union in the country, CUPE represents most municipal employees. Affiliate of the CLC.

GVRD Greater Vancouver Regional District. A coordinating body between Lower Mainland municipalities on such joint concerns as water, sewage, transit and sometimes wages.

GVRDEU GVRD Employees Union. A small union, independent, composed of workers employed directly by the GVRD.

GVRD Labour Relations Department. A private firm with an official-sounding name, which was hired by the Lower Mainland municipalities to conduct their collective bargaining.

SORWUC Service, Office and Retail Workers Union of Canada.
Independent union composed mostly of office workers;
noted for its major attempt to organize bank workers,
and for its feminist orientation.

VMREU Vancouver Municipal and Regional Employees
Union. Independent union of city inside workers, community colleges, school board employees and GVRD
staff; city outside workers are represented by CUPE
1004 (ten-oh-four).

WVMEA West Vancouver Municipal Employees Association. A
small, local, independent union representing the
employees of West Vancouver.

WHERE IT ALL STARTED

We want to tell you people what we've seen and we've heard
That everyone don't understand that union's more than a word
And that's all, I tell you that's all
'Cause we gotta have union, I tell you that's all.

"WE GOTTA HAVE UNION,"
MUSIC BY WASHINGTON PHILIPS,
WORDS BY THE EUPHONIOUSLY FEMINIST
AND NON-PERFORMING QUINTET

Two weeks before we went on strike, many VMREU members were
unaware that such a possibility existed. Strike talk was in the air, but
we didn't really believe it. At issue were wages, health and welfare
benefits, and employer anti-union demands. The four unions involved
in the struggle pointed out that civic workers had fallen grievously
behind in wages over the past few years, as inflation and Anti-Inflation
Board restrictions ate away at our earning power. This year we would
go for a "catch-up."

On the other side, municipal governments, collectively
represented by the GVRD Labour Relations Department, wanted their

employees to accept the responsibility for paying for and administering a total health, insurance and welfare benefits package, without amendment, without discussion, and without adequate time to review the proposal to determine the costs and benefits to the workers. On the surface at least, it appeared that it would cost each of us one and a half percent of our salaries and virtually eliminate the accumulated sick leave of long-term employees. We couldn't accept it.

Moreover, our employer wanted us to agree not to honour other unions' picket lines. We didn't agree.

There were other points of disagreement, a long list of them, but they were not so important. As our executive read out the list, third from the bottom was an item about equal pay, which slid by with no comment and no notice. "Oh sure," I thought wryly, "that's one bird that won't fly."

VMREU (to which I belong) was not voting to go out on strike alone. Some CUPE locals were already out, and the bulk of civic workers were destined to hit the bricks *en masse*. The structure of negotiations would be quite complicated: some locals chose to bargain solo; others started off in joint negotiations decided by a two-thirds majority vote and later switched to consensus; and still another group, including VMREU, was committed to agreement by consensus from the beginning.

Initially the staff and the officials of CUPE called most of the shots. CUPE National has a public relations department, and CUPE locals expected the National to carry on a good public relations campaign. Snazzy brochures exhorted all union members to go for "catch-up." In the newspapers, ads blossomed, informing the public that their civic workers were indeed out to catch up – to the IWA (International Woodworkers of America, and industrial wage leader in B.C.), which came as a bit of a surprise to most of us. City Hall clerk-typists and Parks Board recreation staff had never before been invited to equate their jobs to those of the IWA's fallers and chokermen, and it represented an enormous conceptual leap which neither we nor the public were adequately prepared to make. Not that a good case can't be made for the social value and equivalence of all labour, but that requires more than one newspaper ad in the middle of a strike. Catch-up to the IWA was, in fact, a target for some CUPE locals, mostly of outside workers, and the public relations people seized upon the notion as an inspiration to everybody. It wasn't.

The underlying presumption seemed to be that there is no difference between a private and public sector strike. Workers in either situation will "down tools" (in this case, typewriters and garbage trucks); the employer, turning pale at the loss of revenue, capitulates and signs an agreement. This may actually be a feasible scenario in industry, where the walkout of workers leads to vanishing profits, although in times of recession and overproduction, companies such as INCO may wait out a strike by sitting on their inventory. In the public sector, employers usually save (or appear to save) money in lost wages, simply by not providing public services already paid for in taxes. (The money "saved" may in fact be largely illusory, since often the back-up of work leads to overtime and extra administrative costs at significantly higher rates of pay.) Nonetheless, municipal politicians made political hay of the purported savings and were quite prepared to resist any further wage demands.

"RETROFITTING" THE ISSUES

If we all walk this picket line
We're gonna win this strike
Ain't no way they can ever keep us down.
"IF WE ALL WALK," P. DAVITT

It was cold. Too cold for the garbage to rot and annoy the populace. Too cold for the rats to breed and alarm the populace. Too early for tourists to take umbrage at the garbage in Stanley Park, the rats or the lack of services. There was little public pressure to end the strike. Finally the picket-line perception that we needed an issue to garner public sympathy and support began to be shared by the policy-makers. Our leaders ran a jaundiced eye down the original list of demands, looking for a hot item, and came up with "equal pay." Despite this apparently arbitrary selection, it was a demand that not only engaged the public in debate, but also fired the imagination of VMREU and CUPE members beyond the wildest expectations of the strategists who had targetted it.

Now the strike was a political battle; we were not simply refusing to pick up the garbage.

REACTION IN THE UNIONS

Oh no, you can't scare me, I'm sticking to the union
I'm sticking to the union, 'til the day I die.
"UNION MAID," WOODY GUTHRIE

On the picket lines, not everyone was delighted to find themselves on strike for "equal pay." Many at first did not understand the unions' demand in any precise way; equal pay had not been explained, encouraged or studied in our unions. An explanatory pamphlet was prepared by the VMREU negotiations committee to clarify it for union members, municipal politicians and the public.[1] It disclosed that employees entering the city outside work force (CUPE 1004) started at a wage of $8 an hour, a rate inadequate to meet the financial needs of these workers. By contrast, 74 percent of inside, clerical workers (mainly women) never reached even the *starting rate* for outside workers. "In fact," a VMREU pamphlet explains, "about half the women clerical workers take home less than a single mother with two children on welfare." (Since clerical wages have now gone up and the provincial government has slashed welfare rates, this is no longer true.) VMREU proposed, therefore, that the most common entry position (not necessarily the lowest-paid position) for clerical workers should receive the same wage as the lowest-paid manual worker from their respective first days of work. The union recognized "political and fiscal realities in the public sector" and suggested that equalization of the base or entry rates take place over a three-year period.

Several CUPE locals also issued pamphlets explaining the equal pay demand. However, neither the central negotiating committee, which represented all the striking workers, nor the regional office of

CUPE, which represented the bulk of civic employees, issued explanatory materials. They ran decorative newspaper ads, featuring roses and hammers, but left the actual meaning of the concept unclear.

Among civic workers as a whole, however, there was strong support for the concept. Many female employees felt for the first time that the strike had particular meaning for them. As the issue of equalizing the base rates came to the fore, more women picketers felt personally involved in defending and promoting the idea, and most of their male colleagues supported them. Inside and outside workers, lower- and higher-paid, men and women, "old" and "new" Canadians: virtually everyone agreed on the fairness of the principle.

REACTION IN THE COMMUNITY

My girl, she runs the office; you know that's what girls do
She does her job, yes, very well, and most of my job too
But it's certainly outrageous, it's completely out of line
When she demands a salary commensurate with mine.
"THE BOSSES' LAMENT," TERRY DASH

The strike was becoming more publicly oriented, more "political," if you will. There were mass pickets at half a dozen municipal halls in the Lower Mainland, and confrontations during municipal council meetings. There were rallies at City Hall and on downtown streets, more interviews on radio, TV and in the newspapers. Civic workers were suddenly front-page material, as we slowed commuter traffic over the bridge accesses to the city, disrupted bus service and brought construction in Vancouver almost to a halt. The final economic threat, a tourist "brochure" for distribution throughout the Pacific Northwest and Japan, itemized the decline in amenities of a beautiful city, from the garbage bags rotting in Stanley Park to the dumping of raw sewage in recreational waters. We were deliberately creating a high profile to which we invited the public to respond.

The reaction was mixed.

Some unions, mainly the independents, supported us wholeheartedly – with letters, public statements of support and attendance at rallies. These unions tended to have a high percentage of women workers and/or a strong awareness of feminist issues; they saw clearly the importance of our struggle in relation to their own members. Most of the organized support came from hospital employees (HEU) and downtown and university clerical workers.

The B.C. Federation of Labour agreed that their member unions would honour our picket lines, and told us to be grateful for that support; their president addressed a rally and rousingly declared: ''the gloves are off!'' in the fight between management and labour and that was the last we saw of him. The Fed was far too involved in the aftermath of the Telephone Workers' strike to be bothered with a picayune, 10,000-member civic workers' walkout. CUPE National advised us to keep our strike in perspective; while we might naturally feel that it was a significant event, on the national scene it apparently counted for little. The underlying message was clear: don't expect any help from us.

From the many women's groups in Vancouver, we heard less than we would have liked. Some, but by no means all, attended the Equal Pay Rally at City Hall, with their banners flying. A few groups gave active support. SORWUC organized a noon-hour discussion of the strike issues aimed at unorganized, downtown clerical workers, and passed out leaflets advertising the meeting and the strike issues. The Vancouver Women's Health Collective applied political pressure to their contacts on Vancouver City Council, and the Vancouver Status of Women publicized the strike issues in *Kinesis,* their newspaper.

However, not enough happened, partly because of a lack of initiative in the women's community, but also because of a failure of leadership from the unions. VMREU strategists wanted active involvement from women's groups, but no avenue for that participation was established. CUPE leaders were fearful of such involvement, possibly because of the threat of diminished control. Consequently there was no plan formulated to encourage non-union, community political groups to support us. (After the strike, the lack of involvement was a topic for debate and self-criticism in the women's movement. As a result, there was much more vocal and supportive activity for the postal workers' strike around the issue of maternity benefits. Live and learn.)

The business community's reaction was frenzied. Capitalism would crumble if ever there was a breach in the explicit agreement to keep wages for women down – referred to euphemistically by capitalists as "letting market forces determine wages." The Employers' Council of B.C., representing 150 of the largest and most powerful corporations in the province, strongly and consistently condemned the demand for equal pay and muttered darkly about "the ripple effect" that would occur as one industry after another drowned in the tide of fair pay for women. Not content with airing their views generally, the Council wrote directly to all our municipal councils and local school boards, urging them to stand firm.

Meanwhile, the public was beginning to be drawn into the debate. Increasing numbers of letters to the editor and calls to hotline radio shows dealt with this issue. There was a great deal of confusion about what equal pay really meant, in the context of this strike and over the long haul, and neither side could claim an ideological victory in the news media. Two things were clear, however: one, that equal pay had become one of the major issues of the Eighties in labour-management relations (as proclaimed even by the conservative morning paper); and two, that the concept of equal pay was not widely understood and would need to be a focus for continuing education even after the strike was ended.

THE SETTLEMENT — WINS AND LOSSES

I'm fed up with this rotten typing job
Now we will fight until the day we get fair and equal pay
Or they can STUFF their rotten typing job!

"ROTTEN TYPING JOB," R. THOMPSON,

with L. ROSSELSON and R. BAILEY

There were offers and counter-offers, as usual, and long periods when management refused to negotiate. Perhaps there was some idea of starving us out; thirteen weeks is a long time on the picket line, especially if you've never been on strike before and have no money put aside from your beggarly clerical wage to tide you over. If starvation was a managerial tactic (as it often is), it was felt that it would be the lowest-paid workers, mainly women, who would cave in first, for they were logically the most vulnerable.

But we didn't cave in: not the women, nor the lower-paid workers; nor those more highly paid.

The end came for a number of reasons, but *not* because the picket lines crumbled. It came because municipal politicians, hiding behind the GVRD Labour Relations Department negotiators, took an intransigent stand early on and budged very little and even then, very grudgingly. It came because CUPE National, comptroller of the strike funds for CUPE locals, decided it was time for us to go back to work. And it came, for VMREU at least, because we realized that while management might be coerced into giving more bonuses (one time only pay-outs), they would not raise the actual month-to-month wage rates any further.

Our settlement was disappointing, especially for equal pay. We had seen sister locals – school board locals – in and outside the Lower Mainland win recognition of the equal pay concept and an actual move made toward equalizing base rates for inside and outside workers by the end of 1982. Our contract fell far short of that. Municipal councils acknowledged that clerical workers were systematically lower-paid, but refused to put it in writing – or in basic pay grade changes. Instead, we won substantial percentage increases (which favoured higher-paid workers and especially senior management), and one-time bonuses, which served in the short term to sweeten the inequity for lower-paid employees, but had no lasting effect.

It was not all doom-and-gloom. Our wage increases were hefty enough to make working for the city, even as a low-paid clerk-typist, a more viable option. Significant gains for part-time workers (one-third of the VMREU membership) came into effect in January 1982. Health and welfare benefits were increased for part-timers; there was no change for full-time employees, but at least the all-or-nothing plan was dropped.

THE HERITAGE

These days we're getting organized; this time we won't be beaten
Now it's you lend a hand with the frying pan
I'm off to a union meeting.
You men who cross our picket line; remember you'll get yours in time
The enemy's the same, yours and mine
The scab is the bosses' darling.

"THE BOSSES' DARLING," JEAN HART

A lot of positive results were left to us by this strike, not the least of which was the rise in trade union consciousness among many of the city's inside workers. Bosses were clearly defined by the strike: bosses crossed picket lines, continued to draw pay, did work that striking workers would ordinarily do. Bosses were scabs.

The potential to take strike action is now a very real possibility for our members. Many clerical workers who had never struck before now know they can survive that experience, know that the union can make us strong, know that we will likely be on strike again in 1983. We have experience now: in picketing, in organizing, in surviving. That information is being collected and will be shared; we will be ready for 1983, whatever happens.

Workers made justified criticisms of the strike and the way the union leadership conducted it. Some were angry at the relative ineffectiveness of closing down municipal halls and other city-owned property and want to occupy the buildings next time. Others were frustrated that our leaders bowed to injunction after injunction, when rank and filers wanted to go ahead with mass picketing to close the city down. Out of our frustration at the difficulties encountered in the strike has come an ongoing dialogue within our union and between unions to devise more appropriate strategies.

There were criticisms too of the decision-making process, particularly because many VMREU members felt the timing of the strike was wrong, and the ad campaign inappropriate. These were decisions made by CUPE National, and we felt that we had to go along with them, although they were not wise moves. VMREU, along with GVRDEU and WVMEA, found themselves poorly prepared to share the bargaining table with a giant whose every wish carried considerable financial and political clout.

VMREU learned many useful things from the strike. With our smaller membership, we could keep somewhat better track of what people were thinking. With a less cumbersome bureaucracy, our strike committee could respond to events as they happened, on a daily or even hourly basis. There was easier access of the members to our executive, who were highly visible on the picket lines and in strike committee meetings. Being independent of the CUPE bureaucracy gave us slightly more room to manoeuvre; so although our link to CUPE gave us the advantage of the vast numbers of strikers, we had the freedom to develop strategy independently and carry it through.

We had rallies, demonstrations, confrontations – one a week or more during the last half of the strike. The politicizing of the strike was largely a rank and file decision (particularly within CUPE) with considerable rank and file support, and the encouragement of VMREU executive members and the strike committee. Did it have an effect?

We think so. The Insurance Corporation of B.C. (ICBC) struck before we did and were still on strike when we settled. They ran a very low-key strike, which limped along for upwards of five months. Unless something happened to damage your car, you'd hardly have known this public corporation wasn't hard at work. There was no public interest or support, and they took forever to settle. There's a lesson in that.

We inherited one more thing from the strike. Out of the network of informal, interunion meetings to coordinate rallies and other public activities grew the nucleus of the post-strike EPIC committees: (Equal Pay Information Committees), out to fight an EPIC battle. VMREU has its own EPIC committee internally; some CUPE locals do too, while others decided not to, and still others were never given the opportunity to vote on it. (Equal pay is still a controversial issue even within the unions, and the CUPE brass seems divided on how hard to fight for it.) These committees are crucial. The Burnaby School Board local (CUPE) had an equal pay committee for two years. When the strike came, their members understood the issue clearly and supported it solidly. They got it.

WHEN ALL US SECRETARIES DEMAND
WHAT WE ARE WORTH

These are the lessons of the Vancouver Civic Workers' strike.

1. Ours was the first major strike (11,000 workers) in Canada to stay out for equal pay. This signalled a major change of consciousness regarding female wages both within unions and in the broader community.

2. The strike was positive proof that men will support this concept. As the CAIMAW Kenworth strikers held firm, so too did most of the rank and file male members of the civic unions.

3. The strike showed the need for ongoing public and union education about equal base rates as a first step to a fair wage scale. The EPIC committees will be a major vehicle for this education, helped along by Premier Bill Bennett and the Pope, who have both recently stated that equal pay is fair pay! (Bill later recanted, under pressure from the Employers' Council.)

4. The strike showed the need to develop strategies for public sector unions to keep past gains and to win equality in wages, strategies that go beyond the model of the industrial strike. This need has never been more apparent than now, with the threat of wage controls hanging over the heads of all civil service workers.

5. The strike highlighted the role that feminists inside and outside the trade union movement must play in putting forward the necessity for equal pay as one of the key women's demands for the 1980s. We must encourage the participation of women in this struggle, both as executive members or negotiators for their unions, and in political battles fought outside the trade union arena.

6. The strike showed that when the rank and file are stifled, union activity, especially during a strike, loses militancy and effectiveness. Democratic unions with strong local control are in a much better position to wage a successful struggle.

7. The intransigence of municipal politicians showed us that we should collectively consider action on the civic political front to ensure that we don't meet such reactionary bullheadedness again.

8. Finally, our strike demonstrated our commitment to revive and maintain a labour culture and tradition that gives us an identity, a history, and a strength that has nothing to do with the bosses. We indeed have a community of labour, which we experienced most concretely during the strike, and which we feel again in the songs we sing together.

In our hands is placed a power greater than their hoarded gold
Greater than the might of armies magnified a thousandfold.
We can bring to birth a new world from the ashes of the old
For the union makes us strong.

"SOLIDARITY FOREVER," RALPH CHAPLIN

N O T E S

I would like to thank Aphrodite Harris and Lenna Jones of CUPE, and Gordon Bailey and David Cadman of VMREU, who read an earlier draft, helped straighten out and add to the factual material and queried my interpretation of some events. I of course am responsible for the final draft.

1. "Base Rate Equalization: An Information Brief," prepared by Gordon Bailey and the VMREU Negotiating Committee (mimeo, 8 pp., 1981). Available from VMREU, 300-545 West 10th Avenue, Vancouver, B.C. V5Z 9Z9.

F U R T H E R   R E A D I N G S

Connelly, Patricia. *Last Hired, First Fired: Women and the Canadian Work Force.* Toronto: Women's Press, 1978.

Cornish, Mary and Laurell Ritchie. *Getting Organized: Building a Union.* Toronto: Women's Press, 1980.

Rosie the Riveter

MEETS THE SEXUAL DIVISION OF LABOUR

B Y   D E B B I E   F I E L D

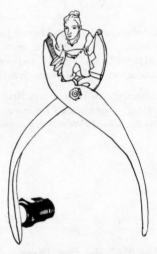

Ten years ago when women spoke about non-traditional jobs, they usually meant careers in medicine, business, law or higher education. But today the emphasis has shifted to the efforts of women to gain access to non-traditional jobs in the trades and heavy industry. This new focus reflects a change in the Canadian and world-wide women's movement over the past decade. Women are still saying that we are tired of lower wages, job inequalities, restricted opportunities and stereotypes that assume our inferiority. Yet, the women's movement has been transformed from being primarily student-based and middle-class to a movement that is increasingly composed of and concerned with the life issues of working-class women. Debbie Field explores the overall economic picture that has created the possibilities for women to move into non-traditional jobs and the problems that await women when they enter these jobs. She presents some tentative solutions to these problems – solutions that involve both the trade union and women's movements.

Helen is a single parent, who supports two children. For years she was the secretary, book-keeper, receptionist and bathroom cleaner for a small auto-repair shop. In 1980 she was earning $4 an hour. Shortly afterwards she began work as a labourer in the Steel Company of Canada's (Stelco's) Hilton works plant in Hamilton. Her starting pay there was $8 an hour. Besides the large increase in money, Helen was thrilled with many aspects of her new work situation. It provided paid benefits, the assurance of job training and advancement and accompanying pay increases, and much to her surprise, a much easier job. For the first time since she and her husband were separated, Helen was able to adequately support her family. And so, during her first week at Stelco, when a shocked foreman stammered at her: "Why are you here? Why would a woman want a dirty job like this?" Helen replied without hesitation, "I am here for the same reasons the men are — higher pay, benefits, the guarantee of regular work."

H ELEN IS NOT a feminist. She finds many of the ideas of the women's movement too radical, "women's libbers" too antagonistic to men. She did not participate in the public campaign that forced Stelco to start hiring women.[1] She does, however, share the feminist belief that women deserve equal pay and equal job access. Though often shy in expressing it, she is proud of her ability to do a job traditionally assumed to be male, proud too of the notoriety she has received from family and friends for being one of the first women to work at Stelco since World War II.

Helen's decision to work at Stelco, like that of other women pioneers in non-traditional jobs,[2] was affected by several related factors. First, the economic reality of life in Canada today forces women to work outside the home, and to find work that pays well.

By the 1970s, the economic boom and expansion of the state sector that had provided thousands of jobs for women had begun to slow down. Within traditional female areas, competition for employment increased, keeping wages low and forcing women to confront the boundaries of the job ghettos by seeking employment outside the line demarcating traditional male and female work. Microtechnology has intensified this process, as clerical jobs are eliminated through the introduction of new equipment.[3]

Second, the technology of the male workplace is undergoing a transformation. Jobs which in the past required extreme physical strength and endurance are now mechanized. The former requirements of muscle, sweat, shovel and sledgehammer are being replaced by the need to operate complicated machines.

The third influence is the women's movement, which gives a conscious organized voice to the desires of women to fight sexual stereotypes and discrimination and unifies women's diverse struggles. Through general education on women's issues, specifically the prominence given the demand for equal job access, and through organized "women into industry" and "women into non-traditional jobs" campaigns, the women's movement has strengthened individual women's critique of sexism and our confidence that we can do jobs we were taught were too dirty, too difficult, too male.

The labour movement and male workers who have broken with their historic resistance to women's equal job access are a fourth influence.[4] Trade union federations have begun to adopt resolutions in favour of women's complete job equality and mobility. Some working-class men see that the sexual division of labour traps them too, as women's exclusion from jobs facilitates our use as a cheap labour pool and we become a factor in driving down all wages. Given the economics of the 1980s, it is clear to men why their daughters, wives, girlfriends and mothers want non-traditional jobs.

There was evidence of this support during my first week at Stelco, when men waved victory fists and shouted encouragement as we two women marched onto the worksite with our shovels over our shoulder. Some wrote WELCOME in big grease letters on the female change-trailer. By forcing Stelco to start hiring women, they saw us as having scored a victory against the company.

Male workers' support is combined with ambivalence and even hostility as they grapple with the potential transformations of both workplace and home that result from a massive entry of women into non-traditional jobs. Nevertheless, union locals, sometimes 99 percent or 100 percent male in composition, have initiated, participated in and endorsed campaigns to get women hired in their own and other non-traditional workplaces.

As a fifth factor, sectors of the business community influence the movement of women into non-traditional jobs. Employers of traditionally male workplaces have generally opposed hiring women. Personnel managers and business executives, reinforcing the dominant sexism of our society, have stressed that women's place is in the home and that high-paying jobs should be left for men.

There are, however, some components of the business community who see potential benefits in hiring women into male areas. Under pressure of public anti-corporate sentiment, and union, women's movement, environmental and community lobbying, corporations began in the mid-1970s, cosmetic campaigns to enhance their corporate image without disturbing their actual structure or activity. Learning from the U.S. example, they realized that hiring a few women willingly would save lengthy and potentially expensive court cases and negative publicity down the road. And so, along with cleaning up the front yards of their factories, planting trees, buying some billboard space, a few token non-traditional women were hired and appeared in the propaganda releases of these farsighted corporations. Token hiring of women had the added benefit of government funding. Small firms could save money by using government training grants to hire women, whether they trained the women or not.

More significantly in the long term, components of Canadian industry are in the process of reorganizing their workplace technology and retooling in an attempt to become more productive and more competitive. This primarily involves the introduction of computerized machinery. Given the history of women being pulled into technologically new areas of the economy, it is possible that lower-paid female, industrial, construction and resource extraction job ghettos will develop. Just as working in a bank or office or for the phone company was transformed from a male profession with relatively high pay and job status to a female job with neither, we can predict a crop of new female jobs.

Numerical control machining equipment provides an interesting example. In contrast to the precision skill of a machinist, numerical control lathes are programmed by experts and operated by a technician who needs little training or knowledge of the entire machining process. The operator loads and unloads the machine, and operating a keyboard ensures that the program is carried out.[5]

Employment counsellors often steer women towards numerical control and away from machine shop training. After all, from their point of view, women are much more responsible when executing routine tasks, more dexterous when punching keyboards, and less likely to quit in an aggressive huff when the boredom of the job becomes overwhelming. Given social acceptance of the views that women will work for less, and that they are potentially more subservient and adaptable to the new technology, we can foresee employers wishing to lay off skilled tradesmen in order to hire women for these new jobs.[6]

Finally, as a sixth factor, the women's bureaus of the federal and provincial governments produce pamphlets, posters and research documents urging women to move into non-traditional areas, and urging employers to halt discrimination against women. In the absence of any affirmative action legislation that would force employers to hire women, these efforts, however well-meaning on the part of women's bureau employees, remain verbal "shoulds" without any force to back them up.

◆

Given all these influences we might suspect a large influx of women into non-traditional areas. However, a number of factors work against this. Though the participation rate is rising, the actual number of women in non-traditional jobs remains very small.[7] Individual women benefit, but for working women as a whole, not much has changed. Low-paying job ghettos continue to be women's main option. No wage spillover has occurred; though small numbers of women receive increased wages, the gap between average male and female wages continues to grow.

The current rise in unemployment is the strongest resistance to the movement of women into non-traditional jobs. Unemployment in Canada continues to rise, and by the end of 1982 will probably exceed a million and a half. As the recession deepens, whole industries are going into crisis, laying off hundreds of workers, and in some cases closing down completely, leaving thousands unemployed. It is probable that the number of women in non-traditional jobs will be lower in 1982 than it was in 1980 as hiring of men and women in traditional sectors declines.[8]

The demand for women's full job access becomes more difficult in times of high unemployment. This is particularly a problem since the union movement has so far failed to counter employer and government attacks on workers with an action program that would halt layoffs, guarantee full employment and protect living standards.[9]

The current economic crisis exacerbates a number of other factors that act as a resistance to the entry of women into non-traditional jobs. Factors such as the sexual division of labour in the home and the nature of the male workplace are critical barriers to women's job mobility.

One woman I know quit her non-traditional job in the coke ovens of a steel plant after a few days because of family responsibilities. Fran and her husband have two young children with plans to have a third in a year or so, and a traditional domestic division of labour in which she does all the child care, shopping, cooking and housework.[10] Her non-traditional job was totally physically exhausting, demanded that she work rotating shifts and exposed Fran to health-damaging gases, things she had never experienced in other jobs. Neither was she prepared to allow potential children to be birth defect guinea-pigs.[11] Her male co-workers arrived with lunches prepared and work clothes laundered. Their dinners were ready when they arrived home, or shortly thereafter when wives, girlfriends, or mothers returned from work. But no one packed Fran's lunch and she had a full shift of domestic work to complete after her paid job.

In addition, for many women, the sexist nature of male workplace culture can be an overwhelming, devastating problem, which drives them out of the workplace. Individually deciding to take on those aspects of male culture that offend women often backfires: the only viable long-term strategy is for groups of women to pose an alternative workplace culture, a culture in which women and men can work comfortably. One woman ripping down nude pin-ups will usually provoke a barrage of pin-ups. An organized group of women, who cover half the wall with pin-ups or pictures of our choice, will usually succeed in having all the offensive pictures disappear.

As women entering non-traditional jobs we have high expectations of ourselves, believing that we will be able to accomplish the work and fit into a completely new environment. We often expect miracles from ourselves, and are disappointed if we have trouble dealing with the sexism of male workplace culture, and are unable to change that culture to suit women. It would help us to remember a crucial lesson of the women's movement — our strength is our numbers, our collective anger, our vision and our activities.

◆

Because of the complexity of the problems facing working women, a precondition for positive changes in women's situation is a strong women's movement, which asserts our refusal to bear the brunt of a social crisis that every day grows more severe, and is capable of organizing coordinated activity around women's concerns.

Women's full job access is an important issue. Campaigns for women into non-traditional jobs must continue, but because this struggle involves only small numbers of women, demands for equal pay and campaigns to improve women's working lives in traditional areas must be central. Efforts to win higher pay and better working conditions, the struggle against the microtechnology replacement of women's jobs and the organizing drives to unionize women in all areas will also continue to be crucial. Taken separately, none of these can alleviate women's workplace inequality. Taken together and combined with other issues — from child care to equal pay legislation and lesbian rights — we can foresee improvements in women's lives.

In the context of fighting to ensure that women do not bear the brunt of current economic problems, demands for preferential treatment for women become necessary. As thousands of workers are laid off weekly, arguments about "defending the family unit" are dug up and revitalized to justify attempts to exclude women from jobs, both traditional and non-traditional. We need a women's movement that can refute the existence of this mythical family unit, pointing out that as working women we need jobs to support ourselves and our families as much as men do. We need to demand affirmative action programs which ensure that employers hire certain percentages of women and continue to do so even when hiring is reduced and unemployment in all areas is rising.

Women are often excluded from non-traditional jobs because we do not have manual or industrial experience. But it is unreasonable to penalize women for a historic division of labour that streamed us from school days on into traditional female skills, jobs and experiences. The women's movement needs to demand preferential hiring to ensure that all skill factors being equal, an employer may hire a woman even though she has less industrial experience than a man. It means giving women special chances to get into apprenticeship and training programs.

A more complicated demand is preferential seniority, whereby women recently hired into traditionally male areas are given extra seniority as a partial rectification of past discrimination, and as protection that women, usually the last hired, will not be the first fired. The demand for preferential seniority is one that needs fuller debate inside the unions and in the women's movement before all its potential implications can be clarified. Those who argue in favour of it point out that without preferential seniority any attempt to get women into non-traditional jobs is erased when the first round of layoffs wipes out all the women who have recently won access. At the same time as they oppose employer or government intervention in the seniority system, supporters of preferential seniority argue that since seniority is an acquisition of the union movement, it can be modified by the unions. For example, after World War II, thousands of women with three or four years seniority were bumped by male soldiers returning from the war. At that time the union movement believed that it was in the interests of the entire society that men be given these jobs. There was little resistance from the unions to tampering with the seniority system then!

On the other hand, many unionists argue that any kind of preferential seniority defeats the goal of the seniority system and makes unions vulnerable to the destruction of seniority rights. As long as strict seniority applies, unions and workers are not involved in deciding who amongst the work force will be laid off — layoffs are done in strict chronological order. Once unions begin to ask for different seniority lists, everything changes. Unions become the ones to decide who has preferential seniority rights and subsequently jobs. Those who object to preferential seniority stress that unions should counterpose a program of no layoffs, jobs for all, and redistribution of the available work to all workers with no loss in pay.

◆

In the late nineteenth century women's existence as a cheap labour pool was used by employers to drive down all wages and create job competition between men and women. In response, the predominantly male labour movement demanded restrictions on women's work and women's access to many jobs was limited.[12] In order to avoid a repetition of this experience, it is critical that the women's movement build an alliance with the labour movement, an alliance whose ultimate goal is full employment for men and women and the explicit rejection of job competition between men and women.

To make it difficult for employers to create low-paying female job ghettos, unions and male workers need to reach out to women, explaining why joining a union could help women get and keep higher-paying jobs. In order to destroy the objective basis of women's use as a cheap labour pool — that is, our lower wage — unions should intensify their support for equal pay and equal job access for women at equal pay rates.

For the women's movement such an alliance means tying "women into non-traditional jobs," or any other specific women's campaign, with the broader goal of jobs for everyone. We must be wary of gaining a few token jobs for women while ignoring the larger question of unemployment. Concretely this means that women into non-traditional jobs campaigns must collaborate with the men and the union (if there is one) of the specific work area to ensure that the men perceive the campaign as directed towards the employer and not against men's jobs. It means joint union-women's movement publicity, campaigns calling for the creation of jobs, training and retraining programs for women and men, and joint strategy sessions on how to organize such campaigns. It means an awareness on the part of women that in the long term, no job solutions for women exist without broader solutions to create full employment and jobs for everyone.

—

The struggle to win non-traditional jobs for women, which appeared difficult five years ago, is today even more complicated. Whatever small gains were possible before are disappearing as the capitalist system once again enters deep crisis. Every time a group raises the demand for justice or equitability, no matter how modest, it confronts political and corporate leaders who explain that the costs are too high. Women, native people, immigrants, lesbians, gays and the working class as a whole — confront a system that is increasingly inflexible in all the areas of social organization.

The choice for women and the mass of working people is becoming clearer and more urgent. Will we tolerate a systematic reduction in our standard of living, our wage levels, the daily conditions of our work and our social and political rights? Will we accept that the system is in debt and we must pay the price? Or will we decide that our demands are legitimate and that a total reorganization of society is necessary to fulfill them?

These questions may appear too abstract or rhetorical, but I believe they bear directly on the issue of women into non-traditional areas. The women's movement has spent fifteen years discovering and analyzing the myriad ways women experience discrimination and oppression. Out of this growing awareness, women have tried, individually and collectively, to rectify our situation by campaigns and rebellions of various kinds. In partial ways we have succeeded in creating a broader social and economic space for women. Our attempts to get non-traditional jobs is one example. But we have been limited by the constraints of the organization of capitalism, and as capitalism's crisis intensifies, our ability to make gains is diminished.

The experience of the women's movement provides three important lessons to women in our struggle for non-traditional jobs, or any other struggle to gain equality. First, against a hostile and inflexible social system, we must have the broadest possible basis of support from women, from oppressed groups, from the working class as a whole. We will not gain non-traditional jobs without this support. Second, even the most profound opposition to the current state of affairs cannot succeed without a strategy to win. Every isolated conflict cries out for a unified movement with clear political objectives and proposals for action. Women will not win access to non-traditional areas unless we develop clearer battle plans to force employers to change their hiring practices, to encourage working-class men to support our efforts, to build a political alliance capable of backing up our demands. Finally, women's full economic and social rights cannot be granted by a capitalist system in crisis. We are compelled to look towards a socialist and non-patriarchal system, which would lay the pre-condition not just for women's equal participation in the work process, but for a more thorough-going equalization of human social relations.

N   O   T   E   S

1. In 1979, Local 1005 of the United Steelworkers of America, representing 13,000 Hilton work employees, and five women, launched a campaign against Stelco for its refusal to hire women. The women, of whom I was one, laid Human Rights Commission complaints and built a support committee which elicited broad union and public endorsation. In March 1980, we were hired and Stelco began hiring one woman out of every ten new employees.

2. Lillian Zimmerman offers a useful definition of non-traditional jobs as "those occupations in which the large majority of workers are male with the normative expectation that this is as it should be." See "Opening Up to Women of Vocational Training and Jobs Traditionally Occupied by Men" (Report to the U.N. Educational, Scientific and Cultural Organization International Seminar, November 1980), p. 3.

3. Patti Schrom-Moffratt and Cynthia Dale Telfer, "Women and Work: Introduction to Non-Traditional Work" (Canadian Research Institute for the Advancement of Women, 1978), p. 2.

4. Working-class men and the trade union movement until recent years have blocked the entry of women into men's jobs. Understanding the relative privilege that accrues to men through the sexual division of labour – of higher-paying jobs, of women's economic, emotional and sexual dependence and our responsibility for domestic labour – they have stressed that women be protected from the "harsh conditions" of male work. Much of male sexism rests on the defence of this privilege.

5. Working on a numerical control lathe is supposedly cleaner and less physically demanding than working on the old machinery, but this is more true in the glossy brochure advertising the new equipment than in fact.

6. A common view of women is that because of our socialization we make "better," that is, more subservient workers. Our history, and particularly the experience of the recent years, disproves this; women have shown increased combativity in workplace resistance and strikes. But when we are a few women in a male workplace, the myth takes on a certain reality. In our concern to prove ourselves we may initially be more inclined than men to follow employers' rules.

7. Taking construction as one example: in 1975, .6% of construction workers were women; in 1980, 1.2% were women. That 1.2% represented 8,000 women all across the country. In 1979, the figures for fishing, hunting and trapping; mining and quarrying; and processing were still too small to record a female participation rate. Women were 5.7% of machinists (16,000 women) and 5.3% of transport equipment operators (23,000). Figures are

from Women's Bureau, *1978-79 Women in the Labour Force,* p. 32 and Carole Swain, *Women in the Canadian Labour Market* (Canada Employment amd Immigration Commission, 1981), p. 29.

8. For example, in December 1981, Stelco in Hamilton laid off over 2,000 workers, including all 200 women, except for a few in the skilled trades, who had been hired the previous year. If we're lucky, these women will return when rehiring occurs, and Stelco will continue to hire new women.

9. Such a program could consist of, among others, the following demands:

   a) wages indexed to inflation and interest rates – so that real income does not fall

   b) 30 hours of work for 40 hours of pay – so that the available work is redistributed more equitably

   c) union ban on overtime – to force employers to create full-time positions when there is extra work

   d) halt the deterioration of the work environment – to ensure that health and safety and workers' lives are not sacrificed in times of economic recession.

10. Helen and Fran are the changed names of two women I worked with at Stelco.

11. While a struggle is being waged to improve conditions for both men and women workers, the fact remains that the health hazards of some traditional male workplaces are more of a problem for women planning to be pregnant than for men, because men don't bring the fetus with them to work. (See article by Marianne Langton in this volume.)

12. Black, native people and immigrants have been used in similar ways.

F U R T H E R   R E A D I N G S

Cohen, Leah. "A Review of Women's Participation in the Non-Traditional Occupations," Technical Study #8 Canadian Employment and Immigration Commission, 1981.

Zimmerman, Lillian. "Opening up to Women of Vocational Training and Jobs Traditionally Occupied by Men," Report to the U.N. Educational, Scientific and Cultural Organization International Seminar, November 1980.

Women in Trades

IN BRITISH COLUMBIA

BY KATE BRAID

Although general consciousness-raising groups are no longer common, there is, at least in the larger cities of Canada, a plethora of support groups organized around specific issues. There are support groups for lesbian mothers, for women writing, for women with addictions, for Third World women. This article by Kate Braid could have been subtitled, "How We Started a Support Group and Took on the World." Women in Trades in B.C. started as just that – a group of B.C. women working in trades who organized themselves to give each other support and break down the isolation they were experiencing by being women doing "men's work." Then, on behalf of other women, they started tackling the difficulties of access to training and the problems of trade schools in the province. Eventually WIT has come to see itself as part of the women's movement in Vancouver and has allied itself with a series of issues that are of concern to all women.

W HAT A SHOCK, to women as well as to men, that women can do "man's work"! The last all-male territory – the construction site, the logging camp, the airplane hangar – where boys were boys, has been (to use a male millwright's phrase) "invaded" by women. Non-traditional work demands and allows that women become competent, confident, assertive, physically strong, mechanically skilled and respon-sible – all qualities not easily acceptable as "feminine" in this culture. Men and women are being forced to question some of their basic ideas about themselves.

But there will be no real long-term changes in the experience of women in the non-traditional workplace until there is one basic change – in numbers. We cannot be the only one on any worksite. We must become more than tokens; we must become at least a minority. It is the only way for us to lose our present isolation and sense of "deviance" and to begin to make the place we work *our* workplace, not just a "man's workplace."

We have begun to tackle our isolation by forming Women in Trades organizations across the country. The first time I was in a room full of tradeswomen was at a workshop at a Women and Work Con-ference held in Vancouver in 1979. Each trade occupation that was called out as we went around the room introducing ourselves was like another window opening on the dingy preoccupations of my isolated self. When forty-seven women showed up at a subsequent meeting, the Women in Trades Association of British Columbia was born.

When we first started meeting, our primary goal was to find others who shared our problems in the trades. We wanted to confirm that we weren't crazy to want to work in trades or incompetent or hopeless in trades work. Initially, for all of us, it had been a major struggle simply to overcome conditioning and *imagine* ourselves as tradeswomen. With vir-tually no role models or encouragement, we had somehow come to realize that we liked mechanical and physical work and that we might become good enough at it to make a living from it.

As we listened to each other's stories, we were able to put together a picture of the very unfavourable odds that women confront both in get-ting into and staying in trades work. One woman in WIT, after several years on welfare with three children, finally got tired of being poor and of chasing the absent father for support money. "I decided that if trades were the only job that gave a woman decent pay, then I was going to be a tradeswoman and I didn't care too much which trade it was. But then my counsellor asked me which trade I wanted and I just asked which had the shortest waiting list to get into pre-apprentice training. He slammed the book shut and said, 'You can't pick a trade like that! If you don't like it we'll have wasted our time and money in training you!' "

The woman grins and continues her story. "So I did a little research on my own and a few days later I went down again and got a different counsellor. This time I said I'd always wanted to be an electrician. I told him that my father was an electrician and I would just love to be able to do that too. I practically said that God had told me to be an electrician. I got into the course." The woman is now, indeed, an apprentice electrician.

Once on the job there are all the difficulties of isolation, lack of confidence and of dealing with men's expectations of a "lady." But the question we are most often asked by other women is, "Were you sexually harassed?" Many people assume that women in non-traditional occupations must suffer more sexual harassment than women in other jobs. Certainly, the men we work with are often rougher and more direct in their language and in certain ways of relating to women but this is not to automatically assume "more" harassment, than say, in offices.

As women in trades, we share stories of real and occasionally severe harassment but we have also found that the nature of our work itself presents us with powerful tools and strategies with which to cope. For example, in the blue collar workplace it is alright to talk back – to shout, curse and express violent feelings when you have been offended. Sometimes you are being specifically tested by a man who wants to know your limits, to know how much he can get away with – or even how much he thinks you might expect.

What is immensely satisfying (and often surprising) is how much respect you gain on a job by saying "no," by getting angry at inappropriate behaviour. As a forklift driver put it, "When I was sitting in an office, I had to sit still while my boss told me what to do. I couldn't talk back or express my feelings or tell him that he was wrong. But on this job I can. I've changed. I think my personality has strengthened a little bit because now I can shoot off my mouth better."

Many of us changed our own attitudes to women. A good example is one woman who, when she first joined Women in Trades, insisted that any woman who really wanted to could make it, that the men on the job were just fine (''considering'') and she was only here because once in a while it was ''nice to talk to other girls.'' Several months later she was overheard describing to a new member how an employer had refused to hire a qualified woman she knew. She was angry. She didn't blame the woman for not trying harder or for not taking a cut in salary just to get her foot in the door. She was angry at an employer who would refuse a woman and hire a man slightly less qualified the following day. She was angry at the systematic blocks he had put in the woman's way, blocks that were winked at and tacitly approved by this society as a whole.

As each of us placed our personal experience of obstruction and inequality into the larger pattern, we began to see systematic discrimination and slowly we came to believe in each other enough to start making demands on behalf of all women. We began to transform our support group into a political organization. But the support function continued to be important. Discovering women who would roll their eyes in perfect understanding before you had finished your story, kept us coming back even when we were burned out and irritated with each other.

For there were tensions in this process of building our organization. As one member said after her first committee meeting and her first major disagreement with another member, ''I'm used to being the most outspoken one in any group and getting my own way. I'm going to have to get used to the fact that this is one very independent and strong-minded group of women!''

Eliciting group opinion has never been a problem, but directing that opinion has been. The chaos of our initial meetings, with their almost total lack of order, was hard on everyone's nerves. Gradually our way of conducting business changed. One of the quiet members finally got tired of not being heard and startled one meeting by speaking up and offering some simple rules she had learned in Quaker meetings. At the following meeting we agreed that the chair would keep a speaker's list and that interruptions would not be allowed. On controversial issues, everyone who wishes to speak must have a chance to speak once before anyone is allowed to speak again.

Another changing and vital thread in the cloth of our organization is the constant and ongoing effort to maintain a sense of responsibility of the group *for* the group. Although we are aware that traditionally there are a small number of members of any organization who shoulder most of the workload, we have fought to avoid a few women taking on most of the work.

What makes this difficult for those few who feel comfortable in a public position, is that in contrast to the slow slogging, of, say, a meeting to carry on daily business or clean up the constitution, are the immediate and exhilarating rewards of high-profile activities such as giving speeches. Speech-making generates more speech-making; someone heard so-and-so give a speech so they phone and ask for that person to do another. Two or three women begin to take on more and more of the public face, the "fame" of the organization. But other women feel that they contribute to the organization in ways that aren't being recognized, or they would like the opportunity to speak and have not been asked or they feel that a group policy decision is being contradicted. In all these cases, there is resentment.

The other unhappy fruit of this "specialization" is that it leads to burnout. Burnout is that now-familiar phenomenon among volunteer groups whereby one eager and committed soul begins to take on too much responsibility. As the volunteer resents the growing load, others are admiring her apparently unlimited capacity until the day she suddenly blows up in anger or simply drops out, disappears from the group and is heard rumbling bitterly about it in other quarters.

We have come to recognize the symptoms of burnout. There are a few phrases that are dead give-aways: "Oh, I can always do one more thing. Why not?" "If I don't do that, nobody else will." etc. We warn each other when we see it coming and women accordingly grant themselves "holidays" from WIT activities. We bear no grudge when a woman who has worked hard for a while gives notice that she is temporarily dropping out. We encourage it, for we think that one of the ways we will keep active members is by allowing each of us at some time or another to recuperate or to focus on other demands such as course work.

We have made progress. Some of the more retiring members have made clear and successful efforts by giving speeches and leading workshops. The more vocal ones have tried to take one step back. It is the theory of collective action meeting the fact of personal limits.

In the end the success of our organization will be measured not just by process (the way we work problems and goals out together), but also by production. The issue that sparked our first set of demands to a public institution came when one of our members was severely harassed at trade school. As well as supporting the woman in a human rights suit, we presented a brief and a list of demands that were met by several concessions such as a women's advocate position and a drop-in centre for women. The school also issued a five-point policy statement ''in support of women seeking access to training and employment in non-traditional occupations.''

Difficulties at trade schools are typical of the problems we have faced in trying to achieve trade skills. It is surprising, to say the least, that in a time of national critical skill shortage, it is difficult for any aspiring tadesperson, male or female, to get into vocational training school. It is particularly difficult for women. In British Columbia there is no one centralized, easily accessible place where a prospective tradesperson can go for all the necessary information. Most often, she accumulates a set of vague and contradictory information from a variety of sources.

Another difficulty for women seeking access to skills training is the basic structure of the apprenticeship program that is primary means of becoming a qualified recognized ''journeyman'' in any trade. In B.C., apprenticeship programs require that the apprentice return to school for from four to eight weeks of theoretical training each year. However, schools are located in only a few centres in the province, so that training usually requires travel away from home. It is so unlikely as to be almost laughable that once every year a woman could announce to husband and/or kids, ''I'm going to Vancouver (Kamloops, etc.) for training. I'll be back in six weeks.'' For single mothers (as for single fathers) the situation becomes virtually impossible, especially as federal training subsidies allow a minimal child care allowance. The provincial government allows none at all.

WIT has been criticized by some women's groups for not having "strong enough politics." I think they are wrong and I wonder exactly what they mean. If at any point we had defined ourselves as feminist or socialist or any of the other "acceptable" labels, it would have scared some women and driven them from the group. Labels are less important than the fact that what we are doing is, in fact, highly political, if you define politics as "personal and public organization for change."

Very slowly, our public position has changed, along with many of our private ones. For example, when we began, the issues introduced at our meetings dealt exclusively with trades. Even then we were very cautious. For example, when the Women into Stelco (see article by Debbie Field in this anthology) asked us to add our endorsement to the long list of private, union and government organizations that protested their exclusion from Stelco jobs, the response of B.C. Women in Trades was to write to ask the company for more information so that we could hear "the other side of the story." We never received a reply to that letter and we never endorsed the women's cause.

Several months later we were informed that women in Quebec who were fighting the Women into CN campaign were in danger of losing their right to a federal Human Rights tribunal that could publicize the issues of women at CN and therefore the ones that many of us were fighting in non-traditional areas of work. We were asked to send a telegram requesting that the tribunal be granted. B.C. Women in Trades not only sent the requested telegram, we also sent telegrams to every other WIT group in Canada suggesting they do the same. (The tribunal was eventually granted.)

Most recently, a member requested that we endorse the struggle of a B.C. Indian band who were demanding the appointment of a federal commission to look into a large mining company's right to dump industrial waste into the band's traditional fishing waters. This was one of the first times we had been asked to take a public statement on an issue that was not directly related to women in trades. There was a pause – and several voices spoke up strongly in support of the request. It was carried. We have since carried our banner in Women's Day rallies, peace marches, May Day and "Women's Right to Choose" parades, among others.

Although the circumstances of each decision were different, it is unlikely that such decisions would have been made a year or two earlier. As a group we are beginning to have a sense of our public place in the world – initially as women in *trades,* then increasingly as *women* facing common problems because of our common areas of work in trades, and lately as *tradeswomen* with a sense of our particular issues in the larger social context of economic recession and government cutbacks.

F U R T H E R   R E A D I N G S

Pierson, Ruth. "Women's Emancipation and the Recruitment of Women into the Labour Force in World War II," in *The Neglected Majority: Essays in Canadian Women's History,* Susan Mann Trofimenkoff and Alison Prentice, eds. Toronto: McClelland and Stewart, 1977.

Wetherby, Terry, ed. *Conversations: Working Women Talk About Doing a "Man's Job."* Millbrae, Calif.: Les Femmes, 1977.

Onto the Streets

THE WOMEN'S MOVEMENT has changed in the past ten years. More women are aware of the struggle to live and work and love as women. More of us call ourselves feminists. And society is more aware of women as strong, independent, courageous and determined. While the issues of a decade ago are still with us, women in the "movement" are in more places and involved in more types of activities than ever before. There is no single description of women who are feminists. We are from different ethnic and racial backgrounds, we are lesbians and heterosexual, we speak many languages and we are of all ages.

We are organizing – and *Onto the Streets* is just a catchy phrase to represent our mobilization. The problems addressed in this section are particularly significant. We've learned, after more than ten years of struggle, that no one is simply going to give us what we want. So we are taking our concerns, special interests and aspirations and organizing around them politically. This group of articles focuses on the vital question confronting us: how best to achieve our objectives. Consistent themes throughout the articles are the possibilities for enlarging the movement and the resources that can be used to help attain our goals.

In the articles grouped under *Double Oppression,* a lesbian, a native woman and immigrant women discuss their priorities in struggling and fighting back in this society. We know that all women are oppressed, but some of us experience an added oppression beyond being women. Those of us who are older, of colour, are lesbians, disabled, are native or Québécoise understand only too clearly that our society oppresses us not only for being women, but also for being old, of colour, lesbians, disabled or non-Anglo.

Just as the women's movement now has a different composition, so too have our energies been concentrated in new directions. Feminists have added a new approach to traditional forms of conveying experience. The articles in the *Tools for Politicization* section explore the political potential of feminist writing and publishing, a feminist way of learning and a feminist art. These articles go beyond the questions of what it means to write, interpret, teach, learn and create in a feminist way – the authors discuss these means as potential tools for politicization.

After so many years of struggle, it is important to stop and ask what we do with all that we have experienced and all that we know. Feminists need to take our history and examine the struggles of the last ten years, evaluating both the mistakes and the inroads we've made. Such analysis is vital, for it is only through a realistic understanding of how far we've come and what got us here that we can rationally develop an effective strategy for the future. The final article of this book attempts to do just that. In it, six feminists address the achievements of the last decade, the obstacles to organizing and potential priorities for the fight ahead.

The necessity for organizing, building and consolidating is stressed in this section as it has been throughout the book. Previous articles demonstrate why feminists have ignored those who tell us to be patient. They also make it clear that our fight is not nearly over. In this final group of chapters, authors explain why we cannot quietly sit back now, but must instead intensify our efforts to build, strengthen and solidify our movement.

◆

Mothers, Sisters, Lovers, Listen

B Y A M Y G O T T L I E B

Lesbian feminism developed as a response to sexism in the gay movement and homophobia and avoidance in the early 1970s in the women's movement. The women's movement no longer seems afraid to raise the issue *of lesbianism and the right to sexual self-determination. But it has often focused on lesbianism as a specific case of civil rights. This article shifts the focus away from lesbianism as just one more issue of the women's liberation movement and asks feminists to address heterosexism as a problem, like sexism, which oppresses all women, regardless of their sexual orientation. Amy Gottlieb calls for an integration into the women's movement of the understanding of lesbians' experience and oppression, and the building of a movement that defines itself in opposition to sexism* and *heterosexism – in order to provide a solid political basis for the creation of unity between heterosexual and lesbian women.*

T HE HERSTORY OF lesbians' struggle for self- and collective identity and against the barren and degrading experience of the closet is a long one. We are only just beginning to uncover who we are – reclaiming a lost heritage of witches, women who lived together in friendship networks, spinsters – all women who have resisted the male right to possession of women.

We are fighting to be and remain independent women, to live our lives free from the economic, social and psychological ties of marriage and subservience to men – and we are fighting for all women to be able to make this choice. Yet at every step along the way we are faced with both a ghost-like invisibility and society's definitions of us as queer, deviant man-haters, men in women's bodies.

In the past decade, many women have come out, declaring themselves as proud amazons. We have built communities and networks, unearthing our potential to transform our lives. We have gained strength and pride from the women's and gay movements, which helped open up the space for us to discover ourselves and explore who we are.

Through our activity with gay men and feminists we discovered many things. Most of all, we began to see that in order to change our lives and those of our many sisters forced into secrecy and silence, we had to reveal our uniqueness and develop our unity with others on a different footing – the basis of which would be an understanding of heterosexism. We would have to define how our common action with feminists and gay men, while still essential, had hidden us in a different closet.

◆

Lesbian feminism is in the process of becoming. It is a theory that is relatively undeveloped, misunderstood and even unknown by many lesbians, gay men and feminists. There are no texts that explain its meaning. If you ask five lesbian activists what lesbian feminism means to them you will get five different answers. But all will acknowledge the potentially radicalizing nature of being a lesbian.

For me, lesbian feminism is not just a personal choice to love other women emotionally and sexually. It is not limited to civil rights protection, although the struggle for job protection, defence of our right to have and keep our children, and against police and state harassment are essential. It is a lot more than a vibrant and inspiring women's culture and community, although that is fundamental to our survival. Lesbian-feminism is primarily a critique of the institutional enforcement of heterosexuality.

In every institution that feminists have shown to be oppressive to women, whether it be the family, organized religion, the educational system or the workplace, heterosexism is prevalent. The assumption that every woman is or would like to be emotionally, sexually and economically hooked up with a man predominates in all institutions of patriarchal capitalism. Heterosexism serves to maintain the discrimination that women experience in the workplace: we are exploited in low-paying, female job ghettos on the assumption that our job is not a primary commitment. Even if a woman works outside of the home her whole life, it is assumed that she is primarily committed to a family and that she has a man who is supporting her financially.

Many lesbians have been forced into marriage in order to survive. A lesbian's position in marriage is similar to that of a battered woman; she is trapped because of economic powerlessness, isolation and nowhere to go. The penalties for rejecting our family and reproductive "duties," for allying with and loving women, are severe: from losing our children, to being fired from our jobs, ostracized from our families and friends, and in many countries, mutilated, imprisoned, tortured and killed. It makes one wonder, as Adrienne Rich does, why "such violent strictures should be found necessary to enforce women's total emotional, erotic loyalty and subservience to men. The tremendous force by which male power is maintained, suggests that an enormous counterforce is having to be restrained."[1]

◆

The gay movement has rarely integrated an understanding of the female aspect of our oppression; of how fundamental women's oppression, the enforcement of our role as wife and mother, is to institutionalized homophobia. The access to jobs, status, economic security that gay men have been afforded because they are men, allows them to make life choices more easily. While they lose a certain kind of heterosexual privilege when they come out, they have been able to survive outside of the nuclear family as a result of their economic independence. This in turn has given gay men a degree of visibility that lesbians have been unable to achieve.

In addition, much of the gay movement's work has been around issues designed to achieve equal status with straight men. The emphasis on equality under the law has excluded lesbians, who can see just how far formal legal equality with men has gotten them. The fight for civil rights has tended to focus on the plight of one individual to the exclusion of how gay men and lesbians are affected by continuous discrimination in our daily lives. For instance, sexual orientation protection would give lesbians at least one avenue in the fight for job security. But it needs mass action to win it, and the male-identified and star-studded approach to gaining support means that many lesbians have difficulty identifying this as part of their struggle. Even in the gay movement's most recent militant activity, in response to the Toronto bath raids in early 1981, the impact of similar, but less focused attacks on lesbians was never articulated. For lesbians, there was an increased level of street harassment and the accompanying fears, but the lack of specifically lesbian institutions meant that the harassment of lesbians remained individual and invisible. The bath raids were a vicious attack on the gay community, but the closing of the Fly By Night, a women's bar, had a much greater social impact on the lesbian community. In one day our only free social/political space was stolen from us.

◆

The role of lesbians in the women's movement has changed dramatically since the lesbian/straight debates and tensions of the early 1970s. Lesbian rights and the defence of lesbians against harassment have been integrated into the central issues addressed on International Women's Day in Toronto. But it is still true that the women's movement as a whole either ignores lesbianism or sees it in terms of "personal choice" or "lifestyle." When the women's movement does take up the issue of lesbian rights it tends to limit its importance to a struggle for the rights of a small minority of women. The deep-seated bigotry that lesbians face is seldom presented as forcefully as it should be – as one of the strongest expressions of sexism in a society that must keep women in our assigned roles, apart from and divided against ourselves. The women's movement's rare attempts to pose lesbian rights as a struggle in the interests of all women have been put forward in a very abstract way. We have been unsuccessful in linking the concerns of lesbians with the concerns of all women, or more specifically, with those of single women. Both lesbians and heterosexual women are responsible for avoidance, confused discussions and the consequent lack of clarity and educational work.

The women's movement must explore the links between sexism and heterosexism. Lesbians and straight feminists must look at how institutionalized heterosexuality has been structured and maintained in the myriad of experiences we go through on a daily and generational level, from the poverty-level wages we get, our double day of labour, the denial of essential services, to the images that confront us in the media and popular culture. It is not just inequality between the sexes, the domination of male culture, or the strong taboos against same-sex love, but the enforcement of heterosexuality that has assured male privilege and men's possession of women's lives. One of the means of this enforcement is the way in which the possibility to be lesbian has been erased and invalidated.

The question inevitably comes up: do lesbians condemn all heterosexual relationships? I think that this is the wrong question, though I understand that it is a genuine one. The point is not to judge whether heterosexual relationships are bad or good, but to understand that all women are limited in the choices we can make. We will continue to be limited until we can define and choose the meaning and place of sexuality in our lives – until we can enter into sexual emotional relationships from a position of freedom and equality.

While lesbian feminism does not condemn heterosexual relationships, it does identify a privilege that heterosexual women derive from them. Heterosexual women do not have to justify or legitimize their existence, which is given by virtue of their connection to a man.

Heterosexual women do not get up each morning wondering how to face a world structurally hostile to their sexual emotional choice. Heterosexual women are not pushed away by their families or refused apartments; they do not have their children taken away from them on the basis that they allegedly cannot create healthy and normal role models for them. Heterosexual women do not live in fear of losing everything, simply on the basis of whom they love.

Heterosexual privilege must be acknowledged within the women's movement, not as a mechanism for guilt or shame, but as a way to understand real differences. Just as we come to terms with white skin privilege, its effects on our movement and the immense struggle necessary to eradicate it, we must come to terms with heterosexism. It is certain that a racist remark would be met with howls and a strong, clear anti-racist response. We must battle against homophobia in the same way. Heterosexual feminists must realize that it is in their own interests to struggle against heterosexism. Therefore they must oppose it not just because they support lesbians' fight, but because they want to create freer, more conscious sexual relations for all women.

In the earlier days of the women's movement, lesbians were often pushed to explain or justify their lesbianism. I think this is not a question for lesbians only.[2] As conscious feminists, whether heterosexual or lesbian, we all have to be aware not only of how society has limited and proscribed our lives, but of the life choices we have made. Lesbian-feminism has begun to articulate an answer to the question "Why are you a lesbian?" It is: "Because we choose to be."[3] There is no natural identity or unity among lesbians based on the fact that we make love with other women. We do not turn lavender when we first make love with another woman or when we come out. Rather, lesbianism involves a conscious choice to acknowledge our love for women, at least to ourselves. It is an identity that we create for ourselves (as well as an identity that is created for us in the form of false and negative images). For me, lesbianism involves a decision to resist, to work towards collective identity in order to survive and move forward to a future of freedom.

A recent TV show in Vancouver, which was taped after the May 1981 Lesbian Conference, is a good example of how we view our rebellion against the imposed feminine norm. The interviewer had done several shows with gay men, and was rendered almost speechless by the response of lesbians to the question, "Why are you a lesbian?" One after another, lesbians spoke of making a choice. Gay men earlier had described their sexuality as being formed at an early age, saying there was nothing they could do about it but accept it and feel pride. Lesbians talked about discovering, some early, some late, that they didn't have to be heterosexual. What these women were saying is that it is important for our sense of integrity and survival to assert our right, every woman's right, to choose to love women. We are not the third sex; we are women choosing as other women have before us to experience love, joy and sensuality in companionship with women.

◆

The gay and women's movements share a misunderstanding about lesbians. It is assumed, for the most part unconsciously, that lesbians are female counterparts of gay men. This conception deprives us of our experience as women and reinforces the idea that we are not full and complete women. Most importantly, being seen as female counterparts of gay men robs the women's movement of the understanding of how the institution of heterosexuality has shaped the lives of all women.

In response to the lack of understanding of our experience as women amongst gay men, and homophobia and avoidance within the women's movement, lesbians have sought common places to meet and antonomous organizations to strengthen our collective identity. The creation of separate spaces has developed in turn different political currents, which have addressed the nature of our oppression, the question of with whom we should ally and the political significance of our fight. For many of us our experience within the lesbian community is an empowering one, both individually and collectively. It has given us a stronger sense of ourselves and a basis to start fighting for lesbians within other movements in which we are active.

It was through our search for political definition in response to feminists and gay men that lesbian feminism was born. Our conceptualization of lesbian feminism began with a fundamental recognition that heterosexuality is not just a sexual preference, but a political institution – an institution that has far-reaching effects on the lives of all women.

The primary place in which an analysis of compulsory heterosexuality will develop is in the women's movement. It is here that the link between sexism and heterosexism will be uncovered. It is here that the double oppression of lesbians, as women and as "homosexuals," can be fully understood, thereby intimately linking the two aspects of our oppression which cannot be separated in the struggle for the liberation of all women.

This is not just a theoretical exercise. The women's movement must increase its support and encouragement to women coming out. It must open itself up to lesbian women. There is a lesbian community beyond the "politically conscious" lesbian feminists that the women's movement must speak to and develop links with. Lesbians are an important part of the constituency that the movement should be reaching out to, educating and learning from, and encouraging to join us. We must put to rest the widespread, often unspoken, assumption that all lesbians, in their heart of hearts, are separatists. We must also acknowledge the existence of lesbians and their particular concerns in other areas of struggle, whether in the trade unions or the day care struggle, for example.

An understanding of the importance of fighting heterosexism can help us respond in a stronger way to the attacks on women, whether they be from anti-choice forces, employers or the state.

Times have been a lot tougher for lesbians in Toronto since the bath raids, since the emergence of vocal anti-gay, anti-lesbian groups in the city. We are becoming more of a "visible" minority. Right-wing organizations have begun to "name" us in their propaganda against the spread of the lavender menace. And lesbians, like all women, are affected by UIC cuts, anti-choice forces, shortages in day care, the push back into the family, union-busting and the reinstitution of dress codes. These attacks, designed to bolster the family and enforced heterosexuality, influence lesbians very deeply as single women living outside conventional norms. The effect on women who are trying to come out is even more devastating.

In any actions against the right, the women's movement must not separate the attacks on women in general from the attacks on lesbians. When the right-wing attempts to isolate and scapegoat lesbians, branding us as "sick perverts," this is an attack on every woman's right to self-determination. When the right-wing attacks women's right to control our reproduction, this is an attack on lesbians as well as on heterosexual women.

By understanding these links and having the courage and insight to integrate lesbian feminism into our analysis and day-to-day activity, we will be helping create a powerful, unified and non-heterosexist women's movement.

In criticizing the women's movement, I do not mean that I intend to sit back and wait for others to come up with an analysis and practice that I can identify with. Lesbian feminists have a prime responsibility for defining our oppression and providing guidance in how to fight back.

We are in the process of doing just this. New lesbian groups have formed recently to fight right-wing and state attacks. Through these groups we will be able to define what issues are most important to us and lay the foundations for an equal partnership with other groups in the fight against the right.

Lesbian feminists are in the process of finding ourselves and our politics. We are in the process of defining the basis on which we will ally with all those fighting sexism, heterosexism, racism and exploitation. What we need within the women's movement is a commitment to honest productive dialogue and activity, a commitment that our existence and our struggles will no longer remain invisible, but will be shared by all feminists.

N O T E S

1. Adrienne Rich, "Compulsory Heterosexuality and Lesbian Existence," *Signs: Journal of Women in Culture and Society*, Vol. 5, No. 4 (Summer 1980), p. 637.

2. Charlotte Bunch, "Not for Lesbians (Gays, Lezzies, Queers, Butches, Toy Butches, Diked Dykes, Ho-Homosexuals) Only," *Quest*, Vol. 11, No. 2 (Fall 1975).

3. While this is true for many lesbians who have come out within the women's movement, this negates the experience of women who feel their lesbianism was inevitable. When I re-read this a year after I wrote it, I realize that this notion of "choice" is an area where my thinking has changed.

A MESSAGE OF

Solidarity

BY
WOMEN WORKING WITH
IMMIGRANT WOMEN

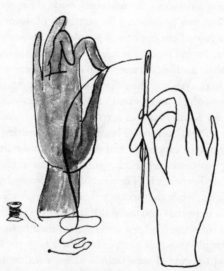

This article was originally a speech presented at an evening focused on women in Central America. It was written by a group of women who are involved with Women Working with Immigrant Women, an umbrella organization of agencies which provide services for immigrant women in Toronto. It is a very clear statement of a consciousness that is feminist and anti-imperialist. The changes that we see as necessary to create a truly non-sexist world involve the changes that will create a non-imperialist world. This article links the struggles of black and oppressed women in other countries with the struggles that occur here in Canada.

W E ARE HERE tonight to speak about struggles of liberation. As immigrant women in Canada, we are committed to the people of Guatemala, Nicaragua and El Salvador and our struggle will continue until the whole Central and South American continent is freed from oppression. As immigrant women we have other commitments to fulfil as well. Though the solidarity work with our countries is crucial for us, we must not forget that we live in a reality where people are also oppressed, where there is a working class fighting against its oppression, struggling against the same system which oppresses people all over the world. Our struggle is therefore international. We cannot remain blind to the reality which surrounds us here in Canada. We must not be insensitive to the oppression that working-class people, native people, Québécois people and we immigrant people face in this country.

As women, we have a third commitment; that is, to the struggles of women. All these struggles – the solidarity work, the commitment to the struggles of Canadian people and the struggles of women – are part of the overall struggle of the oppressed peoples of the world.

We want to focus first on our solidarity work, explaining the role of the multinationals and big businesses in our continent and the reasons for our being here. We will then discuss our reality here in Canada as immigrants, as women and as part of the Canadian working class.

Central and South America are rich lands, with unlimited natural resources and ancient cultures. However, our countries have been for centuries subjected to vandalism and superexploitation from imperialist countries. Big businesses and multinational corporations have large investments in our homelands. They exploit our people by paying them starvation salaries, while they extract enormous profits from our labour power, our raw materials and our natural resources. Repression is used as a weapon to suffocate workers' struggles for their basic rights in order to allow these multinationals to maintain their high profits.

Because of the role of imperialism in our continent, we feel compelled to leave and emigrate to industrialized countries such as Canada. Some of us leave, escaping poverty, looking for better jobs and a better future for our children. Others leave, escaping political persecution, physical repression and torture. Both reasons are political; both are the result of the same thing – the role of imperialism and the voracity of profit-makers in our countries.

Now you know why we leave our countries. Why do we come here? Because we are offered the opportunity to do so, because Canada needs us, because Canada needs our labour power. Immigration policies are closely linked to the needs of the labour market in Canada. Even the selection of refugees in refugee camps is greatly influenced by the criteria.

Some examples of the links between Canadian immigration policy and the needs of the labour market are the Chinese immigration at the end of the nineteenth century, when Chinese men were brought to Canada in order to build the railroad. After the railroad was finished, the Chinese Immigration Act was enacted, making it almost impossible for Chinese people to come to Canada.

During the economic expansion of the 1950s and 1960s, there was a need for highly skilled and semi-skilled workers – Europeans and Americans were brought in to fill these gaps. The late 1960s and early 1970s were characterized by a large immigration of Third World people who were used as a source of cheap labour. Today, because of the economic crisis, they do not need us any longer. Therefore immigration policies are making it almost impossible for us to come.

As part of the working class, we share our oppression with the rest of the workers, both men and women. We produce profits for our employers, but we do not receive anything in return. Many immigrant women work in factories, where we get the minimum wage or less, where we work compulsory overtime, where we suffer sexual harassment from our employers and where we work under unhealthy working conditions.

There are other immigrant women who work on farms, and their reality is not well known to most of us. In Ontario, farmworkers are not covered under the protective health and safety legislation that covers the rest of the workers. As a result, at least one death per week takes place on Ontario farms.

Another area where many immigrant women work is in the field of domestic work. Together with farmworkers, the domestics are one of the most exploited sectors of the working class in Canada. Domestics enter Canada under a work permit, which is, in effect, a contract with a specific employer. Complaining about their employers can result in domestics being fired and later deported. This is why the legal status of domestics puts them in a position where they can be easily exploited by their employers.

Racism is one of the most serious problems faced by immigrant workers in Canada. Racism is often used by employers and big businesses to divide the workers. Immigrants are usually blamed for unemployment, inflation, social services cutbacks and other social diseases.

Unfortunately there are many Canadians who believe this. But we say to them: "Working-class people *do not steal* other workers' jobs. The reason for increasing unemployment is an economic policy which favours the big corporations rather than looking for solutions for the vast majority of the population."

We immigrant workers are not the cause of the problems. In fact, we are in the same boat as the rest of the Canadian working class. It is time for the working class to understand the importance of fighting together, of breaking barriers imposed on us by those who benefit from our divisions. It is time for us to organize and fight together for our common goals!

We have already spoken about our oppression as workers and as immigrants. Let us speak now about our oppression as women. Women are oppressed first because we usually have the double task of working in the paid labour force and assuming most, if not all, of the responsibility for the family and the housework. The system does not recognize women's housework as an important contribution to the economy. The truth is, that without women's free work at home, the system wouldn't be able to function.

Women are also oppressed in the area of our sexuality. The system has converted us into sexual objects for men's pleasure. The use of pornography and sexist jokes humiliate and denigrate women as human beings.

In the area of our political involvement, women also suffer discrimination.We have to *win* our right to participate in the struggles, whereas men are *encouraged* to do so. Also, men have been socialized to fear women's participation in politics, either because this will interfere with our "duties" at home, or because they feel threatened by our development as political beings.

We find within our political organizations that the kind of tasks we are assigned to do are discriminatory. Often these tasks involve not too much thinking but lots of work – cooking for events, distributing propaganda, etc. We recognize that an effort is being made by some organizations to change this situation. However we are just starting to include women's issues in the platforms of our organizations. The creation of an autonomous women's movement within the frame of our political work is essential.

Third World women come from a reality where class oppression is brutal and massive sectors of the population are being exterminated. Given the political and economic reality that our countires face today, it becomes more difficult for us to organize as women. But, this does not mean that we do not recognize our oppression as women. We are aware of it and we are willing to fight against it, but the ways and forms of our struggles will sometimes be different from the ways and forms that Canadian women choose.

We immigrant women often tend to see the Canadian women's movement as being composed of feminists who lack a class perspective. We do realize, however, that the women's movement in Canada is not homogeneous, that there are different sectors within the movement, and that some feminists do have a class perspective.

We think that the movement of women in Canada is growing from its base. Native women, poor Canadian women, Québécoise and immigrant women are organizing ourselves around issues that concern us specifically. There is also the isolated woman at home who knows about her oppression but is not yet linked to any group.

The impact that the Canadian women's movement has made on immigrant women has been important for some of us. We recognize the importance of the issues that feminists have been working for and we support these struggles. However, as immigrants and Third World women, we face a particular kind of oppression and therefore we *must* have political autonomy within the Canadian women's movement. We *must* recognize and accept the differences among us so that real unity can be achieved.

As immigrant women and Third World women, we think that the class struggle and the struggles of women are both essential. We know that we are not going to achieve our liberation within the frame of capitalist society, but we also know that socialism by itself won't liberate us. We have to start fighting for our liberation TODAY! The way we see the family, the role of women in this society, our relationship with men, and the education of our children, are all concepts which have been molded according to the ideals and patterns of a capitalist society. New concepts of the family and personal relationships have to be created, according to the ideals of the new society that we are trying to build. Sexism and male chauvinism are part of the old society, and we, both men and women, have to fight against it.

We share our oppression with Canadian women, with native women, with the Québécoise and with the rest of the working class, both men and women. We call upon the rest of the working class, to fight together against all forms of racial, sexual and class discrimination. We immigrant women will no longer remain silent. We will raise our voices and break the barriers of silence imposed on us by those who benefit from our divisions. Together we shall overcome!

Immigrant Women

THE SILENT PARTNERS OF THE WOMEN'S MOVEMENT

BY WINNIE NG

From time to time, the women's movement takes up the concerns of immigrant women – for example, we have mobilized around the continuing deportation of West Indian domestic workers. And as a movement we increasingly recognize that to resist attacks against us we have to be anti-racist as well as anti-sexist. We know in an abstract way that we have to listen to the experience of all women and be responsive to needs that are different from our own. But it is time we heard of the day-to-day lives of those women who are doubly oppressed, who are put down because they are women and because they are immigrants and/or because they are non-white. We have to learn how we can support the struggles of immigrant women. As Winnie Ng's article demonstrates, immigrant women are organizing and beginning to tell us how best we can work with them to create together a society that is non-sexist and non-racist.

S INCE THE SIXTIES, the women's movement has had a tremendous impact on North American society. Its presence, struggles and gains have affected the welfare of all women. However, the movement has created only ripple effects on the plight of immigrant women in Canada. Immigrant women remain the "muted shadows," the silent partners of our society and the women's movement.

This article is written from the perspective of an immigrant woman who has worked closely with working-class immigrant women in union organizing, community work and English classes. Just as there are various fragments within the Canadian women's movement, the immigrant women's population is also not a homogeneous group. Immigrant women's outlooks and perceptions reflect where they come from, their values, cultural and class backgrounds. In this article, I would like to critically examine the uneasy relationship between the women's movement and immigrant women.

DOUBLE EXPLOITATION

Politically, socially and economically, immigrant women are easy targets for abuse and exploitation. They are exploited both as women and as immigrants. This situation is decidedly not what they were prepared for psychologically when they came to Canada. Most immigrant women come to seek a better future for their families. They come with dreams that are woven with hope and colours. Yet, after the initial excitement of arrival, their dreams are shattered by the cold realities of surviving in this land of "great opportunities."

Immigrants, both men and women, share the same exploitation and job ghettoization in the labour force. They are slotted to "fill the gaps of the labour market," to take up jobs that Canadians refuse. Then, in times of economic recession, they are the scapegoats blamed for taking away jobs and causing unemployment. However, working immigrant women are in worse situations than immigrant men. Very often, they have been sponsored by their husbands as dependents. This bars them from being eligible for government-sponsored language training or skills upgrading programs on the rationale that they do not need English to do housework or work as cleaners or sewing machine operators. For those with professional training and experience from their home countries, but without language fluency, there is usually little hope that they will ever return to their professions. Without language skills, "Canadian experience" and connections, immigrant women are forced to take jobs in the service industries, garment factories and within their own ethnic communities. These low-paying and dead-end jobs will never enable immigrant women to gain equal access to the larger labour force.

The lack of English-language skills further impairs immigrant women's bargaining position as workers. Not only are they unaware of their labour rights, they are also literally "deaf, dumb and blind" because they do not understand, speak or read the language. They are subject to highly oppressive working conditions and a hazardous work environment. Verbal abuse and sexual harassment from their supervisors or employers are not uncommon. The women do not dare to complain, knowing there are people in line waiting to take their jobs. In most of these workplaces 90 percent of the employees are immigrants from various parts of the world. While they share their exploitation, without a common language for communication, the feeling of solidarity among workers that is so crucial to the success of union organizing is never really developed. The employers are fully aware of these handicaps and make good use of them.

At home, the immigrant woman starts another shift of work as she cares for her children and waits on her husband. In many cultures, housework is considered to be the woman's job; thus for most working immigrant women, the day is long and back-breaking. For shut-in housewives, it is a story of isolation and despair: she works at home all day doing domestic labour and sits at home alone all evening while her husband works or goes out with his friends.

In many immigrant families, men control the finances. Bank accounts are usually held only in the husband's name, and, in some cases, men even do the shopping in order to deny their wives access to money. For some immigrant men, the tight control on the finances is the only way to maintain their traditional male role and keep their wife in her "proper place."

Birth control and parenting are the sole responsibilities of women in most immigrant families. The difference in their working hours contributes to the deterioration of the relationships between immigrant women and their husbands and these women are increasingly distanced from their children, who as they learn the new language, become more and more assimilated. Gradually the immigrant woman becomes a stranger in her own home.

Immigrant women, like many Canadian women, are also subject to mental and physical abuse by their husbands, particularly in these times of high unemployment. Where can these women turn? The new social and cultural environment lacks the traditional family support networks and familiar resources. The language difficulty, the need to care for young children and the tight control by husbands all contribute to the immigrant woman's isolation. The result is that many immigrant women rely on tranquillizers for temporary relief – and some, who are pushed beyond their limits, end up in institutions.

The double exploitation of immigrant women in domestic and employment situations is beyond the grasp of the majority of Canadian women. With such an experience, it would seem natural for immigrant women to embrace feminism and for women from the women's movement to seek out their doubly exploited sisters. But few links have been made. The reasons can perhaps be explained by differences in language and priorities, ignorance on both sides and the fact that organizing within the immigrant women's community is just beginning.

THE SILENT PARTNERSHIP

Without the opportunity to learn English or attend orientation programs – due to economic priorities and day care problems – immigrant women are deprived access to the larger community. A lot of basic tasks that Canadian women take for granted – grocery shopping or taking a child to a doctor – are very stressful situations for non-English-speaking women. Thus, one can understand the apprehension and fear an immigrant woman might have attending a meeting of English-speaking women.

Most working-class immigrant women rely on their co-workers, neighbours or family for information and, in many cases, "misinformation." Their social sphere is very limited. To a great proportion of them the women's movement is non-existent. Not only are they not informed, they are not aware of the impact the movement has had on them.

In addition, the cultural values of the different ethnic groups have discouraged immigrant women from associating with the outside community. The needs of their husbands, children and even their employers come before their own personal needs. Besides, feminism threatens the traditional values of many cultures. Even for those who are articulate in English, the fear of being labelled "radical" or "crazy," of being socially sanctioned by their own community, is so great that it outweighs their motivation to find out more about feminism.

Immigrant women are so preoccupied with the daily struggles to meet the survival needs of their families that all other issues seem secondary. How can they demand better health and safety rules in the workplace when they are in constant fear of being laid off? The women's movement is perceived by immigrant women as being essentially a middle-class movement of women in search of self-improvement and access to the top executive world. The perception that is shared by many other activists in the immigrant communities is that the movement tends to attract professional women, better-educated women and women who have some leeway in setting priorities.

The minimal participation of immigrant women in the women's movement can also be attributed to the manner in which women's movement activities are organized. Most of the meetings are highly structured and formal, with rules that lead to the intimidation and exclusion of immigrant women. Meetings are usually held in the evenings or on weekends, when many immigrant women are either too exhausted or too busy to participate. In addition, translations are almost never available, making it pointless for non-English speakers to attend.

Another important block for immigrant women's entry into the women's movement is fear of the consequences of political activism. They may be afraid to come out to rallies and demonstrations for fear of being seen as "subversive" and thereby possibly face deportation or generally put their status in Canada in jeopardy.

There needs to be an ongoing process of building links between the immigrant women's community and feminists. In the last few years feminists have begun marching through immigrant neighbourhoods and leafleting on International Women's Day in Toronto. This is a beginning, and a significant one, but it is not enough to draw immigrant women out. Besides regular promotion in different languages, cooperation should be encouraged through community programs, English as a second language classes and union activities. There need to be opportunities for immigrants to see the connections and the relationships between themselves and other women.

Both English-speaking feminists and immigrant women have misunderstandings and stereotypes of each other. Immigrant women, if they are aware of the women's movement at all, dismiss it, because, as I said earlier, they see it as a middle-class group of women.

And even though the women's movement claims to be non-racist and non-biased, stereotyping is an issue that it should critically examine. A fairly prevalent characteristic among English-speaking social workers, ESL teachers and health professionals who claim to be feminists is a self-righteous and condescending attitude towards immigrant women. Their pity and tears for these "poor immigrant women," in a sense, help to trap immigrant women in this vicious circle. Despite these people's concern, there is often a lack of sensitivity towards the immigrant woman's choice and cultural traditions. An immigrant woman's life does not begin when she lands on Canadian soil! An immigrant woman can benefit from orientation to the Canadian way of life, but that does not automatically negate everything she has done as a contributing member of her home country.

The women's movement appears to make statements against racism and participate in causes only when they are brought to light by the media. When it comes to fighting day-to-day racism, the women's movement is invisible. For example, feminists were involved in fighting the deportation of seven Jamaican women, yet there are racial injustices happening daily in the immigrant communities. Where were feminists when the Chinese community was fighting the anti-W5 issue? Where were feminists when immigrant services were facing funding cutbacks? Where was the representation of the women's movement in the Albert Johnson case?

With all their good intentions, feminists have failed to make links with immigrant women and to recognize the differences in priorities. It is only in the last two years that the movement has really taken an initiative in this area. Of course, it is not a one-way process: immigrant women must also take responsibility for informing the women's movement of their concerns and for building up a network between the two groups.

EMERGING FROM THE SHADOWS

What is obviously needed is improved communication between the women's movement and the immigrant women's community so that the problems of each can be more fully understood and appreciated. At the same time, immigrant women from different cultural and language backgrounds need to organize. We need the human resources, the support from one another and most of all, we need to speak in one voice. Immigrant women must work together to recognize their own strength and then put forward the following demands.

1. English language training must be a basic right with adequate allowance for day care and transportation. Accessibility to language training should not be tied to an arbitrary "settlement period," but be available as a continuous process.

2. The women's movement and the trade unions must prioritize the needs of immigrant women by providing interpreters at meetings, dispensing information in different languages and supporting the struggle against exploitation and discrimination.

3. Feminists must be more consciously aware of and recognize the contribution of immigrant women to the larger society in order to enable a closer partnership in the fight for universal day care, equal pay for work of equal value and other feminist demands.

Within the immigrant women's community, there has been a growing sense of solidarity among women of different cultural backgrounds. Community agencies, such as the Immigrant Women's Centre and the Immigrant Women Job Placement Centre in Toronto, are prime examples of women of different ethnic backgrounds working under one roof, developing cross-cultural links. The strong activist commitment of the umbrella organization, Women Working with Immigrant Women (WWIW), has undoubtedly sparked an initial network between the women's movement and immigrant women. WWIW's participation in the International Women's Day Committee throughout the past year is one important example.

Immigrant women activists have organized workshops and spoken out at meetings to sensitize Canadian women to working-class immigrant women's experience. They have also joined the picket lines of various labour struggles – including the Irwin Toys strike and the postal workers' strike. The large turnout of English-speaking feminists to workshops at

Toronto's 1982 International Women's Day on immigrant women and their workplaces and the struggles in their home countries, have served to improve the understanding among all women. It is only through this kind of solidarity that immigrant women can emerge from the shadows, from being the ''silent partners,'' to become the full participating and equal members of the movement to fight for a just society for all.

F U R T H E R R E A D I N G S

Arnopoulos, Sheila McLeod. *Problems of Immigrant Women in the Canadian Labour Force.* Ottawa: Advisory Council on the Status of Women.

Cross Cultural Communication Centre. *By and About Immigrant Women.* (Available from CCCC, 1991 Dufferin Street, Toronto, Ont. M6E 3P9.)

Multiculturalism Directorate. *The Immigrant Woman in Canada – A Right to Recognition.* Ottawa: Dept. of the Secretary of State.

Beyond Barriers

NATIVE WOMEN AND THE WOMEN'S MOVEMENT

BY CAROLINE LACHAPELLE

Whether it is the Cree demanding compensation for their land flooded by the James Bay hydroelectric project, the Dene fighting for a sovereign nation or the Nishka attempting to protect their fishing grounds from pollution by Amax, Canadian native people have taken an increasingly militant stand in the last decade. Native women are fighting too – alongside men in these issues. Of necessity, the survival of the native community comes before the issue of sisterhood with white women. As Caroline LaChapelle's article notes, one issue that has unified native women is the loss of Indian status due to marriage to a man who is not a status Indian. Native women received some support from non-native feminists on this issue, but a more promising example of feminists understanding the needs of native women took place in Vancouver in 1981 when native women seeking changes on their reserves occupied the Department of Indian Affairs Office. Throughout this action and the court case that followed, native women ''called the shots'' and decided the strategies while non-native women played a supportive, participating role. This is just a first step; LaChapelle encourages non-native women to break the barriers of culture and racism in order to better integrate native women into the Canadian women's movement.

THERE ARE VERY few native women in the Canadian women's movement. This article will attempt to examine why this is so and explore the potential for more active support and involvement between native and non-native women. In order to provide an analysis of native women's lack of participation in the women's movement, I will begin with an historical overview of the plight of native women and then go on to focus on their contemporary struggles. In current usage, the term native is inclusive of all status, non-status and métis Indians as well as Inuit people. The term Indian is often used to designate only status Indians.

THE INDIAN ACT

Although the Indian Act was instituted prior to 1869, it was not until this date that for the first time Indian women were given fewer rights in law than Indian men. Indeed, at that time, many Indian men strongly objected to this legal differentiation, but their objections were ignored by the white men in power. Since 1869, several more revisions have been made to the Indian Act, causing Indian women to suffer further legal repercussions.

The clause which has created the most fervoured response is Section 12 (1) (b). The consequences for Indian women upon application of this clause extend from the point of marriage to the point of death. The clause specifies that if an Indian woman marries a non-status Indian (a person of Indian heritage who is not legally registered under the Indian Act) or a non-Indian man, she no longer has the legal recognition of the status of Indian. In other words, she is no longer an Indian. She cannot live on the reserve, nor can she hold or inherit property on the reserve. The children of her marriage are not considered Indian and have no rights to reserve life.

This denial of her rights as a person inhibits an Indian woman's whole way of being. The oppressive clause deprives her of her cultural roots, creates division within her family (as many of her immediate relatives live on the reserve and are legally defined as Indians) and denies her access to any treaty or reserve privileges. Indeed, should she separate, divorce or become a widow, she still is no longer considered to be an Indian (unlike a white woman who marries a status Indian man).

No such restrictions are provided in the Indian Act for the Indian man. In fact, if an Indian man marries a non-Indian woman, she is automatically given the status of Indian and has conferred upon her all the rights and privileges of an Indian – plus she escapes the racist discrimination. Nowhere in Canada do other women when they marry face such severe penalties as the Indian woman.

REVISIONS TO THE INDIAN ACT

The Indian Act dictates an Indian's entire way of being, ranging from the decision about who is an Indian, to who can hold or inherit property, to the validity of a will. Why then is this offensive piece of legislation still in existence? Many non-Indian people are puzzled by the apparent lack of action by Indians to alter this overt piece of discrimination. The answer for many Indians lies in the belief that aside from the treaties, the elimination of the Indian Act would remove all the rights of Indian people and their desired special status. Thus, for many Indians, any attempt to eliminate the Indian Act or any portion thereof threatens their very existence.

Indian people recall the federal government's White Paper of 1969, which was the first attempt to dissolve the Indian Act without any Indian consultation. The preposterous rationale for getting rid of the Act was to place Indian people on an equal footing with all Canadians. Consequently, Indian people felt that their special status and aboriginal rights would be in jeopardy should parts or all of the Indian Act be superceded.

Is this a reason for maintaining such blatant discrimination? Again, the answer lies in the belief that aside from the treaties, the Indian Act is the one legal claim that acknowledges the rights of Indians, particularly on reserves. Any Indian woman who takes action against the Indian Act is thus viewed as jeopardizing the lives of Indian people in Canada. Pressure is put on these women to remain silent and be martyrs for the cause until Indian people have revised the Indian Act.

In fact, it was not until Indian women protested the application of the Act that anyone verbalized the need to amend it. In 1974, the federal government asked the Indian population to draft a new Act.

Indian organizations, which are male-dominated, vehemently protested any changes to the Act (specifically section 12 (1) (b)), until the Act is entirely revised. And because many Indian women have lost their status, they have been excluded from the very decision-making process that might change the Indian Act. They have no access to negotiations between the government and the National Indian Brotherhood (the male representative voice of Indian people on the revisions to the Indian Act).

STRUGGLES OF NATIVE WOMEN

Although the question of Indian rights for Indian women is the women's issue most visible to the non-native observer, this is just one of the issues of concern to native women. The revision of the Indian Act is an issue around which all non-status Indian women are united. However there is no one issue that creates unity among all Indian women. Status Indian women tend to rally around issues such as poor living conditions on reserves (witness the nine-day occupation of the Vancouver Indian Affairs Office in July 1981 to protest reserve conditions and demand an investigation into Department of Indian Affairs' expenditures), apprehension of Indian children, health care, unemployment and housing.

On some reserves in Ontario and British Columbia, Indian women have begun to fight other sections of the Indian Act, specifically concerning matrimonial property and Indian women's rights to it. But even these cases did not encourage all status Indian women to work together and support each other in attempting to alter the Indian Act.

The majority of Indian women unite around issues affecting the lives of all native people. Thus, the native struggle is a cross-sexual struggle, with the male voice dominating. Indeed, native women are often chastized by male natives, who argue that participation in the women's movement siphons energy away from the native cause and that time, energy and resources should be spent on the battle for the rights of the entire native population.

NATIVE WOMEN AND THE WOMEN'S MOVEMENT

Native and white women have many of the same concerns, such as health care and day care, but sometimes women's groups want native women to identify with the issues that white women have chosen. Consequently, they often do not recognize or validate native women's concerns. In addition, many native women feel that the women's movement is too "comfortable" and that concern for the native struggle is recognized only in a token or abstract way. The problems faced by native women seem to be too far removed from the lives of white women. Many native women believe that they cannot afford to isolate their struggle to deal only with women's issues because of their dual oppression.

The lack of participation by native women in the women's movement is based primarily on four factors: class differences, lack of awareness or knowledge about the women's movement, white racism and fear of dividing the native community.

CLASS DIFFERENCES

The differing socioeconomic status of native and white women is a significant factor contributing to the lack of involvement of native women in the women's movement. The native woman's energy is directed towards survival, whereas often the white woman's energy is aimed at self-fulfillment. An example of this is the equal pay demand. While white women are striving towards ensuring their work is valued as the equivalent of a man's, native women are trying to seek employment in order to feed their families. Native women perceive their motivation to work as being different from that of white women. White women are often perceived as aspiring to be part of the power system that oppresses native people.

Many native women feel removed from the women's movement because it is seen as primarily a white, middle-class movement. White women are less likely to suffer from race and class discrimination and thus it is often felt that there are few women in the movement with whom native women can comfortably relate. And because native women must concentrate on sheer survival, they do not have the time and resources to become involved in the women's movement, particularly to attend meetings or rallies.

Native women probably have a lot in common with that part of the women's movement which is radical, and which addresses itself to grass roots issues and race and class analysis, but because of how they see the movement, this connection is rarely made.

LACK OF AWARENESS

Lack of experience and familiarity with native issues on the part of white women and lack of awareness of feminist issues on the part of native women further contribute to a lack of involvement.

Often feminists are viewed as riding on the coattails of civil rights and as being there only for their own visibility. Indeed, in the past, many white women have not continued contact with native women once the specific native issue was "over." For example, where are all the white women who rallied around Janette Corbière-Laval's Supreme Court case back in 1973?

Tokenism also seems to be a reality in the women's movement. What good is it to invite a native woman to speak, when there are no women of colour in the audience? White women also need to make social contacts, not merely political contacts, with native women.

On the other hand, native women need to be educated about feminist issues. Many native women do not see that they share any oppression with white women. And some native women do not see the necessity of simultaneously eradicating racism and sexism. For them sexual oppression is not as self-evident as racial oppression.

WHITE RACISM

White women are often perceived as being racist, which further alienates native women from the movement. Whether white feminists are cognizant of it or not, their body language, their voice inflection and overall behaviour may subtly communicate that native women have only a "conditional" welcome in the women's movement. In addition, white women are often perceived as feeling that they are superior to native women. Thus native women are often apprehensive about approaching white women. Perhaps for the time being, the onus must be on white women to confront their racism by going beyond an intellectual knowledge of it and by approaching native women.

FEAR OF DIVIDING THE COMMUNITY

Due to the colonialist attempt to break down the native community, native women are very much concerned with solidifying it. Urban white women are viewed as having the luxury to be movement activists without threatening their community, whereas reserve life is like a small town, where lines are drawn according to which side of the issue you stand on. Native women feel that their participation in the women's movement, no matter how well intentioned, would alienate native men, weaken the native family, dissipate the energies of the native struggle and thereby fragment the native community. It concerns some native women that native men, who continue to experience oppression, would receive no direct or evident benefits from native women's participation in the women's movement. To the native woman, there is enough attempted division of the community by the Department of Indian Affairs without creating more disunity by joining the women's movement.

BEYOND BARRIERS – STRATEGIES FOR UNITY

While it is crucial that native women continue to be part of the overall native struggle, there is nevertheless much to be gained through working with the women's movement. Overcoming the obstacles to unity is the first issue that must be addressed.

During the July 1981 occupation of the Vancouver DIA office by Indian women, many members of the women's movement showed their support and concern. For once, there was no switching of priorities. Native women called the shots and decided on strategies, but the presence of the non-native women supporters did not go unnoticed. Indeed, after the occupation ended, white women continued their support of the native cause by assisting in the rallies and by seeking financial support for the Indian women who had been charged. This was a truly emotional learning experience for both the white and

Indian women. Although some of the Indian women expressed their hesitancy about the white women's involvement, in the end the Indian women acknowledged the positive contribution made by the white women.

There is a need for massive reeducation on the part of white women about native women and native issues. The easiest way of transition is for feminists to support native women by informing themselves of issues of concern to native women and passing on this information to other white women. White women need to have an understanding of native culture and an appreciation of native values. They must accept that their set of values are not the only values and that there is much to be learned from the native way of life. White women also need to learn of the effect of white culture on native culture. Most important, white women need to understand the connection between racism, sexism and classism and to confront their own racism.

Although the onus may be on white women to take the initial steps towards unity, native women must accept some responsibility in removing the obstacles to unity. Native women must be educated on feminist issues, in order to understand the experiences that all women share. As difficult as it may be, native women must learn to trust the women's movement, and to share in the concern for the oppression of women everywhere. Barriers will continue to exist unless some of these initial steps are taken, particularly in the areas of trust and respect for each other's culture.

F U R T H E R   R E A D I N G S

Brand, Johanna. *The Life and Death of Anna Mae Aquash.* Toronto: James Lorimer, 1978.

Jamieson, Kathleen. *Citizens Minus: Indian Women and the Law in Canada.* Advisory Council on the Status of Women, Hull, Quebec: Government Printer, 1978.

Vanderburgh, R.M. *I am Nokomis Too: The Biography of Verna Patronella Johnson.* Toronto: General, 1977.

Working with Words

FEMINIST PUBLISHING IN CANADA

BY MARGIE WOLFE

Print media has always been an important part of the women's liberation movement. And the development and dissemination of our political ideas are largely dependent on it. The movement has also created a market – one that other publishers are eager to fill – so that we can no longer say we are printing what nobody else will print. But as Margie Wolfe points out in this article, it is only by controlling our own publishing houses, newspapers and periodicals that we can guarantee the continued publication of material relevant to us and to the growth of the women's movement. By the very nature of our work we focus on the creative and adventuresome – we present writers who have never been published before and we introduce literature that is innovative in form and subject matter. Wolfe advocates that in continuing to write for ourselves and for the increasing numbers of women who are interested in feminism, we must discover more politically effective ways of distributing our work.

I N 1981, WOMEN from the Toronto media invited feminists to a meet-ing at the Press Club. Their aim was to clear up past disputes and generally improve working relationships. Heartened by the news-people's initiative, activists flocked to the session. Yet the media women's explanations of the necessities, demands and power relation-ships of their jobs soon revealed the differences in our positions: the pro-verbial bubble burst when we asked them how they prioritized their feminism. All but one notable exception admitted they were journalists first, and that their concerns as feminists played a secondary role to the demands of mainstream journalism.

This response came as no surprise to activists experienced in deal-ing with newspeople. We already knew that some of them, though well intentioned, weren't feminists; others, more committed, had jobs to protect or advance. The explanations mattered little, what did, was being told once again that our priorities were not priorities for women in the media.

We should not have expected anything more. Mainstream newspaper, periodical and book publishers operate on criteria that are clearly not our own. As commercial, profit-making ventures they res-pond to the demands of the mass market. They must. Profitability depends on keeping corporate advertisers happy with large-scale circulation. Admittedly, many mainstream newspapers and magazines have printed pieces of relevance to women, and some retain writers who consistently do fine work. However, it is unlikely that commitment to the feminist cause is what motivates them. If an issue "makes a good story" and thereby aids circulation, there is a good chance that it will be run; otherwise, it probably will not be. I continually have reporters tell me that they're not interested in an item because the competition has already dealt with the subject or they regard it as no longer timely. When, for example, the first book on day care in Canada was released, a wire service refused to run a story because the issue was "old hat."

The mainstream book industry functions in much the same way. It is a rare commercial publisher that will knowingly take a loss by pro-ducing a book that's not readily marketable. Commercial women's magazines respond to similar demands. Doris Anderson, former editor of *Chatelaine,* argues that the women's movement did not profoundly affect traditional magazines. Maintaining advertising worth many millions of dollars meant that the changes reflected in them were "cosmetic rather than basic." [1] Working-class, rural and older women are not serviced by the magazines. "Advertisers want trendy young couples with two incomes who live in fashionable town houses or high rises and in spite of the fact that good editors know and struggle to run relevant material, the magazines reflect this highly fictitious lifestyle." [2] Even the best of them, *Homemaker's* magazine, not only has a controlled circulation to middle- and upper- income neighbourhoods, but plays it safe by surrounding a serious feminist article with uncritical pieces on beauty and fashion and the ever-present recipes. One gets the impression that the pro-feminist editor of necessity panders to the advertisers in not committing the magazine further. Ultimately, the commercial women's publications are forced to defer to their advertisers. If these money-holders decided that all feminist content should be withheld it probably would be. Concerned readers are given no content guarantees from one issue to the next.

Feminist publishers exist to provide those assurances, to guarantee women's liberation a voice. Primarily non-profit, non-commercial collectives, we articulate and promote the concerns of feminism in print. Our ultimate goal is radical social change. For over ten years now, activists throughout Canada have produced newspapers, books, magazines and journals to further that objective. While our newspapers can't claim the *Globe and Mail's* readership, our periodical publishers, *Maclean's* magazine's circulation, we've made some important inroads. During the Seventies, newspapers like *The Other Woman, Kinesis, Upstream* and *Broadside* addressed issues initially untouched and in some cases, never confronted by the mainstream media. Rural women communicated with each other and with their sisters across the country through the *Northern Woman's Journal, Images,* the *Optimst* and *Prairie Woman. Room of One's Own, Makara* and *Fireweed* explored the creative arts, while *Branching Out* and *Atlantis* provided forums for debate, and *Healthsharing* helped to demystify the care and treatment of our bodies.

At the same time, the book publishers – Press Gang, the Women's Press and more recently, Eden Press – have been filling the void of feminist materials by producing books that deal with the concerns, struggles and history of Canadian women. They, together with the periodical and newspaper publishers, have become information brokers for feminists. By providing this service, by giving us concrete materials to think about, get angry over, discuss, debate and build on, they have helped to build our consciousness. We are continually reminded of the struggles going on, of the work that needs doing, of the obstacles to be overcome.

As the women's movement gained momentum in the mid-Seventies, feminist publishing took on a larger role. Mainstream newspapers that had previously limited their women's pages to fashion and recipes were forced to address a broad spectrum of issues, including day care, non-traditional work and violence against women. The Women's Press book, *Rape: The Price of Coercive Sexuality,* and Press Gang's, *Women Look at Psychiatry,* were featured in magazine and newspaper articles throughout Canada. Similarly, the broadcast media, developing programs on early childhood education, turned to the authors of *Good Day Care* for guidance.

Exposure in the mainstream press allowed feminist publishers to expand their audience and thereby sensitize a considerably larger number of people to the concerns of women's liberation. That readership was further increased as students at colleges and universities, in not just women's studies, but in sociology, history and labour studies, began studying books produced by feminists. At the same time as instructors at those institutions turned to *Atlantis, Resources for Feminist Research* and *Canadian Women's Studies* for additional sources of material, libraries and bookstores began carrying our publications and ministries and boards of education introduced them to their schools. In total, feminist publishers have provided a considerable body of specifically feminist literature that would otherwise never have been produced. For activists, these newspapers, magazines, books and journals have helped to unify, educate and inform. Many Canadians have been at least minimally introduced to subject matter that challenges traditional norms, exposes hidden issues and provides a new history, theory and understanding of our society.

While these accomplishments are significant, they are only relatively so. There is still a large population of women in Canada who have never seen *Broadside,* read a Women's Press book or heard of *Kinesis.* For activist publishers aiming at social change, this fact is of course disturbing. We must ask ourselves: what is the constituency of this elusive audience and why has it remained beyond our reach?

One readily definable group is the significant population of immigrants that do not read or speak English. The majority of immigrants, particularly women, are among the most exploited members of this society, and without language skills, they are prohibited access to our literature. Except for some materials produced by progressive immigrant groups, they have had virtually no contact with Canadian feminist content. Instead, their information comes from mainstream ethnic publishers, who I assume are as unconcerned with feminist issues as their English-speaking counterparts.

There are also large numbers of Canadians who don't read – either for information or for recreation. Educational streaming and the pervasiveness of television, stereos and electric games means there are many English-speaking Canadians who have never been socialized to read. Others simply don't have the time. Working women, for instance, struggling to find and keep a job while caring for home and family, scarcely have the energy or leisure time for reading. Women from working-class backgrounds, in particular, have often not been socialized to read and are characteristically the greatest bearers of the double day.

A non-English-speaking woman cannot decipher *Chatelaine* any better than she can *Hysteria;* a non-reader rarely picks up any kind of literature. But feminists, like other alternative publishers, have particular problems with which to contend. One is credibility. For many Canadians an article in the *Toronto Star* is more believable than an identical story in *Kinesis,* a McClelland and Stewart book more trustworthy than one covering the same subject from Press Gang. Activists challenging the status quo should perhaps expect such skepticism. By proclaiming our feminism we've become vulnerable to criticisms of bias – that we manipulate information to conform to our politics. This would be less problematic if mainstream publications were seen as having their own ax to grind. Instead, they are generally viewed as objective and trustworthy. Few consider that all writers, no matter for whom they write, make subjective decisions about what facts to include; every newspaper and magazine editor determines what truths the reader is allowed simply by selecting which stories to run and which to omit. Without belabouring the myths of objectivity in print journalism, the fact is that feminist publishers face a dilemma, one with no clear solution in sight.

The credibility problem may in part account for our relatively small readership. Feminist periodical and newspaper subscriptions, for instance, vary only from the hundreds to several thousand. Another factor is anonymity. More times than I care to remember librarians, teachers or trade unionists have said they hadn't heard of the Women's Press or didn't know that Vancouver and Toronto produced feminist newspapers. Our publications are not highly visible partly because distribution is limited. Except for alternative and women's bookstores, retailers rarely stock them. While the book publishers fare somewhat better – our literature can more often be found in libraries and stores – none of us have broken into the supermarket and convenience outlets where so many women buy their reading matter.

The problems of credibility and anonymity combined are what – perhaps more than anything else – keep feminist publishing marginal. Our materials are not in demand. Whether we can create that demand is a subject of ongoing debate. At a feminist print media conference held in 1980, one publisher argued that we are doomed to the periphery, servicing a slowly growing, if not fixed market. Those of us who disagree are nonetheless forced to acknowledge the obstacles that have kept us there to date.

We operate on a shoestring. Government and institutional subsidy is becoming harder to get while sales revenue remains low and paper, printing and typesetting costs steadily increase. Periodicals and newspapers cannot attract significant advertising (that's non-sexist, non-racist) because circulation is small. Before it folded, the women producing *Upstream* sold typesetting to supplement their income. Press Gang in Vancouver still runs a print shop full-time. With meagre or no funds available for salaries, we depend on volunteer or underpaid labour. Many of us have full-time jobs elsewhere, only publishing in our spare time. Burnout is consequently always a problem.

Such limited resources have made it extremely difficult for us to adequately concentrate on the facets of publishing that help generate readership. Those tasks – promotion, marketing, publicity and advertising – are not coincidently, also the ones that have traditionally been regarded by feminists as the most "businesslike" and therefore, the most distasteful. While some publishers still disagree, many of us have at last acknowledged that these tasks can be performed with integrity, and that content doesn't have to be compromised to increase sales. After many years we've realized that by professionalizing ourselves in all facets of publishing we have a better chance of securing our existence while furthering the cause of women's liberation.

Marketing and promotion are now being taken more seriously. Through concerted cooperative efforts, advertising and mailing lists are exchanged, publishers display one another's literature, promotional mailings are grouped, and in general, ideas, information and labour are shared. The cooperative activities allow individual publishers access to larger audiences while significantly cutting promotional and advertising expenses and saving womanpower. Although no amount of effort will get a scholarly journal onto a newsstand or a literary magazine into a convenience store, if we can learn to accurately identify our possible markets, accommodate a style and design to suit them, and develop effective marketing and promotion methods, feminists have some chance of creating a demand for our materials.

The economic and political situation of the 1980s leaves us with few alternatives. In the previous decade, starting and maintaining a publishing house was much easier. "Make work" grants and other government and institutional subsidies were more readily available. These are clearly drying up. Public support to the cultural industries is threatened. At a book publishing and public policy conference held in the spring of 1981, a federal spokesperson, openly critical of the so-called "underfunded, oversubsidized" firms started in the 1960s and 1970s, indicated that future financing would be increasingly directed to "commercially viable" companies. These statements imply that the government would not be displeased if a monopoly of three or four profit-making houses comprised the sum total of Canada's book publishing industry. Already a federal Department of Communications program that small and regional publishers hoped would improve their place in the market provides hundreds of thousands of dollars yearly to several large companies and nothing to the very small. Essentially the program is increasing the gap between the profitable and the struggling, and encouraging the kind of industry rationalization that is going on in the newspaper business, for example.

Cutbacks elsewhere have caused the demise of many women's groups across the country. For feminist publishers the problem is compounded by steadily increasing production costs and, perhaps equally important, the shift in life situations of our members. Many of us became involved when we were students or when we had few responsibilities and surviving didn't take much money. Today, our volunteers often have children to rear and jobs that are more important to maintain in the midst of an economic crisis. There's not much time left for extra unpaid work. The kind of self-exploitation that has subsidized feminist publishers can't go on forever. While activists expect to donate time and energy, is it fair to indefinitely compound the exploitation of daily living for people who are doing increasingly demanding political work? Together, the cutbacks, increased expenses and uncertainties of volunteerism threaten the existence of feminist publishing. In recent years several publications have already folded – including *Makara, Branching Out* and *Upstream*. The only realistic solution seems to be increased sales, securing ourselves by reaching that larger audience women's liberation wants and needs anyways.

The changing political situation makes the necessity for survival even more crucial. Government policy is shifting to the right. Cutbacks to social services and women's groups are only one indication; their recent activities – rewarding big businesses while providing little support for small, specialized and alternative firms – are equally telling. In recent years the federal government has also challenged *Canadian Dimension* magazine's charitable status; Between the Lines, a left-wing book publisher, has had its provincial funding placed in jeopardy; and *Makara,* Vancouver's feminist magazine, halted publication soon after its government subsidy was cut off.

With racist, anti-labour, anti-women, anti-lesbian and anti-gay groups emerging on all sides, forums to voice opposition become more and more vital. Mainstream print cannot be trusted to provide us with even the most basic of information. For example, the print coverage of 1982 International Women's Day in Toronto, attended by 8,000 celebrants, was minimal: the *Globe and Mail* overlooked the event completely, while the *Toronto Star* ran a blurry photo and a superficial story that virtually ignored the issues raised. In May 1982, reports of simultaneous demonstrations by pro-life and reproductive rights forces in Toronto focused primarily on the anti-abortion groups.

With an opposition so strong it's naive to depend on the vagaries of a profit-motivated mainstream whose priorities do not match our own. Yet a publishing industry controlled by feminists, producing periodicals, newspapers and books, is itself a potentially powerful force. All the clichés extolling the might of the pen and the power of the press are overworked, but they are nonetheless valid. Why else do book burnings occur? What else but fear of that power motivates repressive regimes to ruthlessly close opposition newspapers and magazines? Now is the time to make better use of our own tools. The work that was started more than a decade ago on a feminist body of literature has helped build and articulate the concerns of a liberation movement. Today feminist publishers are more skilled than ever before, producing a wide range of materials including non-sexist children's books, a women's health periodical, several newspapers, culture magazines, scholarly journals and now, with the *Radical Reviewer,* our own publication of criticism. We have the tools; the challenge is to make them work more effectively for us.

N O T E S

1. Doris Anderson, "Women's Magazines in the 1970's," *"Canadian Women's Studies,* Vol. II, No. 2 (1980), p. 15.

2. Ibid., p. 16.

3. For a closer examination of this magazine see Penney Kome, "Homemaker's," ibid., p. 17.

F U R T H E R   R E A D I N G S

The following is a list of English-language feminist book publishers, the major periodicals and newspapers and a few that are less well-known (several print in French as well). Omitted are the many newsletters produced by provincial and special action committees, political parties, women's centres and single-issue groups. A more complete resource guide, including French-language publishers, can be ordered from the Women's Programme, Department of Secretary of State, Ottawa, Ontario K1A OM5. *The International Guide to Women's Periodicals and Resources* is published by *Resources for Feminist Research* (see address below).

BOOK PUBLISHERS

Eden Press
245 Victoria Avenue, Suite 12
Montreal, Quebec H3Z 2M6

Press Gang
603 Powell Street
Vancouver, British Columbia V6A 1H2

Women's Press
16 Baldwin Street
Toronto, Ontario M5T 1L2

PERIODICALS AND NEWSPAPERS

Atlantis: A Women's Studies Journal
Mt. St. Vincent University
Halifax, Nova Scotia B3M 4K3

Broadside
P.O. Box 494, Station P
Toronto, Ontario M5S 2T1

Canadian Woman Studies/
Les cahiers de la femme
Founders College, York University
4700 Keele Street
Downsview, Ontario M3J 1P3

Common Ground:
A Journal for Island Women
81 Prince Street
Charlottetown,
Prince Edward Island C1A 4R3

Communiqu'elles
3585 St-Urbain
Montréal, Québec H2X 2N6

Fireweed
P.O. Box 279, Station B
Toronto, Ontario M5T 2W2

Healthsharing:
A Canadian Women's
Health Quarterly
Box 230, Station M
Toronto, Ontario M6S 4T3

Herizons:
The Manitoba Women's Newspaper
Box 551
Winnipeg, Manitoba R3C 2J3

Hysteria
Box 2481, Station B
Kitchener, Ontario M2H 6M3

Images: Kootenay Women's Paper
Box 736
Nelson, British Columbia V1L 5R4

Kinesis
Vancouver Status of Women
400A West 5th Avenue
Vancouver, British Columbia V5Y 1Y8

Northern Women Journal
316 Bay Street
Thunder Bay, Ontario P7B 1S1

The Optimst
Yukon Status of Women Council
392 Steel Street
Whitehorse, Yukon T1A 2C5

The Radical Reviewer
P.O. Box 24953, Station C
Vancouver, British Columbia V5T 4G3

Resources for Feminist Research/
Documentation sur la recherche féministe
Dept. of Sociology, OISE
252 Bloor Street West
Toronto, Ontario M5S 1V6

Room of One's Own
P.O. Box 46160, Station G
Vancouver, British Columbia V6R 4G5

Spirale: A Women's Art
and Culture Quarterly
Womanspirit Art and Research
and Resource Centre
359 Dundas Street
London, Ontario N6B 1V5

Status of Women News
National Action Committee
on the Status of Women
40 St. Clair Avenue East
Toronto, Ontario M4T 1M9

More Radical with Age

WOMEN AND EDUCATION

BY SARI TUDIVER

While not denying the very real impact of feminists teaching in educational institutions, Sari Tudiver asserts that women's education does not occur primarily in such institutions. Feminist education takes place mainly in collectives, resource centres and publishing groups that are actively trying to fulfill the advocacy and research needs of particular women's communities. These, together with specific support groups in the community, are the fighting edge of feminist education.

FEMINIST EDUCATION

MY MOTHER, NOT without some sarcasm, used to refer to what happened to young women when they married and had children as a "rude awakening." This awakening of course also occurs when we enter the labour force and find ourselves systematically discriminated against in pay and in access to better jobs and benefits; when we attend university and find little encouragement to pursue advanced degrees; when we try to secure better and more day care facilities, family benefits, more equitable family law legislation, shelters for battered women and children, and confront patronizing, often harassing bureaucrats, politicians or social workers. For many of us, it has taken a very long time to recognize that our dissatisfactions and failures are not the result of deep-rooted personal inadequacies, but of inequalities structured into the nature of the patriarchal class society in which we live.

These insights have come from talking to other women about their everyday lives and discovering common experiences of oppression, from making collective protests against such inequities and from organizing alternate institutions and services. As Gloria Steinem perceptively described it, "Women grow more radical with age."[1]

As a result of the women's movement, women have begun to understand how formal educational institutions have failed to meet our needs. Reforming the institutions means elaborating new learning and teaching methods, identifying non-traditional settings for learning by, for and about women, and researching and developing resources about the history and nature of women's experiences. This feminist approach to education has several broad dimensions: first, it involves us in developing a method to understand how our personal lives are part of a political world – how the work we do at home, our family relationships, our friendships, our images of ourselves, are all shaped by the economic mode of our society, its institutions and dominant cultural attitudes and the social class and gender categories into which we were born. This method turns us into sensitive observers of "gender politics," the power relationships between men and women. Listening to women recount their experiences of dead-end jobs, sexual harassment, rape, chronic fatigue, drug use, or begging their husbands for extra household money, we come to see that our economic dependency, political vulnerability and lack of control over our bodies are expressed almost everywhere – in public settings such as courtrooms, hospitals, offices and on billboards, as well as in the privacy of corporate boardrooms and the intimacy of the bedroom.

This method of analysis leads us to ask critical questions about the nature of Canadian capitalist society: who makes decisions about employment and unemployment, hazards in the workplace, expenditures for military hardware or for social services, control over the new technology – all of which affect the resources and options women and their families have or must do without. This method is historical, because once we start to think systematically about social life, we begin to ask about the conditions from which present-day patterns emerged. Learning that the nuclear family and our notions of femininity evolved in the recent past, we build up confidence in our collective power to change society and our lives.

Secondly, feminist education involves developing organizational skills effective in a variety of settings and integrating feminist concerns into our day-to-day work. For most women, this means gaining the confidence to recognize that we already have a number of useful skills – acquired through years of parenting, running a household, working as a volunteer or in the paid labour force and dealing more or less successfully with schools, hospitals and government agencies. These skills combine with those learned through working cooperatively with other women, as in lobbying for better day care or organizing a support group.

Feminists who hold positions of authority have a particular responsibility to advance feminist concerns through their workplaces. For a primary or secondary school teacher this may involve searching out supplementary non-sexist course materials, showing students how to be critical of traditional texts and organizing a teachers' status of women committee; for a feminist school principal, supporting and encouraging such actions on the part of her staff and speaking out publicly on women's rights. Women need to engage in such activities with care, ensuring that they mobilize, where possible, the support of coworkers and others, because a woman without allies is easily isolated and discredited. Women also need to be part of feminist networks and groups that can provide information, support and critical feedback about ideas and strategies.

Third, feminist education means using our analytic and organizational skills to develop long-term strategies for eradicating social and economic inequalities. A central and inherently difficult task for Canadian feminists is to develop some common vision of a just, non-sexist society and to discover what we need to know and do in order to move towards that goal. It necessitates evaluating the gains of the women's movement thus far, and assessing how its issues and methods have influenced other progressive groups such as those in the labour, anti-nuclear, native and anti-racist movements, in the NDP and the churches. This also means placing the women's movement in its historical and international contexts and analyzing the limits to social and economic reform under conservative, social democratic and contemporary socialist governments. The rise of an organized backlash against civil rights and reproductive choice in the U.S. and Canada underscores the need for the women's movement to draw support from broad-based coalitions of progressive groups and for feminists to be part of such groups. It also warns us to place single issues in the broader context of long-term strategies.

WOMEN'S STUDIES

It is hardly surprising that our formal educational institutions have not encouraged the forms of feminist education discussed above. Historically, such institutions have transmitted conservative values and discouraged critical thought.[2] Despite equal numbers of female and male students in primary and secondary schools, the preponderance of women teachers at those levels and the large numbers of female students in universities, women have had only minor influence in formulating education policies and determining curriculum and budget priorities. Few women occupy senior administrative positions in school systems or universities and fewer still sit on school boards or as governors of universities. Although there are exceptions, those who do, tend to share a common class background and ideological outlook with their male counterparts and rarely see themselves as reformers.

Over the past decade, educational institutions have been a major target of reform for the women's movement. Women have argued against discriminatory practices towards young women in shop classes, sports and career counselling and documented the absence of women in trades training, professional schools and in senior academic and administrative positions.[3] We have shown how curriculum reinforces the dominant values and attitudes towards women by trivializing or distorting the nature of women and their work, whether in the family or in the paid labour force. Women have written or compiled alternate, non-sexist educational materials and pressured school boards to adopt them. Teachers have organized status of women committees to gather information and lobby against sexism in education. Several provincial departments of education, such as B.C. and Manitoba, have curriculum development programs on women's issues. Yet school systems still have a long way to go towards reforming sexist practices.

Since 1970, pressure from concerned faculty and students forced the introduction of women's studies courses and programs in a number of Canadian universities. While there were many administrators and faculty who resisted such developments, these demands came on the heels of heightened Canadian nationalism and a concern with minority group rights. Canadian studies, native and other ethnic studies and even some labour studies programs were thus started during this period of somewhat freer budgets. Women's studies courses were accepted as another ''special interest'' topic. Significantly, except in those very few instances where separate departments were formed, women's studies has not entailed heavy administrative costs: many programs do not have separate budgets and their administration is carried out as part of the normal workload of those faculty members committed to the programs. By the end of the 1970s, more than seventy-five Canadian universities and colleges listed courses related to women's studies, but only ten percent of these had some type of formalized degree program.[4]

Despite their marginalized status, women's studies courses play a vital role in feminist education. They provide a structured setting in which the various disciplines may be closely scrutinized for male bias and for questions pertaining to women that are asked or omitted by researchers in the field. Students learn that it is not sufficient to add chapters or sections on "women" or "women and children" to rectify omissions, but that the very framework, conceptual categories and assumptions with which one began, must be reexamined, taking women and their experiences as the point of departure.[5]

One methodology that has proved particularly important to understanding how the "personal is political" is the use of oral histories. In courses I have taught, students interview their mother, grandmother or another woman they know, focusing on the nature and history of her paid and unpaid work and her feelings about her work experiences. Interviews necessarily take different forms but they offer many insights: into the pressures and stresses on women of the double day; the complex effects of employment or unemployment on family and gender relationships; how women acquiesce to the definitions of themselves offered by church and state, but show incredible resistance and resilience under difficult conditions. Students broaden their understanding of class, gender and history by seeing that women and men in a single household may have different relations to the means of production.

These insights help students appreciate the difficulties of doing good primary research, while at the same time linking individual experiences to objective material conditions. To illustrate:

Gloria, a 37-year-old mature student, interviewed her neighbour Rosa, a 35-year-old Italian immigrant and discovered that she had worked for several years in a soft drink factory in West Germany prior to coming to Winnipeg in 1969. It was only when we listened to the interview in class and suggested that Rosa might have been part of the European guest worker system – about which Gloria knew little – that the deeper significance of Rosa's work experiences began to emerge. Gloria's analysis of the interview broadened; she interviewed Rosa again about visa regulations, living conditions for guest workers in Germany, and the social and economic conditions in southern Italy that led her to migrate. She researched the political economy of the guest worker system and migration patterns of Italians to Canada. Her research raised substantive questions about the positions of working-class women in Italy, West Germany and Canada. Significantly, we all learned how the macro political economy is woven into the personal decisions of women and their families.

Jocelyn, a 40-year-old personnel administrator, told her mother about the assignment and suggested they use the opportunity to record something they had never spoken of together – her mother's abuse by her father. Emma, a 71-year-old Ukranian woman from rural Manitoba, agreed and for two hours painfully recounted highlights of 47 years of a brutal and demeaning marriage. A penetrating and tragic story of why she stayed emerged: her strong religious beliefs that marriage was forever; her shame and despondency over having had a child out of wedlock as a young girl and having given him up – events her husband knew about and often used against her; her economic dependency on him throughout most of their marriage; her isolation from others who might have given her support; feelings of guilt when her husband beat her and identification with her own mother who had also been abused. We see her resilience in starting a small flower business from her home and becoming successful at it as a way to fend off loneliness. The interview is a difficult one, but Emma expresses tremendous relief that someone is willing to listen and does not see her as culpable. For Jocelyn, the course offered a method of probing the unmentionable and a way of beginning to ask why such brutality against women occurs and what can be done.

For many women students, general women's studies courses serve as a sort of "psychic testing ground." Increasingly, the women who take these courses are returning to school after years at home or are in traditional female occupations and contemplating changes. In my experience, few of these students have been active in the women's movement – some are decidedly suspicious about "women's lib" – but enroll in such courses out of curiosity and feelings that they might be sympathetic settings to explore alternatives for themselves. In the classroom they meet young women out of high school and older committed feminists and discover their commonalities and differences.

There are limitations to what can be accomplished in a classroom. Courses are finite in time and in the degree of contact among the participants. Women are stimulated but lose momentum when there is no ongoing support group or when other courses and teachers are unsympathetic to critical, feminist views. Acquainting students with the community resources available for women is often a valuable way of indicating networks of support that extend beyond the classroom walls.[6]

Women's studies courses and scholarship also constitute a "psychic turf" or enclave of mutual support for feminist faculty, who operate in a hierarchical, largely male-dominated, generally conservative workplace. Despite an ideology of academic freedom, such programs operate under serious constraints and feminists often experience harsh consequences. Thus, most male academics (this is true even of politically progressive males) continue to avoid the huge feminist academic literature in their fields or dismiss it, unread, as unobjective. Few integrate questions pertaining to women and their experiences into their course materials. Many remain suspicious, perhaps recognizing that to do so would necessitate rethinking their analytic framework, assumptions and methods of inquiry.

Such individuals sit on tenure and hiring committees, as heads of departments and deans and control the numbers of women (not to mention feminists) hired, given tenure and promoted. The particular danger to women's studies courses is that where they are not taught by progressive feminist scholars, they can easily become special topic courses about women rather than settings for feminist education. Similarly, as research about women gains popularity with funding agencies, conservative academics compete with feminists, often successfully, for funding of research.

But the problem is much larger. Perhaps the most serious constraint to feminist education in the university lies in the non-democratic, authoritarian structure of the university itself. One consequence of this structure is that female faculty often see themselves having interests and concerns different from women clerical and support staff. There have been no sustained attempts to consolidate support among women across these occupational lines, to discuss topics of mutual concern and develop long-term strategies aimed at democratizing the university. Even such hardly radical attempts as encouraging clerical staff to take, audit or participate in women's studies courses as guest speakers and resource persons, might help to bridge this isolation and increase grass roots support for women's studies within the university.

To the extent that academic feminists sensitize themselves and their students to feminist issues and methods, disseminate information and research relevant to the women's movement, and struggle to challenge various aspects of sexism as it affects all women within the university, they are an integral part of the women's movement. Major constraints to their success lie in their lack of control over their workplace and in their failure as yet to develop strategies for increasing that control.

BEYOND THE CLASSROOM

Over the past decade, women's resource centres, advocacy and research groups, publishing collectives, feminist information networks, media groups and other education efforts have proliferated. These organizations are essential to the women's movement. For example, advocacy and research groups have initiated studies of provincial and federal legislation affecting domestic workers and produced information packets about their rights that are accessible to such workers. Health publishing collectives compile information about hazardous products and practices and get the word out regularly to readers in ways that academic channels and the mainstream media do not. Women's resource centres draw together academic and investigative research and provide a place where women can hold courses, seminars, informal groups and counselling. It is these grass roots feminist groups that have brought such practices as rape and battering of women into the public domain as "legitimate" areas of concern for social agencies and the media.

In addition to providing other feminists with information, these groups grapple with the practical issues of organizational democracy, worker control, unionization and new technology. They debate the contradictions of radical organizations accepting state and foundation funds in order to survive. They struggle to develop some common ground among different feminist visions so as to get things done in the short run while considering longer-term strategies. Despite many problems, most of these groups retain their autonomy and offer insights into what non-sexist forms of organization might be like.

Educating ourselves to feminist issues means being observers even as we are practitioners, and finding some time for study, research and discussion in the midst of everything else we do. Formal educational settings can be exciting places to do this, particularly for mature students who come with questions rooted in their experiences and who have a strong desire to learn. However, the future of the women's movement and of non-sexist political strategies depends on the debates, analyses and learning that take place in women's groups and collectives. Such grass roots education reflects the commitment of women to the sometimes painful, sometimes euphoric and always political struggle for our liberation, a struggle from which there is no turning back.

N O T E S

1. Steinem spoke in Winnipeg in January 1982 at the conference, "Perspectives on Women in the 1980s," sponsored by the University of Manitoba's School of Social Work. When she made this comment, 1,100 people cheered.

2. See Samuel Bowles and Herbert Gintis, *Schooling in Capitalist America* (New York: Basic Books, 1976) and Dale Spender and Elizabeth Sarah, eds., *Learning to Lose: Sexism and Education* (London: The Women's Press, 1981).

3. Jill McCalla Vickers and June Adam, *but can you type: Canadian universities and the status of women* (Toronto: Clarke Irwin and Co., 1977).

4. See the *Canadian Newsletter of Research on Women*, Vol. 7, No. 4 (1978) for a major survey of women's studies courses and programs in Canada.

5. Dorothy Smith makes this point particularly well in "A Sociology for Women," paper prepared for the conference, "The Prism of Sex: Toward an Equitable Pursuit of Knowledge" (Women's Research Institute of Wisconsin, October 1977).

6. This proved to be a particularly good strategy for teaching women student teachers, most of whom were suspicious or actively hostile towards "women's lib." I tried to demystify their views of the movement by bringing in resource persons working in areas of relevance to them – family law, rape, wife battering, sex role stereotyping in the schools. Over time, they identified with the movement's goals much more directly and could be critical of those aspects of the movement with which they did not agree.

FURTHER READINGS

Canadian Woman Studies / Les cahiers de la femme.

ISIS Women's International Bulletin (quarterly). C.P. 50 Cornavin, 1211 Geneva 2, Switzerland.

Resources for Feminist Research.

Spender, Dale and Elizabeth Sarah, eds. *Learning to Lose: Sexism and Education.* London: The Women's Press, 1981.

But is it Feminist Art?

BY DAPHNE READ

WITH

ROSEMARY DONEGAN
AND LIZ MARTIN

As feminists, we need art that reveals as well as shapes our experience. We need an art that expresses our anger at the stubbornness of our society to give space to our demands and we need an art that celebrates our delight in our increasing strengths. Through art we can begin to imagine and define the contours of a new feminist reality. In this article, Daphne Read, with Rosemary Donegan and Liz Martin, examines some of the problems faced by artists as they search for expressive voices and forms, and by feminist audiences as they seek to interpret the challenges of the recent flowering of feminist culture. The authors explore the social dilemmas confronted by women as artists, as subjects of art and as a growing self-conscious community. In this context, they touch on recent controversies, such as the politics of feminist "realism" versus the avant-garde and the problems of presenting and interpreting images of women.

> *Dare to imagine, and nothing will ever be*
> *the same again.*
> VIRGIN MARY IN *LES FÉES ONT SOIF*[1]

ONE INDEX OF the growing strength and confidence of women as a group is our ability to lay claim to our own experiences and to name and interpret them in our own terms. Feminist art is on the cutting edge of this process of redefinition and re-vision. It has many functions: consciousness-raising and politicization, affirmation and celebration. Like all art, it moves us to feel, teaches, and gives us pleasure. But because art is born from the artist's psyche and taps into the audience's psyche, it is less susceptible to rigorous political analysis than, for example, struggles in the workplace. The imagination, one might say, defies sectarian analysis.

More analytically, then, how do we define feminist art? We could begin by saying that feminist art is a political art, but the meaning is still obscure: to what do "feminist" and "political" refer? In the practice of art, there are at least three categories to be considered: the artist, the work created, and the audience. To which category or categories do we attach the adjective "feminist" when we talk about feminist art? This is a complex question, to which there are no simple answers.[2]

A single coherent vision of feminist art does not exist. We can't reduce feminist art to a knowable project: it is living, in process, and there are many forms, just as there are many communities of feminists with particular interests. But we can begin to identify some of the challenges and problems faced by artists who consider themselves feminist. We need to clarify the relationship between artist, artwork, and audience. For example, what is the difference between the art created by women politically committed to feminism and other art? What can a feminist audience demand of feminist artists? How can we, in feminist communities, nurture our artists? In untangling these knots, we begin to move towards a political analysis of feminist art and towards fulfilling Robin Morgan's hope and challenge: "No revolution has yet dared understand its artists. Perhaps the Feminist Revolution will."[3]

THE STRUGGLE FOR SURVIVAL

Any analysis of feminist art must take into consideration the economic and social situation in which women artists in general (regardless of their politics) find themselves. A woman artist is doubly cursed: as an *artist* she is in a vulnerable and precarious economic situation, as a *woman* she finds herself on the edge of the mainstream artistic community.

Economic survival is a critical issue for every artist. Unfortunately, in the public mind, being an artist and being poor have come to be identified as natural and just. In this process two distinct images of the artist have been conflated: the sentimental picture of the starving-artist-in-garret and the romantic view of the artist as hero-in-agony. The latter view promotes the equation of art and suffering. The artist is seen as a tormented (male) genius, a visionary, whose isolation and sacrifice combine to guarantee good art. This image in turn gives rise to two variations in attitude: on the one hand, the romantic "suffering is good for the soul and for art," and on the other, the puritanical "if you choose to be an artist and refuse to get a good job, then you deserve to suffer." Although the image of suffering artistry may be attractive to some, appropriately punitive to others, it has little to do with productive creativity.

Artists as a group are marginalized workers, and very few make much money from their art. Unlike workers in comparable low-income brackets, artists themselves are responsible for paying for their tools and materials, and are not eligible for any employee benefits (unemployment insurance, sick leave, paid holidays, accident compensation, employer contributions to medical insurance). Yet artists *subsidize* Canadian culture: the works they create on low incomes become a part of our social wealth.

One of the problems lies in the fact that our society does not have an economic measure for the social value of artists. One proposal has been put forward by a group of artists, the Toronto local of the Cultural Workers' Alliance. They have argued that artists are cultural workers who provide a social service equivalent to educational workers, and therefore they should be integrated into a formalized wage-and-benefits structure.[4] Though not necessarily sharing the same analysis, the National Action Committee for the Status of

Women (NAC) and other Status of Women groups maintain that a guaranteed basic income for artists should be one component of the recognition of their social contribution.

The vulnerable economic situation of the artist is compounded further for women: within the mainstream art community, women encounter the kind of discrimination and ghettoization women workers face in the economy in general. NAC bluntly terms it "censorship." Its 1981 brief to the Federal Cultural Policy Review Committee states: "The under representation of women in Canada's cultural life, and the uneven distribution of women within the arts constitute a hidden, but nonetheless insidious, form of censorship."[5] This censorship ensures that in the arts, as Dorothy Smith has argued for education, "at every level of competence and leadership there will be a place for [women] which is inferior and subordinate to the positions of men."[6] What this actually means for women in the arts is made depressingly clear in the NAC brief: "Discrimination results in fewer women than men regarding the arts as a serious career option, [in women] diverting themselves into audiences, patrons, fund-raisers and perpetual students of evening classes; that is, passive, supportive or behind-the-scenes activity."

If we look at statistics for the visual arts, we can see the effects of a system of discrimination that operates from early sex-role socialization through education to funding. For example, in the visual arts faculties of Canadian universities, more than two-thirds of the students are women, but women comprise fewer than twenty percent of the faculty members.[7] A study of the major government cultural funding agency, the Canada Council, found that there is a direct correlation between the number of women jurors and the number of women artists who succeed in getting grants. Of 229 jury positions between 1972 and 1979, only 28 were held by women; the number of women who were successful candidates for grants was correspondingly low.[8] The NAC brief bitingly draws out the connections between these statistics:

Women. . .are encouraged to attend art schools, to pay tuitions which support the employment of male teachers who are often the same persons who sit on all-male juries awarding fellowships to other male artists who, in turn, view these same women as housewives and whores. The paintings which often appeal explicitly to the prurient interests of male art dealers and male art collectors turn up in the textbooks studied by women as examples of aesthetic achievement of a high order.

To deal with the problem of discrimination against women in the arts, NAC and other women's lobby groups are proposing both economic action (in the form of increased benefits to all artists, including a guaranteed basic income), and affirmative action to rectify the under-representation of women in the arts. These strategies appear to be mere refinements of the liberal principles of equal rights and a fair deal for everyone, but their implementation would require radical changes in the existing economic and political structures. Needless to say, most feminists do not really anticipate that the revolution will be negotiated at the federal level.

Instead feminists have begun to work together collectively and have created alternative institutions and networks for the production and distribution of feminist work. There are now feminist art galleries, such as Powerhouse in Montreal, Women in Focus in Vancouver, and Womanspirit in London. There are feminist publishers – Press Gang in Vancouver, Éditions du Remue-ménage and Éditions de la Pleine Lune in Montreal, The Women's Press in Toronto. There are even feminist record companies. These buttress the struggle of feminist artists for recognition as artists, and encourage their efforts to articulate their vision of the world as women.

FEMINIST ARTIST/FEMINIST AUDIENCE

A receptive, critical audience is crucial for the development of a political artistic community. But too often, political audiences get stuck in a negative critical groove, attacking an artwork or its creator, rather than fostering the political and creative development of the artist. One of the problems with artistic practice, from the point of view of political activists, is that it is difficult to see how art contributes to social change: there isn't a clearly perceived relationship between activism and art. Consequently, political audiences can be very hard on artists, without recognizing their own responsibility. This dialectical relationship of artist-audience accountability is a problem that feminist artists and audiences are just beginning to sort out.

Feminist artists are caught between the conflicting demands of their development as artists and their political commitment to the women's movement. However, recognition within the mainstream or dominant culture carries the risk of political cooptation, at least as far as the artwork is concerned – and this often extends to the artist. Once an artwork is appropriated by the dominant culture, the artist loses control over how it is interpreted and used. Fassbinder's film *Lili Marleen* illustrates both how the artist, a nightclub singer, is appropriated, or controlled, through the star system, and how her song, no longer "hers" once recorded and available for mass distribution, becomes a powerful cultural symbol in fascist Germany. Taken out of the singer's control, it is used for disparate political purposes: by the German government to inspire patriotism, by the German military to torture her Jewish lover, by the Allies to lure patriotic German soldiers to their death.

Obviously the "management" of artists and the perversion of art on this scale are not what we would expect in Canada; however, even here, though more subtly, political art and artists are neutralized. This neutralization tends to be achieved through the marketing and distribution of artworks as items for consumption, a treatment of art which we have come to expect from the mass media and cultural industries. In other words, our art comes processed for us. This has the effect of cancelling the potential political effectiveness of an artist's work. For example, Margaret Atwood, a literary star, has turned her attention to the difficult question of the politics of writing in her two most recent books, *True Stories* and *Bodily Harm*, but the media have ignored this development. Consequently, there has been no debate in the public arena over the political direction in which her work is moving *and* Atwood has been deprived of critical feedback important for her growth as a political writer. Both the audience and the artist suffer from this silence.

One of the sources of misunderstanding and tension that can occur between artists and their audiences lies in what might provocatively be called the audience's "artistic illiteracy." That is, we are more comfortable evaluating an artist's work in terms of its relationship to our own struggles than in perceiving how it works within an artistic tradition. For example, many radicals prefer art with a message that corresponds to their own view of the world. Realism is an acceptable form because it appears to be a transparent reflection of life, accessible to all; thus an audience can evaluate the work without considering its artistic form. But experimental art forms demand some knowledge of the traditions within which an artist is working or against which she is reacting. Although the experience of experimental works may be alienating and disquieting, especially to an untrained audience, the act of finding new forms to express a vision is itself political.

An ideal audience would assume responsibility for educating itself, but even this would not prevent misunderstandings from arising again and again. An artist's meaning can be altered – even subverted – by the context in which the audience receives it. This problem emerged in the controversy over the poster *Fireweed,* a feminist quarterly, used to advertise its National Women's Playwriting Competition in 1980. The image on the poster comes from a photo-cartoon series "SuperSecretary" by Tanya Rosenberg, a conceptual artist. The *Fireweed* collective and the artist understood her intention as a

visual satire of two stereotypes of women – sex object and efficient secretary – and did not anticipate the outraged response the poster generated. In response to their critics, *Fireweed* explained:

> Both Rosenberg and the Collective feel that it is only by strongly confronting the traditional images that are foisted upon women, and the context in which they are presented, that the manipulative nature of these conventional roles can be examined. In using the clown-like image of a woman, parodying the sex-kitten, Rosenberg is asking us to consider how the cosmetized, air-brushed version, seen so often in commercial advertising, is used to exploit. Unfortunately, some people perceive the image not as satire, but as the very thing it meant to debunk and ridicule.[9]

The intentions of *Fireweed* and the artist were to satirize and educate, but *Fireweed* was also using this image to advertise its competition. Because the issues of sexism and violence against women in advertising and the media are so critical, the poster touched a raw nerve in the feminist community at large. In the context of an art exhibit, people would probably have responded to the intended satire, but in the context of public advertising which reaches a wide audience, the image appeared to reinforce the offensive stereotype.

The hostility directed at *Fireweed* and the denunciations of its use of the poster point to another significant problem: how to develop a nurturing community for feminist artists. By ''nurturing'' we don't mean uncritical adulation for every feminist effort. We mean struggling to find ways to express support without losing critical perspective, encouraging excellence without undermining the efforts to achieve it – in short, developing a feminist critical practice. The kind of feminist criticism we envisage will be rooted in the principles of feminist practice: non-hierarchical, non-competitive, non-aggressive, collective and consensual.[10]

One aspect of developing this critical practice is becoming aware of the various ways in which mainstream – or *male-stream*[11] – criticism isolates, denigrates and trivializes feminist art. Feminist art is often reviewed by unsympathetic critics (frequently male), who have little knowledge of the feminist arts community or of the goals of feminism, but draw on popular, glib distortions of the women's movement. A typical way of dismissing a work by a self-defined feminist artist is to describe it as ''feminist.'' This signals to the critic's audience that the critic thinks the work is polemical or propagandistic and not worthy of serious consideration. This tactic is the anti-feminist equivalent of a more general phenomenon: the denigration of all self-professed political art. In the vocabulary of mainstream critics, "political" is a pejorative adjective. Good art, it is argued, is "above politics," which means that "good" art does not openly proclaim any politics. When a critic describes a work as political, it generally means that she or he does not agree with the artist's intention or point of view – and if a work is overtly political, then how can it possibly be good art?

"Feminine" is another loaded term within male-stream critical vocabulary. Though a more subtle epithet than "feminist," nevertheless it is often used patronizingly to imply inferiority, and is one instance of a larger cultural phenomenon: the linguistic derogation of women and things associated with women. In the arts, "feminine" means small, delicate, intuitive, emotional. "Feminine" materials are those found in the home, used by women. The "feminine" arts include dance and the fine arts. "Feminine" is appropriate for women, pro-blematic when applied to men, whereas the universal, to which we have been taught all good art aspires, is generally a form of the masculine. To describe a work as "feminine," therefore, is to imply that it does not measure up to universal/masculine standards of excellence. This anti-feminist bias automatically defines and condemns *women's* fiction, *women's* art – even *women* artists – as the limited case, second-rate, and suitable only for *women* audiences.[12]

◆

Feminists are, however, reclaiming the feminine and proclaiming the feminist. Artists across Canada, working in every medium – visual art, film, theatre, dance, video, performance art, fiction, poetry, music, poster art, photography – are building a feminist culture.

Some are involved in working feminist themes into traditional genres. In novels, films and theatre, for example, women's experiences are being named and scrutinized. An important aspect of much feminist art is this process of naming the world from women's perspective – affirming the world as women experience it. When feminists name, they identify experiences and feelings in new and provocative ways – an essential process in consciousness-raising groups. It can be as straightforwardly significant as giving an experience a name – such as wife-beating – and making it visible, or as complex as treating artistically the experiences of groups not traditionally recognized in art: lesbians, Third World women, working women. Recognizing ourselves in art affirms our lives and struggles and helps us make connections with each other.

Some feminists are experimenting with new forms to express a feminist content. In poetry and fiction, writers are attempting to turn language inside out – exposing its sexist bias – and to create a feminist language. New fields, like video and performance art, are attractive because there is greater freedom for women to experiment with form and content and to learn technical skills. In fact, working in avant-garde areas attracts many feminists precisely because these areas are more in flux sexually and socially, less rigid in formal terms, and more investigative in relation to content.

Other feminists are moving into traditionally male-dominated areas, such as rock. Feminist rock singers and performers are discovering a feminist version of machismo – "machisma." Expressing a strong feminist sensuality in performance is a far cry from the sexualized-bunny stereotype popularly associated with women in rock.

Many women are reclaiming traditional crafts and validating them as art forms. At the level of high art, Joyce Wieland, in *True Patriot Love,* and Judy Chicago, in *The Dinner Party,* have subverted male-stream conventions by incorporating feminine crafts into their works of art.

There are other tasks, other projects, too: recovering women artists and women's art from the past; critiquing stereotypes of women and imagining new "heroes"; fashioning stories and images of a feminist world. These all contribute to challenging the ways we are taught to see and interpret the world. Feminist artists are creating new images of what women are and can be; they are giving us new forms – a new language. They speak to us, about us, for us, with us. Together we move towards a feminist vision.

N   O   T   E   S

We would like to thank all those who contributed both directly and indirectly to the development of this article. Some of these people include: Himani Bannerji, Jody Berland, Carole Conde, Kate Lushington, Lorraine Segato, and Rhea Tregebov, who generously participated in early discussions with us; Jan Patterson, whose splendid support qualifies her as a literary midwife; and Connie Guberman and Jane Springer, who nurtured us through the various stages of editing.

1. *Les fées ont soif,* by Denise Boucher (Montreal: Les Éditions Intermède, 1979), is a feminist play about three women – the Virgin Mary, Marie the housewife, and Madeleine the prostitute. This line is quoted in translation in Patricia Smart, "Culture, Revolution and Politics in Quebec," *Canadian Forum,* Vol. LXII (May 1982), p. 10.

2. In our original outline for this article, we attempted to delineate major areas of concern for the feminist art community. We then used this outline as the basis for our discussions with feminist artists. Clearly, these questions and issues need more discussion and analysis.

   a) The relationship between form and content:
      • artistic vs. political intention
      • high/fine art vs. folk/hobby/domestic art
      • materials, style, form

   b) Practice:
      • the economics of being an artist
      • method: e.g., collective, individual, individual with support group

   c) Politics and aesthetics:
      • is there a feminine sensibility?
      • how does "the personal is political" translate into art?
      • particular perspectives: e.g., the specificity of being a non-white or working-class or lesbian woman in the Canadian cultural community

   d) Audience:
      • the relationship between the artist and her work and the community (how is the community defined?)
      • who is the audience – the artist's own political community or those outside it?

   e) The relationship between the women's movement (in all its forms) and feminist art:
      • how has the women's movement affected women's art practice?
      • how has feminist art affected the women's movement?

   f) Is art a political tool?

3. Robin Morgan, *Going Too Far: The Personal Chronicle of a Feminist* (New York: Vintage Books, 1978), p. xii.

4. The Cultural Workers' Alliance makes this argument in their brief to the Federal Cultural Policy Review Committee. An extract from the brief, "Service or Commodities?" appears in *Fuse* (May/June 1981), pp. 175-76. The Federal Cultural Policy Review Committee, as its name indicates, is conducting a public inquiry into culture and the arts in Canada. It held public hearings in 1981 and is expected to present its final report in 1982.

5. National Action Committee for the Status of Women, "Canadian Cultural Development with Equity for Women," Toronto, 1981. We also consulted briefs presented to the Federal Cultural Policy Review Committee by other Status of Women groups.

6. Dorothy E. Smith, "A Peculiar Eclipsing: Women's Exclusion from Man's Culture," *Women's Studies International Quarterly,* Vol. I (1978), p. 293.

7. Sasha McInnes-Hayman, "Contemporary Canadian Women Artists: A Survey," prepared for Womanspirit Art Research and Resource Center, London, Ontario, and Status of Women Canada, Ottawa, 1981, and submitted to the Federal Cultural Policy Review Committee.

8. Jane Martin, "Women Visual Artists on Canada Council Juries, Selection Committees, and Arts Advisory Panels; and Amongst Grant Recipients from 1972-73 to 1979-80," prepared for Canadian Artists' Representation/Le Front des Artistes Canadiens (CARFAC), and submitted to the Federal Cultural Policy Review Committee, 1981. See also: Avis Lang Rosenberg, "Women Artists and the Canadian Art World: A Survey," *Atlantis: A Women's Studies Journal,* Vol. 5, No. 1 (Fall 1979), pp. 107-26. For an analysis of the situation of women poets in anglo Canada, see: Sharon H. Nelson, "The Sexual Politics of Poetry," *League of Canadian Poets – Newsletter,* No. 32 (July-August 1981), pp. 15-18.

9. *Fireweed: A Feminist Literary & Cultural Journal,* Nos. 5 and 6 (1979-80), p. 15.

10. An exciting step in this direction has been taken by the Women's Cultural Building, a collective of women in Toronto (as yet without a home), who are working to provide a forum for women artists in all fields and to develop a new audience for women's cultural work. In June 1982, they held a public panel discussion of Judy Chicago's *The Dinner Party,* which was then showing at the Art Gallery of Ontario. The panel addressed in depth the aesthetic, economic and political issues raised by *The Dinner Party.* Criticism of this kind – committed and constructive – is essential for understanding the problems of the making and the reception of feminist art.

11. This is Mary O'Brien's phrase. See her book, *The Politics of Reproduction* (London: Routledge and Kegan Paul, 1981).

12. This is an oversimplified and condensed explanation of the linguistic derogation of women. For an introduction to this concept see: Dale Spender, *Man Made Language* (London: Routledge and Kegan Paul, 1980).

F U R T H E R   R E A D I N G S

Canadian Woman Studies / Les cahiers de la femme, Vol. 3, No. 3 (Spring 1982).

Fireweed: A Feminist Quarterly.

Fuse: The Cultural News Magazine.

Heresies: A Feminist Publication on Art and Politics.

Room of One's Own.

What Are Our Options?

COORDINATED
BY NANCY ADAMSON

In addition to groups that focus on one specific issue of feminism, there are a few groups that fight for a set of issues – that have a platform of immediate and long-term goals. Some of these groups are organized nationally, such as the Feminist Party of Canada and the National Action Committee on the Status of Women. A few are organized provincially, such as the B.C. Federation of Women. A group that has functioned locally is the International Women's Day Committee in Toronto. Nancy Adamson coordinated the following discussion with five other women who are active in IWDC: Carolyn Egan, Sandy Fox, Sue Genge, Mariana Valverde and Lynda Yanz. In selecting this format, we wanted to reflect the non-hierarchical nature of much of the Canadian women's movement, where decision-making, organizing and strategizing result from group discussion and debate. We therefore asked these women to talk about options for feminist organizing. Although they share certain assumptions, coming from a common socialist feminist perspective, they do not always agree. This piece is an example of the kind of discussion that occurs in all groups that are attempting to turn feminist theories into practice.

NANCY: There are a number of different ways of defining the women's movement in Canada. For example, we're often accused of being a small group that addresses the concerns of only white, middle-class women. How do *you* describe the women's movement?

CAROLYN: The women's movement is no longer the small grouping that it was 10 or 12 years ago, and to maintain, as the media does, that the very small politically active feminist community is the extent of the women's movement is wrong. To me, the women's movement includes the women working with immigrant women, the women in the trade union movement, lesbians, sole-support mothers and all the women who are struggling for women's rights.

SANDY: Yes, in the last year or two we've been on demonstrations or pickets for first contract fights, for day care, for equal pay, for abortion, for the right to non-traditional jobs; we've been involved in union women's caucuses – how can anybody say that that list represents only middle-class women?

MARIANA: It's important to recognize that women are oppressed in different ways, apart from all being oppressed as women. Immigrant women, as the article in the anthology argues, have to be organized as immigrant women, and *then* plug into the women's movement. It would be very alienating for individual immigrant women to join a group that was primarily anglo. They need their own groups, which fight for specifically immigrant women's issues and identify their own concerns, so that when they come into the general women's movement they can set their own demands. Similarly, lesbians or native women, or any woman who faces a separate oppression, needs her own organizations and her own groups. We have to recognize the existence of different groups within the women's movement.

LYNDA: But isn't it also important to look at the way the development of different groups represents divisions in the women's movement? For example, in Vancouver and certainly in the States, the need for immigrant, Third World and lesbian women to form their own groups is posed as a criticism of the women's movement, as an indication of how the women's movement has not addressed aspects of their oppression. The anger of Third World and lesbian women is only beginning to surface; hopefully the critiques they are making will have the long-term effect of strengthening our capacity as a movement to represent minority and working-class women's interests.

MARIANA: We have to work towards unity in the women's movement, and I think oftentimes people have this mistaken conception: they think that unity means that everyone has to be in the same organization and all have the same ideas. Well, that's not what *we* mean. You can be aware of your differences and yet work together for common goals.

NANCY: We all work together in a socialist feminist organization in Toronto called the International Women's Day Committee. Let's talk about IWDC and how we see it fitting into the larger women's movement.

SANDY: IWDC began in the late 1970s, during the period that the media was full of news of the ''death'' of the women's movement. And certainly, in Toronto at least, there seemed to be no highly visible ongoing women's organizations, apart from service groups like the YWCA. We first came together to plan a celebration of International Women's Day 1978, decided we wanted to continue working together and here we are today! Of course, we've had our ups and downs.

Our basis of unity statement defines us as anti-capitalist and anti-patriarchal. In simpler terms, we define ourselves as socialist feminists. We are an activist group and over the past five years have been involved in strike support work, demonstrations for abortion rights, day care and against violence against women. We have co-sponsored forums with other groups on issues such as lesbians in the women's movement, capitalism and patriarchy, nuclear power and the rise of the right. I see IWDC as a place where we can be part of the independent women's movement and come together with other socialist feminists to get support, to develop ourselves as feminists and as individuals.

CAROLYN: IWDC has enabled us to continue our activities on single issues and at the same time to come together with women involved in other areas. I think the way IWDC tries to integrate our overall analysis into so-called single issues is important. For example, last year we did a fair amount of work in the area of reproductive rights. When we spoke of it we referred to a whole range of women's issues: the right to have children when and if we choose is central, but beyond that, we need support services such as free universal day care and paid parental leave, the right to safe and effective birth control, the right to free abortion, the freedom to choose our own sexuality, and an end to coerced sterilization. It's not enough to just have some legal right, if we lack the economic means and the social support to exercise that right: and this is where we see that women's demands really do pose a tremendous challenge to the system. In our work, we presented reproductive freedom as one of the most basic of women's rights, and outlined how the women's movement and all we are struggling for was really under attack in this area.

SUE: The other role IWDC plays in Toronto is to bring single issue groups together to support each other's struggles. And in particular we do that around International Women's Day. We bring groups together partly because our members work in those organizations and partly because of our analysis, which says that if we're going to win gains anywhere we have to build unity in various sectors of the women's and progressive movements.

NANCY: How does the current social and economic situation affect the women's movement?

SUE: It seems to me that we're in the middle of a really massive economic crisis, and, in terms of women's issues, we haven't felt it yet. We've felt the rise of the right, the attack on lesbians and gays, on abortion, and the beginning of the attack on the labour movement politically, but we haven't yet felt the full brunt of the economic crisis. What I'm afraid of is that, as the crisis unfolds, the issues of women are going to get lost. It's going to be a situation where the major fight is the fight for jobs, and that means the fight for jobs for *men*. So if you live in Windsor, you're not going to be fighting for non-traditional jobs in auto, you're going to be fighting to have the auto plants reopened. Right? And my concern is that we learn how to argue that women's issues are not divisive, that they're not secondary, but that they're absolutely essential to the fight against the economic crisis. We have to insist that the putting down of women, and the undercutting of women's jobs and wages is an attack on the whole working class. The right wing's attack on our right to choose our sexuality is an attack on everybody. Unless we're prepared for that, we're going to lose women's issues in the general struggle for survival.

MARIANA: Yes, it's important to remember that when there's an economic crisis we are not just affected economically. Most people don't understand how the economy works, so they look for explanations in other places. For example, I was listening to a program about unemployment on "Cross Country Checkup" a few weeks ago. People were phoning in from all over the country to express their concerns. Many of them were saying things like this: "It's really unfair in hard economic times for two people to work in a family when there's another family where no one works." Or "It's unfair for women who don't have children to have good jobs, if men who have kids/don't have any jobs."

SUE: Women on their own should starve!

MARIANA: We have to understand where that comes from. It's based on a traditional idea of men and women in the family – that the man works for wages and the woman stays at home. We can say that women into jobs is an economic issue, but if we don't do the educational work around things like the family and women's position in the family, we're going to lose on the economic issues.

The struggle for economic independence is not separate from the struggles for reproductive rights, lesbian rights and a freer sexuality for all women. The same women who are fighting for jobs or for day care are also engaged in a perhaps less vocal but just as vital struggle to build sexual and emotional relationships that are non-sexist and satisfying. The movement as a whole is not saying that just because we're in a recession we are going to quit worrying about issues like violence against women or lesbian rights.

In IWDC we've been having a very good discussion about the concept of compulsory heterosexuality. Basically, we've said that, while it's of course important to defend lesbian and gay rights, it's perhaps even more important, in the long run, to realize that the way we are brought up to find a "handsome prince" to take care of us is oppressive to *all* of us, regardless of our sexual orientation – the way that everything in this society pushes us into a traditional family is what is at the root, both of lesbian oppression and of independent heterosexual women. We've also been saying that, no matter what our sexual preference, we are united in the struggle for women's independence. So that when women choose to have relationships with men, they'll do so from a position of equality and autonomy, not because everyone tells them they're worthless if they're not with a man, and certainly not because they need a man to survive economically. If the women's movement really took up the issue of compulsory heterosexuality it would be an important step forward, both in terms of our understanding of women's oppression and in terms of our political strategy. Of course, we're not going to immediately yell at everyone we meet on a picket line that they must struggle against heterosexism – as we know, changing people's consciousness takes time, and we ourselves have to do more thinking and talking about how to integrate this perspective into our practice. But slow changes are sometimes the most durable.

LYNDA: That's in part why the political/educational role that IWDC plays is so important. Not only does a socialist feminist analysis of the current economic situation make sense to people, but we have a mass action and coalition approach to practice.

For example, microtechnology is a very important issue for women right now. Thousands and thousands of clerical and service jobs that women have counted on are going to be wiped out over the next 15 years. It's absolutely essential that a massive campaign be developed to respond to the potentially devastating effects of microtech. And that campaign will have to involve women's and community groups in alliance with the entire union movement. The union movement has begun to move on this issue and different women's groups have begun to try and grapple with what it's going to mean for women. But in the conferences that are taking place in different cities across the country you hear very little about how central a major attempt at organizing the unorganized is to this issue or about the need for alliances between these different movements.

SANDY: That's the incredible position IWDC finds itself in after almost five years of work, because we have built real links between the women's movement and the trade union movement. I think that of all our allies, the trade union movement is potentially the largest and most powerful. As socialist feminists we can, and *must*, play a key role in the general discussions the trade union movement is now engaged in about how to fight the current attacks on the union movement and how to fight for jobs. We have something particular to say about women and their work situation. For example, here in Ontario, the Ontario Federation of Labour set up a major day care campaign. And nationally, the CLC recently passed a resolution supporting free-standing abortion clinics. That linking of broader issues to the more traditional economic concerns of trade union conventions was the result of a lot of hard work by union activists with the help and support of feminists outside the union movement. As I see it, those are important ways of ensuring that women's issues don't get tossed aside in hard economic times.

CAROLYN: What IWDC hasn't been able to do is really harness the energy and power of women into a mass movement in the way it should be, the way it can be, done.

LYNDA: Are you saying that organizing women is the issue?

CAROLYN: Well I think that, yes, organizing women and building a mass movement of women that has an analysis of fightback is absolutely key. And I think women are doing it, the consciousness is there, it's a question of how to focus that consciousness.

NANCY: So, how can we focus that consciousness? How do we organize women to fight back?

SANDY: I often hear people say that we need to sit down and work out a long-term strategy, that is, figure out what the issues are and how to act on them. Nine or ten years ago we wouldn't have predicted that we would be fighting first contract struggles and dealing with workplace issues like sexual harassment, affirmative action and women into non-traditional jobs. Nor would we have guessed that the anti-nuclear movement would have become *the* international grass-roots issue of the 1980s. General economic, social and political conditions determine the issues. So, in a sense, we will always be responding to issues that arise out of those conditions.

NANCY: The fact that we are responding or reacting to issues is often seen as a negative thing. But we should remember that that response is developed from certain "organizing principles," which guide our actions and reflect our politics. IWDC has laid out some of these in our basis of unity.

MARIANA: Yes. One of the things we stress as we struggle to end women's oppression is that the state is not neutral. That's a polite way of saying that we think the state is against us. The state has a nature of its own and part of that nature is to control and repress any demands that would upset the system. The demands of workers can be accommodated up to a point, but past that point they become too upsetting for the system, so the state has to repress them. Similarly, in terms of women, there are some reforms that we may be able to win, but generally if we win them it's because they happen to be convenient. For example, if we are able to win certain concessions on family benefits it's probably because the unemployment rate is so high that they don't want us all to be looking for jobs. So when the state gives us a reform we always have to ask: what is the role of the reform that we have won? Is it really for us, because they have our best interests at heart – or is it because it's convenient for them? And these reforms of course are not to be sneezed at, because they can be very beneficial. Family benefits are important, and now in Ontario they're in danger of going out the window, so we have to fight for them. But we have to remember that these reforms are not there for us, they're there because they serve a function in the system, and if they don't continue to serve that function, they'll go out the window whenever a depression hits.

So it's not just a matter of winning a particular thing, it's also a matter of radicalizing all the people who are supposed to be benefitting from the reform. That's why mass actions are good; they have the effect of radicalizing people. Plus it teaches us a lot of skills. If we have to put on a demonstration, it teaches us a lot about how to reach different groups; we have to leaflet, go and do outreach, talk to people we wouldn't ordinarily talk to, try and convince people that women's rights are really worth fighting for.

SANDY: Mass action can mean anything from ten women or ten people on a picket line to thousands of people on a street; it means people who are putting their foot on the sidewalk or on the road to protest something – not begging or saying please give us something, but demanding their rights. A demonstration is inspiring because it means that lots of other people share our concerns: it means that we're not speaking alone, that there are other people who feel the same things we do. And that's why the state's so afraid of demonstrations – because it gives people a sense of their collective strength. Some of the most powerful demonstrations I've been on were Take Back the Night marches, where women protested our lack of safety on the streets. We really did "take back the night" by taking over the streets and the police were powerless to stop us.

LYNDA: A demonstration shows the power of people, it gives people a sense of what they collectively can do. Sometimes they're successful and sometimes they aren't; sometimes you'll actually get a result from a particular demonstration, sometimes you won't; but even when you don't, the organizing effort isn't a failure; it's a part of a larger process.

NANCY: In addition to mass action, a recognition that the state is not neutral, the struggle to build unity within the women's movement, and a commitment to work in coalitions, *how* we organize our groups is important. Right from the start, feminists insisted on the importance of non-hierarchical structures. Many women's groups operate collectively. I think our efforts to develop each woman's strengths, to share decision making, to recognize every woman's importance to her organization is crucial to building and expanding the women's movement.

While we all struggle in individual ways to change ourselves and our lives, many of us also work for change within an organization. Do you think political parties are an effective mechanism for bringing about the changes the women's movement advocates?

SUE: The only party which is at all concerned with women's issues is the NDP. And the problem with the NDP is that they think the world can be changed by changing the government. It's the question once again of whether or not the state is neutral, and I don't think it is. What happens when the NDP gets into power is that they have the job of running the country within a certain set of rules, because it's a capitalist system – and they are stuck with administering those rules. They can't introduce all the reforms that we want them to introduce, because the reforms we want change the nature of society. That's why it doesn't work.

CAROLYN: There's an assumption in a social democratic point of view that, through electoral change, people will simply give up capitalism, that the bourgeoisie will give up their power and say "Okay, you people have democratically decided to change society, thank you, we'll retire!"

But that is not the case, and I think we've seen it illustrated in enough nations around the world.

SANDY: But there is a significant difference between the NDP and the Conservatives and Liberals, and that difference is that the NDP is a labour party. It's based on the trade unions. I'm a member of the NDP and I've gone around canvassing and trying to convince people to vote NDP. I try to explain that the Liberals and Conservatives represent the boss, and by voting for the NDP you vote for yourself – you vote for labour and not big business. For a lot of people it's an important first step to take a political stand at the ballot box and to say "I'm a worker, I'll vote for a party that says it represents workers."

CAROLYN: In terms of the women's movement, at least from my perspective on it, the NDP certainly involves a lot of women who have a feminist consciousness, who are fighting for the liberation of women. In IWDC we work with NDP women's committees, and with the NDP in coalitions. We urge them through their riding associations to come out and support joint activities, etc. It makes sense to have strategic alliances with people in the NDP, but whether I would work in the NDP is another question entirely.

SUE: I think that if you live in any small town across the country you probably would go to the NDP because it tends to group together the progressive people in an area and also the progressive people in the labour movement. If I lived in a small town, the NDP is probably the place I would work.

LYNDA: I worked in the NDP in Manitoba and the experience left me very disillusioned. The issue isn't just the limitations of the NDP in the long term; it's not so great in the short term either. In Manitoba, we managed to get some good policies passed at conventions but getting those implemented by an NDP government was a whole other story. The NDP was very important to me; it was the place where I got politicized and where I first came into contact with feminists and the women's movement. But I sure wouldn't encourage other people to go through the same process. There are areas in which an NDP government can make a difference so I might vote for them but I would never go out knocking on doors again, trying to convince working people that they have a lot to gain from the NDP. I'd rather put my energy into working to build different kinds of political organizations.

Women who have been in social democratic parties have, I think, also been radicalized as feminists, have been active in the autonomous women's movement and have urged and pushed their organizations and parties to take up women's issues. But we've seen historically that without an autonomous women's movement that isn't possible. The changes we have to make will not be made unless there is pressure from some sort of women's movement, a mass women's movement.

NANCY: Well, we seem to be in agreement that unless there are autonomous women's organizations our demands will be put on a back burner. Fortunately, there are now a wide variety of women's organizations in this country.

CAROLYN: Yes there are. The National Action Committee on the Status of Women (NAC) was established to give Canadian women one national voice, to be a forum, a network for women's organizations. It has a conference once a year to which all of its member organizations can send delegates. Mostly NAC uses a lobbying approach – they pressure various levels of government to pass or change legislation. IWDC has rejected the lobbying approach because we don't feel it is effective. However, I think that it's very important that there is a national organization of women in this country. Socialist feminists should be part of it and speak to it and put forward suggestions for strategies that may be more effective than the ones that have been developed so far. It is one of the few ways in this huge country that women from all over get a chance to come together and talk about issues, like violence against women or economic rights or reproductive rights.

LYNDA: And that coming together is very important; it's part of how we develop politically – whether it's NAC's annual conference, or rape crisis centres across the country meeting to assess their work or a bi-national lesbian conference. We're not a movement that has the same kind of intellectual tradition as, say, in Britain. Most of us don't sum up our political experiences in writing, we tend to develop more through practice and talk – getting involved in doing and trying things and then thinking that through with other women.

If you look back you can see a point about five years ago when women, in almost every province, and with very different experiences, started new sorts of organizations. It's not an accident that socialist feminist study groups began independently of one another in every province. The economic crisis was pushing back the gains we'd made and we were faced with reassessing what kind of political action was going to work. Women made different choices and built different kinds of organizations. IWDC is one example of a long-lasting socialist feminist activist group. The British Columbia Federation of Women (BCFW) is a different kind of organization that attempts not just to link but to bring together women's groups from across the province to discuss strategy collectively. Lesbian groups have held two bi-national conferences to discuss common problems and develop common strategies. And various single issue groups have also come together to discuss issues and strategies; for example CARAL (Canadian Abortion Rights Action League) meetings or national day care conferences.

NANCY: I think what we're saying is that we need both "single issue" groups working intensively on individual issues and the more broad-based groups. The single issue groups have the time and the information to develop detailed strategies for their issue. The more broad-based groups: IWDC, NAC, NDP women's committees, immigrant women's groups or whatever, link the issues together and facilitate cooperation between groups.

We in IWDC see as one of our important roles, building unity in the women's movement and building support for all of our struggles as women. One way we do this is by building and working in coalitions. The March 8th Coalition which plans the International Women's Day events in Toronto is the most regular and largest example of this – last year about 75 women's, political and community groups participated. And we work in coalitions dealing with a wide range of issues: day care, abortion, solidarity work, anti-nuclear work, strike support work, etc.

CAROLYN: Indeed, there are many things that we have to do, issues that we have to fight for – but when you think of what the early Sixties were like, compared to the early Eighties, when you think that's only twenty years . . . The changes in the average woman's consciousness, of her possibilities, what she will *not* put up with, what she would have put up with then, are remarkable. We have a long long way to go, and we have to learn how to harness the incredible energy and awareness of women so far. But there have been really significant changes in the consciousness of women. And it would not have happened, I don't think, unless there'd been an autonomous women's movement to do it.

The women's movement is still strong, growing and influential. If we work together to build a mass movement of women – with the support of the trade unions, anti-racist groups, immigrant groups, gay and lesbian groups and other progressive groups – and continue to build mass actions and put forward our analysis, then we will figure out, not just how to fight back, but how to move forward, in spite of these hard economic times.

F U R T H E R   R E A D I N G S

BOOKS

Barrett, Michele. *Women's Oppression Today: Problems in Marxist Feminist Analysis.* London: Verso and New Left Books, 1980.

Delacoste, Frederique and Felice Newman, eds. *Fight Back! Feminist Resistance to Male Violence.* Minneapolis, Minn.: Cleis Press, 1981.

Huws, Ursula. *Your Job in the 80's: A Woman's Guide to New Technology.* London: Pluto Press, 1982.

Rowbotham, Sheila, Lynne Segal and Hilary Wainwright. *Beyond the Fragments: Feminism and the Making of Socialism.* London: Merlin Press, 1970.

JOURNALS

Feminist Review, Vol. 11 (1982).

Quest: A Feminist Quarterly, Vol. V, No. 4 (1982).

C O N T R I B U T O R S

NANCY ADAMSON is a graduate student in history and has been active in the International Women's Day Committee in Toronto.

JACKIE AINSWORTH is a bank clerk and founding member of SORWUC and AUCE. She helped write *An Account to Settle* and is active in the Bank and Finance Workers Union, Local 4 of SORWUC.

KATE BRAID spent several years as a writer, secretary, child care worker, student and teacher. Then, after a summer working in a lumber planer mill, she discovered how much she enjoyed physical labour. She is now a third-year apprentice carpenter and in July 1983 will be a journeywoman carpenter.

SUSAN G. COLE is a freelance writer and a member of the collective for *Broadside*, a feminist newspaper published in Toronto. She is currently writing a book on pornography in Canada.

PATRICIA DAVITT has been active in the women's liberation movement in Vancouver, particularly around issues concerning women and work. As a member of the Corrective Collective she helped to produce *She Named it Canada* and *Never Done*. She did the graphics for *An Account to Settle* and sings with The Euphoniously Feminist and Non-Peforming Quartet. A Renaissance woman, in short.

ROSEMARY DONEGAN is a founding member of the Women's Press, works in Canadian art history and as an arts administrator.

CAROLYN EGAN has been an activist in the women's liberation movement in Toronto for the past twelve years. She works at the Birth Control and Venereal Disease Clinic in Toronto and is involved in the International Women's Day Committee.

DEBBIE FIELD is a socialist feminist, present of no fixed address. She was active in the Women Back Into Stelco Campaign in Hamilton and worked in the coke ovens at Stelco steel plant for one year.

MAUREEN FITZGERALD maintains an illusion that she lives in Toronto and Vancouver. She is a member of the Women's Press Collective and has also worked with Press Gang Printing and Publishing. She teaches at the University of Toronto and is the co-author of a children's book, *The Day the Fairies Went on Strike*.

SANDY FOX has been active in the women's movement for the past thirteen years. She was a member of the early Toronto Women's Caucus and a founding member of the International Women's Day Committee. She is currently studying computer programming.

DEIRDRE GALLAGHER helped found the Toronto Women's Caucus, a socialist feminist formation, and worked on *Women Unite*. She has worked for Organized Working Women and was instrumental in the establishment of the Ontario Federation of Labour's women's committee. Presently editor of Steelworker's national newspaper, *Steelabour,* and responsible for women's affairs in the union, she is a member of the women's committees of the Ontario Federation of Labour and the Canadian Federation of Labour.

SUSAN GENGE is a library worker and active in her CUPE local. She is also active in the International Women's Day Committee in Toronto.

AMY GOTTLIEB is a red diaper baby who is now part of the lavender and red menace; typesetter and paste-up artist by day, political and sexual activist by night.

CONNIE GUBERMAN is an editor, writer and freelance organizer of conferences and literary events. She is currently working on a video about writers and human rights. She is a member of the International Women's Day Committee and the Women's Press in Toronto.

ANN HUTCHISON has been a library worker at the University of British Columbia for eighteen years. She is the founding member of AUCE, past president of AUCE Local 1 and presently an active member of that local.

BARBARA JAMES is a lesbian socialist feminist, active in Halifax, Nova Scotia.

MARLENE KADAR is a member of Alliance Against Sexual Harassment and has taught a course on the topic of sexual harassment at the University of Alberta, Edmonton. She is presently completing a dissertation on literature and politics in the 1930s. A freelance writer and editor, she recently edited a book on the history of the Ukranian theatre.

JOANNE KATES survived childhood in Toronto and went to Wellesley College where they train women to be ladies. She has been rebelling ever since, as a feminist journalist and in the women's liberation movement. She has just completed a book on Algonquin Park and is working on a book about single people.

MYRNA KOSTASH is a full-time writer who lives in Edmonton. She has written on feminist issues in various magazines and is the author of *All of Baba's Children* and *Long Way from Home.*

DENISE KOURI was president of Saskatchewan Working Women until her departure for Mozambique, where she is currently working with Canadian University Services Overseas. In Saskatchewan she was active in abortion campaigns, day care organizing and in her union, CUPE. She was the provincial coordinator of the SORWUC bank organizing campaign in Saskatchewan.

CAROLINE LACHAPELLE is an Ojibwa who lives on Vancouver Island. Caroline works with the Women's Self-Help Network, whose program entails teaching women self-help skills for social action. She has worked with the Indian Friendship Centres Program and Employment Issues for Native Women.

MARIANNE LANGTON is vice-president of Times Change Women's Employment Service and studies occupational health at the Faculty of Environmental Studies, York University.

MEG LUXTON is the author of *More Than a Labour of Love: Three Generations of Women's Work in the Home.* A sociologist at McMaster University, she is currently studying working-class families in Hamilton, Ontario. She is the mother of two.

SUSAN MARGARET is a clerical worker in a Vancouver law firm. She is a founding member of SORWUC and is active in SORWUC Local 1.

LIZ MARTIN is responsible for design and production at the Women's Press and also teaches art in a Toronto high school.

KATHLEEN MCDONNELL is a journalist, playwright and writer of fiction who lives in Toronto. She has had a longstanding involvement in women's health and reproductive rights, and is a founding member of *Healthsharing* magazine. She is the mother of one child.

WINNIE NG is originally from Hong Kong. She has been a community worker, union organizer and English as a Second Language teacher. She presently works at the Toronto Immigrant Women's Centre as a health counsellor.

SHEILA PERRET was a clerical worker at Capilano College. She has held various positions on the provincial executive of AUCE.

MICHELE PUJOL is a founding member of TSSU (Teaching Support Staff Union) Local 6 of AUCE. She is presently teaching economics at the University of Manitoba.

MARY JEAN RANDS is a steno with the Bank of British Columbia. She is a founding member of SORWUC and AUCE, helped write *An Account to Settle* and is active in the Bank and Finance Workers Union, Local 4 of SORWUC.

DAPHNE READ is a member of the Women's Press and a graduate student in English at York University.

JILLIAN RIDINGTON worked at Vancouver Transition House from 1974-78. She has been an executive member of the Vancouver Status of Women and is currently a vice-president of the National Action Committee on the Status of Women. She has written on pornography and prostitution, family law, native women and is writing and doing research on the Vancouver Civil Service, violence against women in the family, native and pioneer women in B.C.

STAR ROSENTHAL is a library worker at Simon Fraser University and currently president of AUCE Local 2. She does research and writing on women's trade union history.

PATRICIA SCHULZ has been involved in day care advocacy for the past eight years, as a parent, as a volunteer day care worker, as a parent board member of a day care and as a teacher of Early Childhood Education in a community college. She is currently involved with Action Day Care and is the vice-president of the steering committee of the Ontario Coalition for Better Day Care. She has written articles for both *Women at Work in Ontario* and *Good Day Care.*

JANE SPRINGER is a freelance editor and active socialist feminist in Toronto. She copyedited this anthology.

SARI TUDIVER is Project Officer for Women and Development with the Manitoba Council for International Cooperation, a non-governmental organization which coordinates funding of development projects in Third World countries. She has taught anthropology and women's studies at the University of Manitoba and is completing a dissertation on political economy and family relations in eastern Kentucky. She is the mother of a two-year-old son.

MARIANA VALVERDE is working on a book on socialist feminists in nineteenth-century France. She is active in the Toronto International Women's Day Committee and is a member of the Red Berets singing group.

SUE VOHANKA works on the staff of the CCU. She is a freelance writer most involved now in *This Magazine.* She lives in Toronto.

WOMEN WORKING WITH IMMIGRANT WOMEN is an umbrella organization composed of twenty-five agencies that work with immigrant women in Toronto. Over the last two years, WWIW has focused its discussion on immigrant women's roles as immigrants, as workers and as women in Canadian society.

LYNDA YANZ works for the Participatory Research Group in Toronto and is active in the International Women's Day Committee. She is also involved in New Star Press, Toronto/Vancouver and is the editor of *Sandino's Daughters* by Margaret Randall.

NAOMI WALL is a member of the Women's Press Collective and co-edited *Come With Us.* She is a typesetter and also teaches English as a Second Language. She is a member of Women Working with Immigrant Women in Toronto.

MARGIE WOLFE, a staff person at the Women's Press, also teaches English as a Second Language and does freelance broadcasting work. Besides a number of articles, she has authored guides for teaching women's history.

EVE ZAREMBA has been an activist in the women's movement throughout the last decade. She has produced an anthology called *Privilege of Sex: A Century of Canadian Women* and is the author of *A Reason to Kill,* a thriller featuring detective Helen Keremos. She lives in Toronto with her lover and works on *Broadside,* a feminist newspaper.